Data Governance

by Jonathan Reichental, PhD

Data Governance For Dummies®

Published by: **John Wiley & Sons, Inc.,** 111 River Street, Hoboken, NJ 07030-5774, www.wiley.com

Copyright © 2023 by John Wiley & Sons, Inc., Hoboken, New Jersey

Published simultaneously in Canada

For general information on our other products and services, please contact our Customer Care Department within the U.S. at 877-762-2974, outside the U.S. at 317-572-3993, or fax 317-572-4002. For technical support, please visit https://hub.wiley.com/community/support/dummies.

Wiley publishes in a variety of print and electronic formats and by print-on-demand. Some material included with standard print versions of this book may not be included in e-books or in print-on-demand. If this book refers to media such as a CD or DVD that is not included in the version you purchased, you may download this material at http://booksupport.wiley.com. For more information about Wiley products, visit www.wiley.com.

Library of Congress Control Number: 2022946780

ISBN: 978-1-119-90677-3 (pbk); 978-1-119-90678-0 (ebk); 978-1-119-90679-7 (ebk)

Contents at a Glance

Table of Contents

Introduction

I n the 21st century, data really matters. Some even claim it's the most important asset organizations possess today. Reviewing the evidence, I think they might be right.

Although all organizations use and manage data, far too many don't do it well. As a consequence, they are missing out on opportunities to grow their businesses, increase revenue, and leverage valuable insights. In addition, they're putting their organization at greater risk in a world of complex regulatory requirements and punishing cyberattacks.

Today, an increasing number of leaders recognize that managing data well and increasing its quality can deliver remarkable results for their organizations. They're discovering the value behind data governance.

Unfortunately, implementing data governance is no walk in the park. Research from Gartner suggests that up to 90 percent of organizations fail at their first attempt. This book can help fix that. Proven, high-quality guidance is required and that's what this book is all about.

I wrote this book to help you succeed at managing and optimizing your data in better ways than you do today. Understanding data governance will empower you to increase the value and quality of your organization's data and manage the risks and obligations associated with it.

About This Book

Despite the title, this isn't a book for dummies. It's for those smart people who recognize that managing data well is the right thing to do. But you already knew that.

Data governance may not be the most exciting topic of our times, but in terms of importance and positive organizational impact, it's certainly hard to beat. The increasing demand for data governance is a direct result of the rise in the value and volume of data and the attendant opportunities and risks this presents.

Since you're reading this book, my assumption is that you generally get this. Ahead of many, you recognize the value of data governance and that attaining the skills and methods to implement a successful program will benefit you and your organization.

That said, I wrote this book for those with no data governance knowledge and for those with existing skills but with a desire for more insight and detail. In other words, whether you know a little or a lot on the topic, this book is designed to help you. In practical terms, like all *Dummies* books, you can read it from cover to cover, or you can just jump to a certain section.

Data governance is often a confusing and complex topic. It also has a lot of unfamiliar terminology associated with it, particularly if you don't have a technical or data background. As an educator, I like to explain things simply. In fact, I like to explain things the way I would like them explained to me. This means I've gone to great efforts to eliminate the confusion and complexity of the topic while also providing easy-to-understand explanations. You may also find some repetition in chapters, and this is deliberate. Repeating some concepts, in a variety of contexts, reinforces the core ideas.

If you decide to read the book from cover to cover, you'll notice it has five parts that are designed to take you from concepts to planning and right through to implementation and support:

>> **Part 1, Data Everywhere:** The chapters in this part provide a detailed background of data governance and explain why it's important in a world of increasing volume, variety, and velocity of data.

>> **Part 2, Discovering Data Governance:** The chapters in this part explain how to build the business case and get approval for your data governance program. It also explains the value data governance can bring to different functions in your organization.

>> **Part 3, Developing Data Governance:** The chapters in this part detail the steps to planning, designing, and developing your data governance program.

>> **Part 4, Democratizing Data:** The chapters in this part cover how to support and maintain your data governance program once it is implemented, including monitoring it and measuring results.

>> **Part 5, The Part of Tens:** The chapters in this part provide two lists — one that identifies best practices and the other that covers the essential stakeholders involved in data governance.

Foolish Assumptions

I made the following assumptions about you, dear reader, when writing this book. You:

>> Have little patience for unnecessary jargon and deeper explanations and just want what's necessary to get the work done and be successful.

>> Want a comprehensive guide to data governance that can be read cover to cover or used to provide the answers you seek.

>> Know that this book doesn't provide information and details about specific technology vendors.

>> Understand that data governance is focused on people and their behaviors. You won't be learning how to write a database query.

>> Recognize that data governance is not the same as data management.

>> Appreciate that data governance can appear easier to implement than in reality. The tips and best practices in the book will help.

>> Acknowledge that some repetition is deliberate in order to reinforce important concepts and to describe them in different contexts.

>> Understand that data governance is evolving, so you're best to supplement these topics by exploring current best practices and research online.

>> Understand that you cannot implement data governance alone. It requires collaboration across the enterprise. Your colleagues may need to read the book too!

Icons Used in This Book

You'll see a few icons scattered around the book. These icons highlight bits of information that are of particular importance to you.

TIP

The Tip icon shares an insight or lesson that I've learned the hard way — so you don't need to — or it's been gleaned from extensive research and suggests a good way to approach an issue.

REMEMBER

The Remember icon highlights information that's especially important to know. This is key information that you'll want to reference later.

WARNING

The Warning icon tells you to watch out! It highlights information that may save you headaches. Don't skip over these.

Beyond the Book

You can complement everything in this book with additional research online, including some excellent written and video content. You might also enjoy watching my "Learning Data Governance" video series on LinkedIn Learning. It's an hour and a half and is a light summary of some of the key areas in this book. You can also check out this book's online cheat sheet by searching for **Data Governance for Dummies Cheat Sheet** at dummies.com.

Where to Go from Here

You don't need to read this book from cover to cover. You can, if that strategy appeals to you, but it's set up as a reference guide, so you can jump in wherever you need to. Looking for something in particular? Take a peek at the table of contents or index, find the section you need, and then flip to the page to get your answer.

1
Data Everywhere

Chapter **1**

Defining Data Governance

Today, the topic of data governance suffers from a public relations problem. In the pages ahead, I explain how data governance is one of the most valuable programs that an organization can implement right now. The trouble is that many business leaders have an entirely different perception, assuming they even know what data governance is.

Although the momentum toward adoption is picking up pace, far too many organizations don't understand what data governance is. Many executives admit it's not showing up on their list of top priorities. They perceive data governance to be bureaucratic, complex, expensive, and largely discretionary.

Leaders soon change their views when they understand that data governance, done right, can help unleash the remarkable power of data, drive business growth, and enable successful digital transformations, all while reducing significant business risk.

What's not to like?

Solving this public relations problem begins with growing the number of people — in every role and level — who understand what data governance is and the value it brings to all organizations. That's why, in this chapter, I'm starting at the beginning, by defining governance and explaining what it means relative to the growing volume and complexity of data that confronts every business.

This book is dedicated to changing perceptions and helping more organizations succeed. When data governance is fully understood, your organization can enjoy its powerful results. Managing data well is a big deal and it must be a priority for every business leader.

In the second half of this chapter, I delve into the importance of determining whether your data culture — the level of commitment to data-driven decisions and actions — is ready for data governance.

Understanding Data Governance

The topic of data governance seems abstract to far too many people without a full appreciation of its definition, role, and value. You may have experienced puzzled looks from friends, family, and colleagues when you told them that your work involves data governance. They want to be happy for you, so they smile and congratulate you, but there's a reasonable chance they don't know what you're talking about.

I want to help fix that.

If you're going to communicate the importance of data governance to your organization so you can, for example, build a business case and get approval to design and deploy a program, you need to explain the topic clearly. Your senior leaders will appreciate it. So will your colleagues. I start by answering the most fundamental question.

What is meant by governance?

When first presented with the phrase *data governance*, most people immediately understand the data part, but can be quickly confused by the use and context of the word "governance."

Governance is not a word that most of us use on a regular basis. Sure, you create data. You use data. You store data. These concepts make sense. But governing data? That's not something that comes up too often. It sounds abstract, a little exotic, and frankly, complicated.

Fortunately, it's not nearly as complex as it appears. Understanding what it means right now, in the context of data, will put you at ease as you immerse yourself in the world of data governance.

Governance is the manner in which an entity chooses to oversee the control and direction of an area of interest. It typically takes the form of how decisions are made, regulated, and enforced. When entities grow and increase in complexity, formal governance becomes important. Left ungoverned, the possibility of devolving into chaos is all too probable. I'm reminded of what used to happen when the teacher briefly left the classroom in my elementary school. Anarchy!

Governance is a relatively straight-forward concept, but in so many contexts, it's extremely important and impactful.

REMEMBER

To some degree, everything in life is governed. It's just a question of its degree of formality. Parents may have a loose set of rules that govern how they raise their children, whereas our national government has a more rigorous governance system to enable, support, and enforce our democracy and its laws.

The formality and structure that governance takes depends on context and intent. For example, given their goals as organizations, governance in a public agency such as a city will differ greatly from that of a private enterprise. Each of these entities has different purposes and responsibilities.

REMEMBER

Governance is the system that formalizes control, processes, and accountabilities, so that specific results such as meeting goals or sustaining standards can be attained.

The many domains that have adopted the term *governance* apply it relative to intent. Project governance, for example, is focused on a process for how project decisions are made and how communications are managed between stakeholders. Another area, land governance, concerns itself with issues relative to land ownership and the rules under which decisions are made around land use and control.

This book is concerned with exploring techniques and approaches for deriving as much value from your data as possible while also managing any associated risks. The priority of data value and risk management has escalated in recent years, as data continues to grow rapidly and flow with velocity into the organization from a large number of sources. Today, the average data volume in an organization is growing at over 30 percent a year, and many are growing at an even faster rate.

These factors create urgency for many organizations to build a formal system for data control and oversight, and that includes structured processes and accountabilities.

Organizations want to reap the benefits of data abundance while managing its growing risks. In other words, organizations are now demanding data governance.

What is data governance?

To be effective at their jobs, staff want to find the data they need quickly, and they want it to be high-quality data. This means the data needs to be accurate and current. Leaders want data to provide the basis for rich insights that enable timely and informed data-driven decision-making. The legal department requires data to be handled by everyone in a manner consistent with laws and regulations. Product designers want data to inform creative decisions that align with marketplace demands and customer trends. Security professionals are tasked with ensuring that the data is appropriately protected.

Undoubtedly, a wide range of stakeholders want to harness the remarkable power of data.

To achieve these and other increasingly common business demands, you need some form of data control and accountability in your enterprise. Quality results require the diligent management of your organization's data.

Data governance is all about managing data well.

Today, when data is managed well, it can drive innovation and growth and can be an enterprise's most abundant and important lever for success.

Well managed data can be transformational, and it can support the desirable qualities of a data-driven culture. This is when decisions at all levels of the organization are made using data in an informed and structured manner such that they deliver better outcomes internally and to customers. Research confirms that most business leaders today want their organizations to be data-driven, but, according to a survey by NewVantage Partners, only around 32 percent are achieving that goal.

Successful data governance also means that data risks can be minimized, and data compliance and regulatory requirements can be met with ease. This can bring important comfort to business leaders who, in some jurisdictions, can now be personally liable for issues arising from poor data management.

Every organization manages data at some level. All businesses generate, process, use, and store data as a result of their daily operations. But there's a huge difference between businesses that casually manage data and those that consider data to be a valuable asset and treat it accordingly. This difference is characterized by the degree in which there are formalities in managing data.

Broadly, the discipline in which an organization acts in recognition of the value of its *information assets* (a fancy term for data with specific value to an organization, such as a customer or product record) is called *enterprise information management* (EIM). Governing and managing data well is a central enabler of EIM, which also includes using technologies and processes to elevate data to be a shared enterprise asset.

Data governance versus data management

Within the EIM space there are many terms that sound like they might mean the same thing. There is often confusion about the difference between data governance and data management. Data governance is focused on roles and responsibilities, policies, definitions, metrics, and the lifecycle of data. Data management is the technical implementation of data governance. For example, databases, data warehouses and lakes, application programming interfaces (APIs), analytics software, encryption, data crunching, and architectural design and implementation are all data management features and functions.

Data governance versus information governance

Similarly, in EIM, you may want clarity on the difference between data governance and information governance. Data governance generally focuses on data, independent of its meaning. For example, you may want to govern the security of patient data and staff data from a policy and process perspective, despite their differences. The interest here is on the data, not as much on the business context. Information governance is entirely concerned with the meaning of the data and its relationship in terms of outcomes and value to the organization, customers, and other stakeholders.

You might experience obvious overlap between the two terms. For sure, as a data governance practitioner, to some extent you'll be operating in both the data and information governance worlds each day. This shouldn't present an issue as long as the strategy for data governance is well understood. My view is that understanding the context of data, a concept known as *data intelligence,* and the desired business outcomes, complement data governance efforts in a valuable manner.

The value of data governance

If an organization considers data to be a priority — and an increasing number of businesses believe just that (in fact, according to Anmut, a data consultancy,

91 percent of business leaders say that data is a critical part of their organization's success) — and it puts in place processes and policies to leverage the data's value and reduce data risks, that organization is demonstrating a strong commitment to data controls and accountabilities. In other words, that organization values data governance.

REMEMBER

Fundamentally, data governance is driven by a desire to increase the value of data and reduce the risks associated with it. It forces a leap from an ad hoc approach to data to one that is strategic in nature.

Some of the main advantages achieved by good data governance include:

>> Improved data quality

>> Expanded data value

>> Increased data compliance

>> Improved data-driven decision-making

>> Enhanced business performance

>> Greater sharing and use of data across the enterprise and externally

>> Increased data availability and accessibility

>> Improved data search

>> Reduced risks from data-related issues

>> Reduced data management costs

>> Established rules for handling data

TIP

Any one of these alone is desirable, but a well-executed and maintained data governance program will deliver many of these and more.

In the absence of formalized data governance, organizations will continue to struggle in achieving these advantages and may, in fact, suffer negative consequences. For example, poor quality data that is not current, inaccurate, and incomplete can lead to operating inefficiencies and poor decision-making.

WARNING

Data governance does not emerge by chance. It's a choice and requires organizational commitment and investment.

Creating a data governance program

The basic steps for creating a data governance program consist of the following (these steps also form the basic outline of this book):

1. Defining the vision, goals, and benefits
2. Analyzing the current state of data governance and management
3. Developing a proposal based on the first two steps, including a draft plan
4. Achieving leadership approval
5. Designing and developing the program
6. Implementing the program
7. Monitoring and measuring performance
8. Maintaining the program

Depending on the level of sophistication and the nature of the business, the design and implementation of a data governance program can vary greatly. Unfortunately, there's no one-size-fits-all approach. One business may implement data governance with an emphasis on realizing greater revenue growth, while another may be more concerned with the regulatory requirements of their industry. Each organization will approach data governance in a manner that best reflects their desired outcomes.

As a discipline that has matured over a number of years, data governance is achieved through a set of common elements. Figure 1-1 illustrates many of the most common areas. You can think of these as a good representation of data governance scope. Right now, several of the terms in the illustration may not be familiar to you. Don't worry, because this book explores each one of these and suggests approaches that may work for you.

In summary, data governance is about managing data well and helping to deliver its optimum value to your organization. It includes ensuring your data is available, usable, and secure. It's the actions that team members take, the policies and processes they must follow, and the use of technologies that support them throughout the data lifecycle in their organization.

It's safe to say that for a growing number of organizations, data governance is becoming a very big deal.

(c) John Wiley & Sons

FIGURE 1-1:
The most
common
elements of a
data governance
program.

Developing a Data Governance Framework

You can't buy a data governance program off-the-shelf. That's actually good news. Organizations must implement a program relative to its level of interest, as well as its needs, budget, and capabilities. Even a modest effort can produce meaningful results. Glancing at all the areas in Figure 1-1 may seem overwhelming, but not all these elements need to be addressed (certainly not at first), and there are different degrees in which each can be pursued. As you read and learn about them in this book, you can decide what makes most sense for your organization.

Regardless of how and to what degree you implement the elements of a data governance program, you'll need a basic set of guiding concepts and a structure in which to apply them. This is called the data governance framework.

REMEMBER

While there are many framework variations to choose from, including ISACA's Control Objectives for Information and Related Technologies (COBIT) IT governance framework, they share some common components that address people, process, and technology.

I've done the hard work of distilling down the most important qualities of a data governance framework and captured them in Figure 1-2. In addition, these components are explored in detail throughout this book. You'll learn everything you need to know about how to implement a basic data governance framework. This is a foundation that will serve you and your organization well and enable you build upon it over time.

Leadership and Strategy

• Ensuring senior leadership support and aligning data governance efforts with the vision, mission, and strategy of the organization.

Roles and Responsibilities

• Identifying and empowering the right team members with responsibilities for the data governance program and others with accountability for data.

Policies, Processes, and Standards

• Developing and enforcing the policies, processes, and standards for governing and managing data.

Metrics

• Measuring and reporting on the performance of the data governance program and the broader outcomes of data management activities.

Tools

• Deploying and utilizing a range of software-based tools to support data governance and management.

Communication and Collaboration

• Adopting specific methods for high-performance communications and collaboration in support of data governance and management.

FIGURE 1-2: Common components of a data governance framework.

© John Wiley & Sons

The data governance framework in Figure 1-2 is not in a specific order, with the exception of leadership and strategy, which is a prerequisite for the rest of the framework.

Leadership and strategy

Your data governance program must be aligned with the strategy of the organization. For example, how can data governance support the role that data plays in enabling growth in specific markets? Data plays a role in many aspects of organizational strategy, including risk management, innovation, and operational efficiencies, so you must ensure there's a clear alignment between these aspects and the goals of data governance.

The disconnect between business goals and data governance is the number one reason that data governance programs fail. When mapping organizational strategy to data governance, you need the support, agreement, and sponsorship of senior leadership. I'll be blunt about this: Without full support from your organization's leaders, your data governance efforts won't succeed.

Roles and responsibilities

Your data governance program will only be possible with the right people doing the right things at the right time. Every data governance framework includes the identification and assignment of specific roles and responsibilities, which range from the information technology (IT) team to data stewards.

While specific roles do exist, your organization must understand that data governance requires responsibilities from nearly everyone.

Policies, processes, and standards

At the heart of every data governance program are the policies, processes, and standards that guide responsibilities and support uniformity across the organization. Each of these must be designed, developed, and deployed. Depending on the size and complexity of the organization, this can take significant effort.

Policies, processes, and standards must include accountability and enforcement components; otherwise it's possible they will be dead on arrival.

Metrics

The data governance program must have a mechanism to measure whether it is delivering the expected results. Capturing metrics and delivering them to a variety of stakeholders is important for maintaining support, which includes funding. You'll want to know if your efforts are delivering on the promise of the program. Based on the metrics, you and your team can make continuous improvements (or make radical changes) to ensure that the program is producing value.

Tools

Fortunately, a large marketplace now exists for tools in support of data governance and management. These include tools for master data management, data catalogs, search, security, integration, analytics, and compliance. In recent years, many data science-related tools have made leaps in terms of incorporating ease-of-use and automation. What used to be complex has been democratized and empowered more team members to better manage and derive value from data.

Communications and collaboration

With the introduction of data governance and the ongoing, sometimes evolving, requirements, high-quality communications are key. This takes many forms, including in-person meetings, emails, newsletters, and workshops. Change management, in particular, requires careful attention to ensure that impacted team members understand how the changes brought about by the data governance program affect them and their obligations.

REMEMBER

A large number of disparate stakeholders need to work together in order to effectively govern data. Collaboration is essential and can be the difference between success and failure. Good collaboration requires a positive culture that rewards teamwork. It also requires clear channels between teams, such as regular meetings. Online collaboration platforms are increasingly being used too.

Preparing for Data Governance

It might seem a good idea just to form a team, create a plan, buy some tools, and then implement data governance. That would be a mistake. Data governance requires careful treatment, beginning with understanding whether an organization is ready to accept it. As the following sections make clear, there are some traps that you can avoid if you and your team are diligent.

Being ready as an organization involves determining the extent to which a data culture exists. Intuitively you can conclude that an immature, reactive data culture, where data is simply handled in an ad hoc manner, is an entirely different experience than a sophisticated data-driven culture.

There are other prerequisites for data governance success. These include ensuring that the organization's strategy is fully aligned with the proposed program. As mentioned, any misalignment here is the number one reason data governance program deployments fail.

At the end of the chapter, I provide a basic checklist that will help you evaluate your organization's overall readiness for a data governance program.

What is data culture?

In my over 30 years as a business and technology leader, I've had the chance to observe at close range hundreds of projects and initiatives, some that have succeeded and some that have failed. I've been deeply interested in why so many efforts miss the mark. After all, most teams work thoughtfully and diligently to deliver a quality result. Of course, much has been researched and written about this topic, but there's one area in particular that's worth exploring relative to your mission to design and deploy a successful data governance program.

I've seen well-designed projects and initiatives fall flat and fail even though their teams seem to have done everything right. Too often, the work gets deployed into an environment that is either not ready for change or doesn't have the optimum conditions for success. A study by IDC noted that organizations are spending trillions of dollars on technological upgrades — digitally transforming their businesses — and 70 percent are failing because they don't have the prerequisite data culture to support these efforts.

Yes, data culture. In a boxing match, culture defeats strategy almost every time.

Imagine for a moment designing and deploying a data governance program for an organization that has little or no data culture. Intuitively this sounds like a disaster in the making. To be fair, every organization has some form of a data culture; it just might not be pretty.

Assessing the data culture

If you want to increase your chances of success — and I think you do — you need to understand the data culture of your organization and determine how to broaden and mature it if necessary. You need an environment for success.

REMEMBER

On a basic level, data culture is how your organization values data and how it manages and uses it. There's a wide chasm between companies that simply manage data as a consequence of doing business versus those that consider data central to how their organization operates and makes decisions (the latter being the qualities exhibited by a mature data culture).

Effective data cultures support and empower all employees, from the newest intern to the CEO, to access and use meaningful and timely data for their work. Such cultures ensure that employees have attained the skills they need to use data analytics and can make good data-driven decisions. It's not an overstatement to say that these types of organizations are often defined by their enlightened and competitive use of data.

In a data culture, decisions don't rely on gut feelings, guesses, or the opinion of the highest paid person in the room (admit it, this is all too common, right?). Rather, decisions are based on data and the insights they can produce.

It's been said that data culture is decision culture.

In Chapter 2, I go to great lengths to describe why data is an organization's most valuable asset today. In a world undergoing rapid digital transformation, data is the metaphorical oil that is powering and enabling it all. To be competitive, a progressive data-driven strategy is no longer optional. It's a central concern. Data culture can be now considered a new way of doing business in the digital age.

Leaders in all types of organizations are recognizing that to succeed in the third decade of the 21st century and beyond, they must leverage the enormous power and value of data. This acknowledgement, and the actions that senior leaders take to foster the use of data, is the primary success factor in the development and maturity of an effective data culture.

Trust comes in a close second. This means that team members will only make data-driven decisions if they trust the data they're using. Trust is built when data is high-quality, its origin and value is understood, and team members know how it can contribute to the goals of the business.

To start, you need to assess the maturity of your organization's data culture. You and your team can interview leaders and team members. You can also observe how people make decisions, how decisions are communicated, and the degree to which data is currently governed and managed. It won't be just one thing that provides a score for your data culture, but a mix of inputs. If the conclusion is that your data culture is sufficient for the introduction of a data governance program, you're in good shape.

What you shouldn't lose sight of here is that implementing data governance will be a positive and important contributing factor to building a data culture.

Maturing the data culture

If you decide that you need to better prepare the organization for data governance by maturing the data culture, consider these items to start (good news! many of these items are covered in detail in this book):

>> Help leaders communicate the value of data and model the type of behavior that demonstrates that data is a priority. This must include communicating the positive results of using data.

>> Provide basic tools and education for data use that includes manipulating data, analytics, data cleansing, basic query commands, and visualization. Don't overlook the remarkable capabilities of common applications such as spreadsheets.

>> Do something, even if it's small, to show progress. A successful data culture doesn't begin with the deployment of complex, far-reaching solutions. Rather, it can be eased into the organization via basic data-management skills offered in a classroom setting or online.

>> Recognize that resistance and frustration is part of the journey. Rather than fighting it, find ways to bring comfort and rewards to team members. At a minimum, provide a channel for feedback and positive discussion.

Assessing data governance readiness

So, you've either determined your organization has a good data culture, or you've put into action some steps to help move it forward, and now you've decided it's time to roll up your sleeves and begin designing a data governance program. Right?

Wait. Not so fast. There are a few other items you should consider in order to determine if your organization is ready for a data governance program. If the right conditions don't exist, you may be walking into a minefield, only one step away from disaster.

WARNING

Unfortunately, the success rate of data governance programs on the first try remains low. That's me being nice. It's important to maximize the conditions for success. You may not even get a second chance.

This book walks you through all the steps for designing and creating a data governance program, but you also have to consider the readiness of your organization prior to beginning the journey.

The following basic checklist of items will help you determine the data governance readiness of your organization:

☐ The basis of a data culture exists.

☐ The program is 100 percent aligned with business strategy.

☐ Senior leadership is 100 percent committed to the program and its goals.

☐ Senior leadership understands this is a strategic, enterprise program and not the sole responsibility of the IT department.

- ❑ One or more sponsors have been identified at an executive level.
- ❑ The program has a commitment to fund its creation and to maintain it in the long term.
- ❑ The organization understands this is an ongoing program and not a one-off project.
- ❑ You have documented the return-on-investment (ROI).
- ❑ Legal and compliance teams (internally or externally) understand and support the goals of the program.
- ❑ Fundamental data skills exist for the data governance journey.
- ❑ The IT organization is capable and resourced to support the program.

Of course, this list is not exhaustive and there may be other items you consider relevant to your organization.

TIP

As you read through this book and begin planning your data governance program, return to this list often and assess the status of each item.

Chapter **2**

Exploring a World Awash in Data

'’ve had the fortunate opportunity to work in private industry, government, and academia. Regardless of the sector, I observed that almost all actions were taken in the context of constraints. There are always limitations around budget, skills, time, and more. Of course, that's no big revelation. Scarcity is the central basis of economics. How resources are used and allocated is of great concern to everyone and largely drives societal behavior.

My observation about constraints was elevated — and to me particularly noteworthy — because it contrasted so greatly with the abundance of data that was available. Each organization had resource limitations that dictated the terms of their decision-making and actions, but also had such quantity of data, that abundance, rather than constraints, was a source of concern.

Recognizing the issue of data abundance, many questions arose in these organizations, such as could they take advantage of it? Could they protect it? Could they simply manage it?

Today, most organizations exist in an environment awash in data. The volume of data amassing may be the result of their day-to-day activities, their products and services, the data they have access to, or the data created and delivered by their customers and partners. Whatever the reason and source, this is the age of big data.

Governed and managed correctly, data has the potential to improve an organization's operations and performance and increase profits and market share. To fully understand the potential of data abundance and learn how you can leverage its value, you need to understand what data is and how it fits into the larger business landscape.

Defining Data

You and I create and use data all the time. We usually take it for granted. It's part of our daily personal and business vernacular. Like so many things, if I were to ask you to define data, you'd give me your definition and it may not be the same as mine. In fact, it may not even be entirely accurate. It's not so much a criticism as a statement of how much we take data for granted, and perhaps don't stop and pause to ensure each of us is on the same page.

WARNING

For example, your colleague may ask you to gather *data* on a topic. Seems straightforward. But might they actually be asking you to gather *information* instead? They're different things. If you gather data and then produce it for them, they're going to be disappointed when their expectation was information.

We have to be on the same page. Data has a specific meaning and it's really important to be clear on the definition, particularly as we start talking about information, knowledge, and insights. But it's even more important as we consider data in the context of governance and management. After all, as I will soon make clear, data governance is not the same as data management.

TIP

A solid definition of data and its role today gets us on the same page and sets the stage for delivering on the promise of data governance.

What's all the fuss about data?

Data refers to collections of digitally stored units, in other words, stuff that is kept on a computing device. These units represent something meaningful when processed for a human or a computer. Single units of data are traditionally referred to as *datum* and multiple units as *data*. However, the term data is often used in singular and plural contexts and, in this book, I'm going to simply refer to both as data. I'm happy to get that out of the way.

Prior to processing, data doesn't need to make sense individually or even in combination with other data. For example, data could be the word *orange* or the number 42. In the abstract and most basic form, something we call raw data, we can agree that these are both meaningless.

Data is also defined based on its captured format. Specifically, at a high level, it falls into one of the following categories:

>> **Structured:** Data that has been formatted to a set structure; each data unit fits nicely into a table in a database. It's ready for analysis. Examples include first name, last name, and phone number.

>> **Unstructured:** Data that's stored in a native format that must be processed to be used. Further work is required to enable analysis. Examples include email content and social media posts.

>> **Semi-structured:** Data that contains additional information to enable the native format to be searched and analyzed.

REMEMBER

Units of data are largely worthless until they are processed and applied. It's only then that data begins a journey that, when coupled with good governance, can be very useful. The value that data can bring to so many functions, from product development to sales, makes it an important asset.

To begin to have value, data requires effort, a theme I will keep returning to throughout this book. If we place the word *orange* in a sentence, such as "An orange is a delicious fruit," suddenly the data has meaning. Similarly, if we say, "The t-shirt I purchased cost me $42," then the number 42 now has meaning. What we did here was process the data by means of structure and context to give it value. Put another way, we converted the data into information.

This basic action of data processing cannot be overstated, as it represents the core foundation of an industry that has ushered in our current period of rapid digital transformation. Today, the term *data processing* has been replaced with *information technology* (IT).

Figure 2-1 illustrates how you can think of data units at a basic level.

Welcome to the zettabyte era

I have an admission. Until just a few years ago, I didn't know what a zettabyte was. My excuse? I didn't have to know what a zettabyte was. Few people did. There was little to no use for the term by the general population.

But then something changed. As we entered the 21st century and the volume of data being created and stored grew rapidly, we needed to break this term out from the vault. A hyperconnected world accelerating in its adoption and use of digital tools has required dusting off a seldom used metric to capture the enormity of data output we were producing.

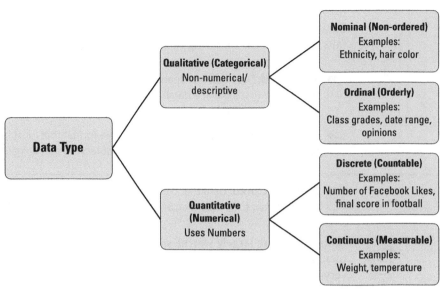

FIGURE 2-1:
The qualitative
and quantitative
nature of
data types.

Today, we live in the zettabyte era. A zettabyte is a big number. A really big number. It's 10^{21}, or a 1 with 21 zeros after it. It looks like this: 1,000,000,000,000,000,000,000 bytes.

By 2020, we had created 44 zettabytes of data. That number continues to grow rapidly. This *datasphere* — the term used to describe all the data created — is projected to reach 100 zettabytes by 2023 and may double in 3-4 years. If you own a terabyte drive at home or at work, you'd need one billion of those drives to store just one zettabyte of data. You read that right.

Here's a simplified technical explanation of what a zettabyte is. Consider that each byte is made up of eight bits. A bit is either a 1 or 0 and represents the most basic unit of how data is stored on a computing device. Since a bit has only two states, a 1 or 0, we call it *binary*. Some time ago, computer engineers decided that 8 bits (or 1 byte) was enough to represent characters that we, as mere mortals, could understand. For example, the letter A in binary is 01000001.

It was a mutually beneficial decision. We understand the A; the computer understands the 01000001. A full word such as "hello" converted to binary reads: 01001000 01100101 01101100 01101100 01101111. Stick around with me long enough and I'll have you speaking in bits.

With more data being produced in the years ahead, we'll soon begin adopting other words to describe even bigger volumes. Get ready for the yottabyte and brontobyte eras!

From a more practical perspective, in this book I'll occasionally refer to the size of data. Knowledge of data volume will be useful. Table 2-1 puts bits and bytes into context.

TABLE 2-1

Quantification of Data Storage

8 bits	1 byte
1024 bytes	1 kilobyte
1024 kilobytes	1 megabyte
1024 megabytes	1 gigabyte
1024 gigabytes	1 terabyte
1024 terabytes	1 petabyte
1024 petabytes	1 exabyte
1024 exabytes	1 zettabyte
1024 zettabytes	1 yottabyte
1024 yottabytes	1 brontobyte

REMEMBER

Understanding that we are in an era of vastly expanding data volume, often at the disposal of organizations, elevates the notion that managing this data well is complex and valuable.

Managing a small amount of data can have challenges, but managing data at scale is materially more challenging. If you're going to glean value from data, it has to be understood and managed in specific ways.

From data to insight

Creating, collecting, and storing data is a waste of time and money if it's being done without a clear purpose or an intent to use it in the future. I don't rule out the logic of collecting data even when we don't have a reason because it may have value at some point in the future, but this is the exception. Generally, an organization is on-boarding data because it's required.

WARNING

Data that is never used is about as useful as producing reports that nobody reads. The assumption is that you have data for a reason. You have your data and it's incredibly important to your organization, but it must be converted to information to have meaning.

Information is data in context. I explore more of the differences between data and information in Table 2-2.

TABLE 2-2

The Differences Between Data and Information

Data	Information
Raw	Processed
Items such as characters, words, pictures, and numbers that have no meaning in isolation	Data that is organized and given context to have meaning
No analysis dependency	Dependent on the analysis of data
Unorganized and not dependent on context	Organized and dependent on context
Not typically useful alone	Useful alone

When we apply information coupled with broader contextual concepts, practical application, and experience, it becomes knowledge. Knowledge is actionable. Dare I say it, knowledge is power.

It doesn't end there. When we take new knowledge and apply reasoning, values, and the broader universe of our knowledge and deep experiences, we get wisdom. With wisdom, we know what to do with knowledge and can determine its contextual validity.

We could have stopped at knowledge, but wisdom takes us to the ultimate destination derived from data. All wisdom includes knowledge, but not all knowledge is wisdom. Dummies books can be deep too.

Finally, insight is an outcome that can emerge from knowledge but is best demonstrated through a combination of knowledge and wisdom. With insight, we've gained a deeper understanding of something and have the skills to think or see it differently.

To summarize, consider the following:

>> John Lennon is *data*.

>> The fact that John Lennon is in the group, The Beatles, is *information*.

>> The fact that The Beatles are looking for a record deal is *knowledge*.

>> The fact that The Beatles are very talented and popular and should get a record deal is *wisdom*.

>> Avoiding the decision-making processes of Decca Records is *insight*.

(I'm a Beatles fan. That's information.) Figure 2-2 illustrates the journey from data to insight.

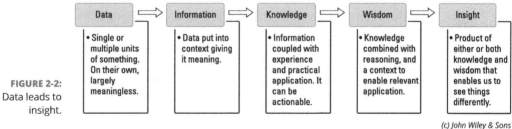

Data	Information	Knowledge	Wisdom	Insight
• Single or multiple units of something. On their own, largely meaningless.	• Data put into context giving it meaning.	• Information coupled with experience and practical application. It can be actionable.	• Knowledge combined with reasoning, and a context to enable relevant application.	• Product of either or both knowledge and wisdom that enables us to see things differently.

FIGURE 2-2: Data leads to insight.

(c) John Wiley & Sons

REMEMBER

It's no surprise then that data has enormous value when considering it through the lens of delivering wisdom. However, this journey from data to wisdom is full of challenges. These are significant issues that organizations struggle with every day. For example, it's not a stretch to imagine what the outcome of using bad data could be. Transforming good data into valuable information and beyond is no simple task. It requires tools, skills, and processes.

Every day, different organizations with access to the same data have different outcomes. While the best outcome can't be guaranteed no matter which processes, tools, or skills are used, good practices such as the right level of data governance can absolutely lead to better results.

The Role of Data in the 21st Century

Since the early days of data processing in the 19th and 20th centuries right through to digital transformation in the 21st century, data has played many important roles. It's helped us understand the world in completely new ways, improved our ability to make better informed decisions, and supported our efforts to solve all manner of problems. In this way, it's fair to say that data has always been important.

Something is quite clear though. The value data has been adding over the course of many decades has not remained flat. On the contrary, since the mid-20th century, as more computer systems came online, the role of data has grown. It's not just that the quantity of data began to increase rapidly, but it was also the quality of the data and the availability of it to so many people. In particular, the arrival of the Internet in the mid-1990s resulted in the reality of the Information Industry Association's 1970's motto, "Putting information at your fingertips."

In the late 1980s, Bill Gates, co-founder and former CEO of Microsoft, would later build on this and champion the idea that eventually, "any piece of information you want should be available to you." Prophetic, indeed.

REMEMBER

In these early decades of the 21st century, we are producing more data than we can handle, and the depth, breadth, and quality of the data that is being used is reshaping not just the tools and capabilities of our industries and cities, but the nature of how we learn, socialize, and entertain ourselves. It's also elevating risks that we may previously have characterized as annoyances to a world today where a cyberattack can result in millions of dollars of losses in hours.

There's an argument that data has become the most valuable asset in the world. If we believe that to be true, we truly have entered a new era for data.

Could data be the most important asset in your organization? Since you're reading this book, you're either contemplating the answer or you already have the answer.

Data-driven decision-making

Perhaps one of the greatest values of data is its ability to help us all make better decisions. You know intuitively that reading the customer reviews of a restaurant on a website such as Yelp! can help you decide whether you want to eat there. It's valuable to you, but it's also valuable to the restaurant owner. Those reviews can make a big difference, including being a motivation for action. Perhaps the bathrooms should be cleaner.

Deciding on a restaurant based on reviews is an example of data-driven decision-making, but it's also on the less complex end of the decision-making spectrum.

Deciding to enter a new market with an existing product or service requires a deep understanding that can come from rich sets of data. If the data exists and you have the tools to process and interpret it, you may be well positioned to make the right decision. It may also be easier to decide because you're able to get the answers to your concerns. Conversely, without good data and the skills and tools to analyze it, a bad and costly decision may result. This happens far too often.

WARNING

The availability of abundant good quality data has been a boon for decision-making. You should note that I said *good quality data*. Consider this; if you make a decision based on bad data, your challenges will be entirely different. Abundant data is a product of the 21st century, but quality data is the product of deliberate actions. Turns out, data governance plays a central role when aspiring for data quality.

Data as the new oil

A popular refrain coined by the mathematician Clive Humby in 2006 is that data is the new oil. Just as oil drove and grew economies in the past, data is doing that now. Some have subsequently added that just like oil, data has value but must first be processed to be useful. Specifically, oil is refined to make gas, plastics, and other useful chemicals. In a similar fashion, data must be organized and analyzed to understand patterns, make decisions, identify problems, and feed other systems.

Without these additional steps of organizing and analyzing, oil and data are similar in that they are notably messy and unusable in their raw form.

As oil powered the industrial economies of the 19th and 20th centuries, data is powering the digital economies of the 21st century. The big economic powerhouses are being powered by data, such as the technology firms Facebook and Google. While they dominate, every other industry from banking to government and beyond is being reinvented by digitalization and data. Many are moving data management from a cost center to a profit center by making data power their businesses and generate new sources of revenue.

Like oil, those who control large repositories of high-value data have disproportionate power. The challenges and results of our dependency on oil through the 20th century are well known. There are lessons here that should inform us and warn about the risks of personal data being managed by just a few big market players.

Data ownership

For something to be properly managed, someone needs to be responsible. We create accountability in job descriptions and projects. Without that, how will we know that something will get done? If this strikes you as self-explanatory — and it should — the idea that there should be accountability for every data set in an organization should also not come as a surprise.

Data ownership describes the rights a person, team, or organization has over one or more data sets. These rights may span from lightweight oversight and control to rigorous rules that are legally enforceable. For example, data associated with intellectual property — items such as copyrights and trade secrets — will likely have high degrees of protection, from accessibility rights to who can use the data and for what purpose.

Ensuring that the right organizational roles and responsibilities are applied to data to ensure that its value is leveraged and that the appropriate controls are in place is a central requirement of good data governance. Chapter 9 explores data ownership in detail.

Data architecture

Today, it's not an exaggeration to state that almost every organization is a technology business. After all, what business can function without having systems to support their operations and deliver their products and services? It's possible of course, but not practical. In the 21st century, digital beats analog every time.

When designing the technical needs of an organization to support their business strategy, this practice is known as enterprise architecture (EA). Using standards and established principles, organizations can analyze, design, plan, and implement the right technologies, policies, and projects to support business goals.

A subset of EA is data architecture. In the same manner in which you can consider the holistic nature of EA in support of the organization's strategy, data architecture is the manner in which data design and management decisions are being made to align with EA and in turn, with the business. Simply stated, data architecture is the agreed blueprint about how data supports an organization's functions and technologies.

When high-quality enterprises and data architectures both exist, organizations run more smoothly, and they can transform as conditions (either internally or in the marketplace) dictate. The absence or poor implementation of both can stifle digital transformation efforts, create high levels of complexity, and increase the possibility of failure.

At a minimum, data architecture considers and typically supports the following:

>> Ensuring data is available to those who need it and are approved to use it

>> Reducing the complexity of accessing and utilizing data

>> Creating and enforcing data protections to support organizational policies and obligations

>> Adopting and agreeing to data standards

>> Optimizing the flow and efficient use of data to eliminate bottlenecks and duplication

Data architecture is a direct reflection of data governance. An established and functioning data architecture immediately signals that an organization values data, manages it as a critical business asset, and has controls in place to ensure that it aligns with business needs. Indeed, like EA, data architecture is not the exclusive realm of technologists but a cross-organizational responsibility. In most medium to large organizations, data must efficiently flow across business silos, such as sales and product development, and serve many different audiences in multiple forms.

Chapter 4 covers aspects of data architecture in support of data governance.

The lifecycle of data

All data goes through phases during its lifecycle. Figure 2-3 illustrates a typical lifecycle.

1. **Creation:** This is the stage at which data comes into being. It may be manual or automated and get created internally or externally. Data is being created all the time by a vast number of activities that include system inputs and outputs.

2. **Storage:** Once data is created and assuming you want it available for later use, it must be stored. It most likely will be contained and managed in a database. The database needs a home, too as a local hard drive, server, or cloud service.

3. **Usage**: Hopefully you're capturing and storing data because you want to use it. Maybe not immediately, but at some point, perhaps for analysis. Data may need to be processed to be useful. That could include cleansing it of errors, transforming it to another format, and securing access rights.

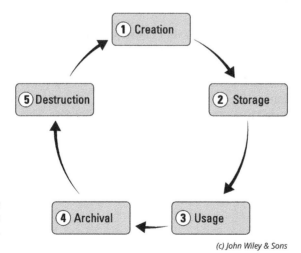

FIGURE 2-3:
The lifecycle of data.

(c) John Wiley & Sons

4. **Archival:** In this stage, you identify data that is not currently being used and move it to a long-term storage system out of your production environment. If it's needed at some point in the future, it can be retrieved and utilized.

5. **Destruction:** Despite a desire by some to keep everything forever, there is a logical point where destruction makes sense or is required by regulation or policy. Data destruction involves making data inaccessible and unreadable. It can include the physical destruction of a device such as a hard drive.

REMEMBER

The idea that data is in different states at different times is an essential context of data governance. Depending on the stage of its life, data may be treated differently and have unique requirements. For example, the security needs of data being regularly used will differ from data in an archival state.

Data quality matters

Perhaps one of the most important takeaways from this book is the relationship between data governance and data quality. It turns out that while quality is something we intuitively understand, it's remarkably hard to define. In the broadest sense, it's a form of judgment on the excellence of something. Data quality is certainly about excellence, but it does have a more defined meaning.

REMEMBER

Data quality is the degree to which data is fit for its purpose. A quick example of this would be whether records you've requested are kept up to date. Let's say you want your salespeople to call customers from a list. If that list is not current and a high percentage of the phone numbers are no longer functioning, that's what we call bad quality data.

I know, we've all been there.

Data quality is also concerned with data requirements such as timeliness, relevancy, correctness, and completeness.

To run a great organization well, to ensure it is set up for success, that it can ensure compliance with policies, regulations, and laws, that it manages risk, and that it is optimized to succeed, you need high-quality data. This kind of data takes attention and effort.

Chapter 7 explores data quality in more depth.

Understanding the Impact of Big Data

Data isn't some kind of new phenomenon. In fact, we've been capturing and storing data in an analog fashion for thousands of years. The Romans, for example, used ledgers to keep track of their various activities across their expansive empire.

Fast-forward to the 20th century and the Cold War was instrumental in the technological leaps that resulted in microprocessors and the classical computing we use today. One by-product of the Cold War, the space race between the United States and the Soviet Union, accelerated innovation in computing and telecommunications.

THE ROLE OF THE U.S. CENSUS IN THE INFORMATION REVOLUTION

Processing data on some form of computing device has been around since the late 1800s. In fact, the need for a mechanism to better tabulate the results of the U.S. constitutional requirement to conduct a population census every ten years is said to be the origin of data processing. Counting all the people and other data points in the 1880 census took almost eight years. It's assumed it was full of errors. It was also a boring, tedious process. Credit for the first company to automate and commercialize the processing of this data goes to the Tabulating Machine Company, founded in 1896.

To count census results, handwritten results were converted to punched holes in cards. For example, if a result for an individual was a "man," then this was represented by a punched hole. A rod would attempt to pass through the hole to make an electrical connection with a pad on the other side. With the electrical connection made, a counter would progress with an addition of one. These punch cards could be considered a form of data storage.

The Tabulating Machine Company was later renamed International Business Machines, IBM. The rest, as they say, is history.

Over the next few decades, IBM and its many data processing cohorts began to infiltrate more and more aspects of life. Most often in the desire to increase automation in the office, but also the military, academia, and factories.

These major developments and others culminated in what we now know as the *third industrial revolution*: the information age. Data quickly became the raw material feeding a new generation of productivity and ideas. Connectivity provided the arteries for information to freely flow across devices, organizations, and geographies with few limitations.

The result? Data creation, storage, and use exploded. By the turn of this century, we were creating data at unprecedented levels. Data volume and velocity had become so unwieldly that it was creating a *data swamp* — a term for out-of-control amounts of data — that made it difficult for traditional software applications to manage. Observing this notable phenomenon, someone smart came up with a term to describe the scale and challenge of all the data. They called it *big data*.

I agree, not exactly inspired. And probably the understatement of the century.

This isn't *big* data. This is *huge* data. Enormous. Gargantuan. Humongous. You get the idea.

Defining big data

REMEMBER

Big data is structured and unstructured data that is so massive and complex in scale, that it's difficult and often impossible to process via traditional data management techniques.

One way to define and characterize big data is through these five Vs:

>> **Volume:** The sheer scale of data being produced is unprecedented and requires new tools, skills, and processes.

>> **Variety:** There's already a lot of legacy file formats, such as CSV and MP3, and with new innovation, new formats are emerging all the time. This requires different methods of handling, from analysis to security.

>> **Velocity:** With so many collection points, digital interfaces, and ubiquitous connectivity, data is being created and moved at increasing speed. Consider that in 2021, Instagram users created, uploaded, and share 65,000 pictures a minute.

>> **Variability:** The fact that the creation and flow of data is unpredictable.

>> **Veracity:** The quality, including accuracy and truthfulness, of large volume of disparate sets of data can differ considerably, causing challenges to data management.

The drivers of big data

At a technology conference in 2003, I recall one particular quote attributed to then CEO of Google, Eric Schmidt. At the time he said that every two days the world was creating more data than all the data created since the dawn of civilization. A stunning and vivid statistic.

REMEMBER

Big data was a thing even before Android and Apple smartphones and apps started generating data. This was before we had connected billions of devices, called the Internet of Things (IoTs), which would eventually begin collecting all manner of data. Big data even predates videos of cats published every day on social media platforms.

By the third decade of the 21st century, with so many devices connected and the world in a state of digital transformation, the volume of data being created had experienced a *Cambrian explosion* — a term the data science community has adopted from an early period in history notable for the rapid introduction of life into the natural environment. We were regularly well into the zettabyte range of data and its hockey stick growth curve was continuing relentlessly (see Figure 2-4).

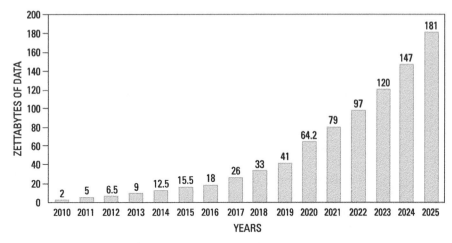

FIGURE 2-4:
Data growth in zettabytes from 2010 to 2025.

In 2021, global technology use generated 79 zettabytes of data, and it is anticipated to hit 180 zettabytes in 2025. A reader picking up this book in 2040 might read the previous sentence and smile at such small numbers, the same way I do when I recall thinking I'd hit the jackpot with a massive 100MB (megabyte) disk for my Iomega Zip drive back in 1995.

Consequences of big data

WARNING

While these big data statistics are impressive, they don't really paint the full picture. It might be easy, for example, to assume that all the data is good quality. You might believe it is easy to analyze. You may even think it is easily accessible. Most of these assumptions and many related ones will likely be incorrect. For starters, up to 80 percent of data is unstructured. That's a challenge right there. The vast majority of organizations struggle with unstructured data. In addition, a lot of this data is duplicative. Some of it will be bad data, which means it can't be trusted, has errors, or includes some other substantive challenge.

REMEMBER

I've called out just a few of the issues with big data, but the truth is that data at scale is providing incredible value to all types of organizations. It's also the source of remarkable innovation, from self-driving cars to optimized supply chains.

An over-used quote attributed to the 19th century U.S. retailer John Wanamaker stated that half his advertising budget was wasted but he just didn't know which half. In a time when advertising was mainly billboards and newspapers, it was nearly impossible to know which advertising resulted in a sale. Today, a combination of hyperconnectivity and data has upended this predicament. Marketeers using the latest technology can better understand the marketplace in granular detail. They can target specific audiences, and even specific individuals, where the chance of a sale is highest.

Big data is making this happen.

What about small data?

All this talk about big data might suggest that small amounts of data just aren't as interesting or valuable. I don't want to suggest that, as it would be wrong.

REMEMBER

While so many of our business activities in the digital economy are driven by big data, there's still a lot of small data sets that are instrumental in decision-making and day-to-day operations. Think about all the spreadsheets that come by your inbox, or the short surveys, or those go-to lists that we've all compiled and can't live without. It's not nearly as glamourous as big data, but in some cases, it may be arguably as valuable.

Big questions can be answered in small data.

In fact, big data is often more meaningful when broken into smaller, more manageable chunks — an increasingly popular definition of small data. Smaller, logically arranged data can be the way to make sense of big data. In some circumstances, it may be the only way.

Here comes smart data

Smart data has emerged as a new term that defines big data that's been optimally prepared for use to deliver the highest business value. Instead of being overwhelmed by the distractions inherent to the volume, velocity, and variety of data in big data sets, processes are applied to big data to prepare it for specific uses. For example, marketing teams can target potential customers with precision. Analytics applications can use high-quality real-time data generated in a manufacturing setting.

Smart data uses new processes and tools to make the data most useful. For example, the increasing use of artificial intelligence (AI) is now being applied to find patterns in unstructured big data and extract the data that is most relevant for a given application. Using new methods such as AI reduces time, lowers errors, and enables the creation of data subsets that may not have been previously possible. In addition, smart data solutions are often applied at the point of collection rather than a post-processing solution.

REMEMBER

In the 21st century we must recognize that all data can have value — big, small, and smart. Data governance is concerned with data no matter what form it takes.

Chapter **3**

Driving Value through Data

This chapter explores many of the ways that data is used in organizations. It's not a comprehensive survey, but it covers the most important areas. I also share the essential ways that data can be leveraged to bring value and better outcomes.

Identifying the Roles of Data

To fully appreciate the value that data brings to every organization, it's worth exploring the many ways that data shows up on a day-to-day basis. Recognizing the incredible diversity of data use and the exposure it has across all business functions reinforces its importance. It's critical to ensure that data is high quality, secure, compliant, and accessible to the right people at the right time.

Data isn't something that just concerns the data analytics team or the information technology department. It's also not something that is limited to decision-makers and leaders.

REMEMBER

Data matters to everyone.

Operations

Business operations concern themselves with a diverse set of activities to run the day-to-day needs and drive the mission of an organization. Each business has different needs, and operational functions reflect these specific requirements. Some core functions show up in almost every organization. Consider payroll, order management, and marketing. At the same time, some operational support won't be required. Not every organization needs its own IT organization, or if it's a service business, it may not have a warehouse.

REMEMBER

Operations run on and are powered by a variety of data and information sources. They also create a lot of both, too.

The performance of operations is often easily quantified by data. For example, in a human resources (HR) function, they'll want to know how many openings there are, how long openings are taking to fill, and who is accepting offers. There's a multitude of data points to quantify the answers to these so that relevant decisions can be made.

In HR, data is also created by the activities of the function. For example, candidates enter data when they apply for a position, data is entered when evaluating an applicant, and all along the way the supporting systems log a variety of automated data, such as time, date, and how long an application took to complete online.

In this HR example, and frankly, in any other operations teams explored, data is created in abundance as a result of and in support of functions.

Operations use data to make decisions, to enable systems to run, and to deliver data to internal and external entities. For example, a regional sales team will deliver their monthly results to headquarters to be presented to vice presidents or the C-suite.

Many data functions in support operations are automated. For example, a warehouse inventory system may automatically generate a replenishment order when stock drops to a certain level. Consider all the notifications that systems generate based on triggers. Who hasn't received an email notifying them that they haven't submitted their time and expense report?

REMEMBER

As you'll notice in almost all data scenarios, there are skilled people, dedicated processes, and various technologies partially or wholly focused on handling operational data.

Strategy

Every organization has a strategy, whether it's articulated overtly or not. At the organizational level, this is about creating a plan that supports objectives and goals. It's essentially about understanding the challenges to delivering on the organization's purpose and then agreeing on the proposed solutions to those challenges. Strategy can also be adopted at the department and division levels, but the intent is the same: understand the journey ahead and make a plan.

Strategy leads to implementation and requires the support of operations to realize its goals. In this way, strategy and operations are two sides of the same coin. Done right, a data-driven strategy delivered with operational excellence can be a winning ticket. (On a related note, Chapter 4 covers creating a data strategy.)

Creating a strategy typically comes down to a core set of activities. It begins with an analysis of the environment followed by some conclusions on what has been gathered. Finally, a plan is developed, driven by some form of guiding principles. These principles may be derived from the nature of the work, the values of the founders, or some other factors.

TIP

Deeply tied to all these steps is the availability of good quality data that can be processed and analyzed and then turned into actionable insights.

Certainly, data and information won't be the only mechanisms in which the plan will be constructed. There must be room for other perspectives, including the strength of belief that people with experience bring to the discussion. The right mix of data and non-data sources must be considered. Too much of one or the other may not deliver expected results.

REMEMBER

A best practice for strategy development is to consider it an ongoing process. This doesn't mean updating the strategy every month — that is a recipe for chaos — but it may mean revisiting the strategy every six months and tweaking it as necessary. Revisions to strategy should be guided by new data, which can mean new knowledge and new insights. While a regular process of strategy revisions is encouraged, new information that suddenly presents itself can trigger an impromptu update.

In the 21st century, organizations need to react quickly to environmental conditions to survive. Data will form the backbone of your response system.

Chapter 4 discusses the related role of creating and implementing a data strategy.

Decision-making

It's generally accepted in business that the highest form of value derived from data is the ability to make better informed decisions. The volume and quality of data available today has no precedent in history. Let's just say it as it is: we're spoiled.

Without even creating a single unit of raw data, there's a universe of existing data and information at our fingertips. In addition, increasing numbers of easy-to-use analysis capabilities and tools are democratizing access to insight.

Popular consumer search engines such as Google and Bing have transformed how we make decisions. Doctors, for example, now deal with patients who are more informed about their symptoms and their causes. It's a mixed blessing. Some of the information has reduced unnecessary clinic visits, but it's also created a headache for physicians when the information their patients have consumed is incorrect.

Within organizations, access to abundant data and information has resulted in quicker, more timely, and better-quality business decisions. For example, executives can understand their strengths, weaknesses, opportunities, and threats closer to realtime. For most, gone are the days of waiting until the end of the fiscal quarter to get the good or bad news. Even if the information is tentative in the interim, it's vastly better than being in the dark until it may be too late.

While there's little surprise that data-driven decision-making is a fundamental business competency, it all hinges on decision-makers getting access to quality data at the right time. Abundant and out-of-date data are not synonymous with data value. Bad data may be worse than no data. Bad data processed into information and then used as the basis for decisions will result in failure. The outcome of decisions based on bad data could range from a minor mistake to job termination right up to the closing of the business.

I'll revisit the theme of data-driven decision-making throughout this book.

Measuring

Organizations are in a continuous state of measurement, whether it's overt or tacit. Every observed unit of data contributes to building a picture of the business. The often-used adage, *what gets measured gets managed*, is generally applicable. That said, some things are hard to measure and not everything gets measured.

The aspiration for every leader is that they have the information they need when they need it. You might not always think of it this way, but that information is going to be derived from data that is a result of some form of measurement.

TIP

Data measurements can be quantitative or qualitative. Quantitative data is most often described in numerical terms, whereas qualitative data is descriptive and expressed in terms of language.

My favorite way of distinguishing the two is described as follows: When asked to describe a journey in a plane, a person could answer it quantitatively. For example, the flight leveled off at 35,000 feet and travelled at a speed of 514 mph. Another person asked the same question could answer it qualitatively by saying the flight wasn't bumpy and the meals were tasty. Regardless, the data and information tell a story that, depending on the audience, will have meaning. It might be worthless, but nevertheless, meaningful.

REMEMBER

The type of information desired directly correlates to measurement approach. This is going to inform your choices of at least what, when, where, and how data is captured. A general rule is only to capture and measure what matters. Some may argue that capturing data now to measure later has value even if there isn't a good case yet. I can buy that, but be careful with your limited resources and the potential costs.

Finally, it seems fitting to end this section with a quote from the author, William Bruce Cameron, "Not everything that can be counted counts, and not everything that counts can be counted." Let's not forget this by being too zealous with data.

Monitoring

Monitoring is an ongoing process of collecting and evaluating the performance of, say, a project, process, system, or other item of interest. Often the results collected are compared against some existing values or desired targets. For example, a machine on a factory floor may be expected to produce 100 widgets per hour. You engage some manner of monitoring in order to inform whether, in fact, this expectation is being met. Across a wide range of activities, monitoring also helps to ensure the continuity, stability, and reliability of that being supervised.

REMEMBER

Involved in monitoring is the data produced by the thing being evaluated. It's also the data that is produced as a product of monitoring. For example, the deviation from the expected result.

The data produced through monitoring feeds reports, real-time systems, and software-based dashboards. A monitor can tell you how much power is left in your smartphone, whether an employee is spending all their time on social media, or if through predictive maintenance, a production line is about to fail.

Monitoring is another process that converts data into insight and as such, exists as a mechanism to guide decisions. It's probably not lost on you that the role of data in measurement and monitoring often go hand-in-hand. Intuitively you know you have to measure something that you want to monitor. The takeaway here is not the obvious relationship they have, but the fact that data is a type of connective tissue that binds business functions. This interdependence requires oversight and controls, as stakeholders often have different responsibilities and permissions. For example, the people responsible for providing measurement data on processes may belong to an entirely different team from those who have to monitor and report on the measurement data. Those that take action may again belong to an entirely different department in the organization.

This is not the only way to think about monitoring in the context of data. Data monitoring is also the process of evaluating the quality of data and determining if it is fit for purpose. To achieve this, it requires processes, technologies, and benchmarks. Data monitoring begins with establishing data quality metrics and then measuring results over time on a continuous basis. Data quality monitoring metrics may include areas such as completeness and accuracy. (Data quality is discussed in detail in Chapter 6.)

TIP

By continuously monitoring the quality of the data in your organization, opportunities and issues may be revealed in a timely manner. Then, if deemed appropriate, actions can be prioritized.

Insight management

Data forms the building blocks of many business functions. In support of decision-making — arguably its most important value — data is the source for almost all insight. As a basic definition, business insight is sometimes referred to as information that can make a difference.

WARNING

It's not enough to simply collect lots of data and expect that insight will suddenly emerge. There must be an attendant management process. Thus, insight management means ensuring that data and information is capable of delivering insight.

Insight management begins with gathering and analyzing data from different sources. In order to determine what data to process, those responsible for insight management must deeply understand the organization's information needs. They must be knowledgeable about what data has value. In addition, these analysts must know how information flows across the organization and who it must reach.

With the data gathered and processed, analytics will be applied — this is the interpretation of the data and its implications.

Finally, insight management involves designing and creating the most effective manner to communicate any findings. For different audiences, different mechanisms may be required. This is seldom a one-size-fits-all. Some people will want an executive summary while others may want the painful details. You'll know whether your organization's insight communications are working if those that receive it can make decisions that align with the goals of the organization.

TIP

For insight to be most valuable, it must be the right information, at the right time, in the right format, for the right people. That's all. Of course, I kid. This is no simple task.

As you've probably guessed, there's a strong overlap between insight management and knowledge management. For simplicity, you can think of knowledge management as the organizational support structures and tools to enable insight to be available to employees for whatever reason they need it.

Reporting

Perhaps the most obvious manifestation of data and information management in any organization is the use of reports. Creating, delivering, receiving, and acting on reports are fundamental functions of any organization. Some say they are the backbone of every business. That sounds overly glamorous, but it does speak to the importance of reporting and reports.

The content of a report, which can be summarized or detailed, contains data and information in a structured manner. For example, an expenditure report would provide some basic overview of the purpose of the report and then support it with relevant information. That could include a list of all expenditures for a department over a certain period or it could just be a total amount. It will depend on audience and purpose. The inclusion of visuals are popular.

For example, a chart, considered a visual form of storytelling, is a way to present data so that it can be interpreted more quickly. With so much data and complexity in today's business environment, data storytelling is growing as both a business requirement and as an in-demand business skill.

The report may have a discussion of the findings and will conclude with a summary and sometimes a set of recommendations.

Reports are typically online or physical presentations of data and information on some aspect of an organization. For example, a written and printed report may show all the sales of a particular product or service during a specific period. Sometimes a report is given verbally in person or via a live or recorded video. Whatever the format — and that's less important today as long as it achieves its objective — a report is developed for a particular audience with a specific purpose.

With so many uses of data and information, the purpose of reporting is largely about improved decision-making. With the right information, in the right format, at the right time, business leaders are empowered to make better decisions, solve problems, and communicate plans and policies.

While reports do empower leaders and give them more tools, they don't guarantee the right decisions. Knowing something is not the equivalent of making the right choices at the right time.

Other roles for data

While I've provided a number of the most visible uses of data in organizations today, it was not my intent to list every conceivable way that data is used. That said, here's a short list of some other important areas that I don't want to omit.

>> **Artificial intelligence (AI):** Data is considered the fuel of AI. It requires a high volume of good data (the more, the better!). With huge quantities of quality data, the outcomes of AI improve. It's from the data that AI learns patterns, identifies relationships, and determines probabilities. In addition, AI is being used to improve the quality and use of data in organizations. The use of AI in data governance is discussed in Chapter 10.

>> **Problem solving:** Acknowledging the close association with decision-making, it's worth calling out problem solving as a distinctive use of data. Data plays a role in how a problem is defined, determining what solutions are available, evaluating which solution to use, and measuring the success or failure of the solution that is chosen and applied.

>> **Data reuse:** While we collect and use data for a specific primary purpose, data is often reused for entirely different reasons. Data that has been collected, used, and stored can be retrieved and used by a different team at another time — assuming they have permission, including access and legal rights (notable controls within data governance). For example, the sales team in an organization will collect your name and address in order to fulfil an order. Later, that same data set may be used by the marketing team to create awareness about other products and services. These are two different teams with different goals using the same data. Data reuse can be considered a

positive given that it reduces data collection duplication and increases the value of data to an organization, but it must be managed with care so that it doesn't break any data use rules. (*Note:* High-value shared data sets are called master data, and in data governance, they are subject to master data management, a topic I cover in detail in Chapter 11.)

Improving Outcomes with Data

Now that the diverse roles of data have been identified and discussed, it's useful to understand how data can be leveraged to glean its maximum value. It begins with recognizing that data is an organizational asset. This simply means that it's something that brings economic value to the organization. It's clear to see this when its pointed out, but many team members don't yet look at data this way. When data is considered an asset — in fact, specifically a high-value asset — it often gets treated differently.

REMEMBER

Perhaps the function that is most associated with data is the process of exploring it and looking for insights. Called *data analytics,* this is a comprehensive organizational function that requires skilled staff and tools. With the emergence of big data, data analytics has become more complex and requires deeper skills, but it's also made data more valuable and important to the business.

Ultimately, as the following pages reveal, to get the best outcomes from your data assets, you need to create or further develop your existing data management and governance processes.

Approaching data as an asset

An asset is something that is owned by a person, an organization, or a government with the expectation that it can bring some economic benefit. This includes the generation of income, the reduction of expenses, or an increase in net worth.

REMEMBER

An asset can be tangible or intangible. Tangible assets are physical things such as inventory, machines, and property. That's stuff you can see and touch. An intangible asset is the opposite; it's a non-physical thing like software, copyrights, a brand, and goodwill. Data is an intangible asset.

Organizations care about both types of assets because they typically get captured in their financial accounts. Listing the value of assets presents the true state of any organization and reflects its financial health. In addition, capturing and valuing assets is required for determining tax obligations and for acquiring loans.

After it is processed from its raw form, data has the potential to create enormous economic value for all manner of stakeholders. Here are some examples of the economic value of data:

>> Improves operations

>> Increases existing revenue

>> Produces new forms of revenue

>> Builds relationships with customers and other stakeholders

>> Improves the quality of products and services

>> Contributes to competitive advantage

>> Enables innovation

>> Reduces risk

It's notable that data isn't typically captured overtly on an organization's balance sheet. The discussion about whether and how data should be reflected as an asset in financials is an ongoing debate. For one, it depends on the accounting standards of a country. It's a topic best left for another book and perhaps an opportunity for your own future research.

The net result of knowing that data is an asset, but not treating it the same way as other financial assets, means it often doesn't get the attention and respect it deserves. In practical terms, this may mean that data is often taken for granted, not leveraged nearly as much as it could be, and not protected to the extent it must be.

TIP

Recognizing that data is an asset is the first step to good data governance.

You've seen that data has value and you're ready to take steps to manage it that way. Just like assets on the balance sheet, you need to know what you have and where it is, as well as have an expression of its value. It may not be a dollar amount, but you can probably measure it in terms of how essential it is to the success of the business. By the way, if data has no value, seriously consider whether you should be managing it.

When you think of data as an asset, you'll be concerned with whether it is good or bad data. You'll pay attention to the data's accuracy, completeness, validity, and more. It means the organization will be mindful of whether data is being used as an organizational resource or being hidden in silos. This will mean understanding how the data is being managed and who has responsibility for it. Without roles and accountabilities, data can't truly be managed well.

Bottom line: Data is an asset and for its value to be leveraged, it must be governed. This may be one of the most important motivations for good data governance.

Data analytics

Raw data is largely useless. If you've ever briefly glanced at a large data set that has columns and rows of numbers, it quickly becomes clear that not much can be gleaned from it.

In order to make sense of data, you have to apply specific tools and techniques. The process of examining data in order to produce answers or find conclusions is called *data analytics*. A formal and disciplined approach is conducted by a data analyst, and it's a necessary step for any individual or organization that's trying to make good decisions for their organization.

The process of data analytics is varied depending on resources and context, but generally follows the steps outlined in Figure 3-1. These steps commence after the problem and questions have been identified.

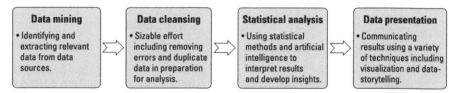

FIGURE 3-1:
Basics steps in
data analysis.

(c) John Wiley & Sons

Data analytics has four primary types. Figure 3-2 illustrates the relative complexity and value of each type.

>> **Descriptive:** Existing data sets of historical data are accessed, and analysis is performed to determine what the data tells stakeholders about the performance of a key performance indicator (KPI) or other business objective. It is insight on past performance.

>> **Diagnostic:** As the term suggests, this analysis tries to glean from the data the answer to why something happened. It takes descriptive analysis and looks at cause.

>> **Predictive:** In this approach, the analyst uses techniques to determine what may occur in the future. It applies tools and techniques to historical data and trends to predict the likelihood of certain outcomes.

>> **Prescriptive:** This analysis focuses on what action should be taken. In combination with predictive analytics, prescriptive techniques provide estimates on the probabilities of a variety of future outcomes.

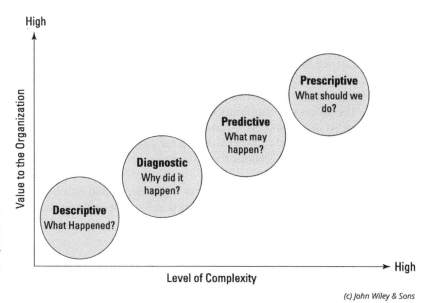

(c) John Wiley & Sons

REMEMBER

Data analytics involves the use of a variety of software tools depending on the needs, complexities, and skills of the analyst. Beyond your favorite spreadsheet program, which can deliver a lot of capabilities, data analysts use products such as R, Python, Tableau, Power BI, QlikView, and others.

If your organization is big enough and has the budget, one or more data analysts is certainly a minimum requirement for serious analytics. With that said, every organization should now consider some basic data analytic skills for most staff. In a data-centric, digital world, having data science as a growing business competency may be as important as basic word processing and email skills.

Data management

WARNING

No, data management is not the same as data governance. But they work closely together to deliver results in the use of enterprise data.

Data governance concerns itself with, for example, defining the roles, policies, controls, and processes for increasing the quality and value of organizational data.

Data management is the implementation of data governance. Without data management, data governance is just wishful thinking. To get value from data, there must be execution.

At some level, all organizations implement data management. If you collect and store data, technically you're managing that data. What matters in data management is the degree of sophistication that is applied to managing the value and quality of data sets. If it's on the low side, data may be a bottleneck rather than an advantage. Poor data management often results in data silos across an organization, security and compliance issues, errors in data sets, and an overall low confidence in the quality of data.

Who would choose to make decisions based on bad data?

On the other hand, good data management can result in more success in the marketplace. When data is handled and treated as a valuable enterprise asset: insights are richer and timelier, operations run smoother, and team members have what they need to make more informed decisions. Well-executed data management can translate to reduced data security breaches, and lower compliance, regulatory, and privacy issues.

Data management processes involve the collection, storage, organization, maintenance, and analytics of an organization's data. It includes the architecture of technology systems such that data can flow across the enterprise and be accessed whenever and by whom it is approved for use. Additionally, responsibilities will likely include such areas as data standardization, encryption, and archiving.

Technology team members have elevated roles in all of these activities, but all business stakeholders have some level of data responsibilities, such as compliance with data policies and with realizing data value. I discuss the essential roles and responsibilities in data governance and management in Chapter 8.

REMEMBER

In summary, good data management provides the opportunity for significantly enhanced organizational performance.

Governing data

You knew I'd come back to this. After all, convincing you that governing data is important to your organization and helping you implement it is the purpose of this book. Governing data means that some level of control exists to support a related policy. For example, an organization may decide that to reduce risk, there needs to be a policy that requires data to be backed up every day. The control would be the documentation of the process and enforcement of that policy. If, in the review of policy adherence, data wasn't getting backed up, then you'd quickly know that governance, for whatever reason, was not working.

REMEMBER

To fully realize the potential of data in your organization means that data must be governed. Any time an organizational resource or asset is left unmanaged, it's either a recipe for disaster or a missed opportunity. Even a small amount of governance beats no governance every single day.

The success of governing data can be reduced to three essential factors:

>> **People:** While recognizing that data is increasingly created and used exclusively by machines without human intervention, handling and benefiting from data is still a highly people-centric exercise. Even in a machine-centric context, it's people who are most often defining, designing, and maintaining data use. In governing data, people are the subject matter experts, they are responsible for quality, and they oversee and manage all related processes and responsibilities.

>> **Policies:** A data policy contains a set of adopted rules by an organization that apply to the handling of data in specific conditions and for particular desired outcomes. These policies apply in areas such as quality, privacy, retention, and security. The number of policies is typically a reflection of the size of the organization, the industry, and the degree to which data is considered a high priority asset. As you can imagine, the healthcare and financial industries, for example, which manage high volumes of sensitive data, are replete with data policies in support of their data governance programs.

>> **Metrics:** It's largely true, what gets measured gets managed. In developing policies in support of data governance, you have to consider how each is measured. For example, if a policy states that there shouldn't be more than five risk events per month such as a regulatory requirement being out of compliance, then, assuming the metric is high to begin with, it should decrease over time. If it doesn't decrease or it does and then fluctuates widely, there's an issue with the relevant data management procedures. Metrics must be in support of both technical and business needs. I discuss data governance metrics in more detail in Chapter 12.

Chapter **4**

Transforming through Data

This chapter discusses the challenges of searching for and finding data in the enterprise. The emergence of *data catalogs* has provided a viable solution to understanding what data is available, where it is, and how to access and use it. Having a current and easy-to-use data catalog is an excellent basis for higher value data performance. After all, how valuable is data that can't be found?

When you acknowledge that data is an asset, you expect that data to bring economic benefits. This is called *data monetization* and I discuss it in depth, including how to put a price on data.

The chapter concludes with an overview of what a data strategy is, how to create one, and how to increase its chances of success. If your plan is in any way related to elevating the role of data in transforming your organization, creating and delivering a data strategy is required.

Examining the Broader Value of Data

In small organizations or when a business is first created, only a few systems are used, and team members know the type and location of most of the data that is available. You can imagine, for example, basic repositories for customer data, invoices, and marketing materials.

The ability of team members to access data that they need for their work, without having to rely on specialists, is called *data democratization*.

WARNING

As organizations grow and more systems are employed, eventually no single person knows what data is available and where it is in the enterprise. Without this knowledge, the ability to properly govern your data and leverage its value is greatly hampered. Without deliberate actions, data democratization becomes elusive.

Unfortunately, over time, the situation often deteriorates. Whether because of culture, strategy (or lack of strategy), systems design, budgets, mergers, or any number of other dynamics, data sets get siloed. A *data silo* is a data repository controlled by an entity in an organization but not frequently shared or known by other parts of the business. Data silos hinder business efficiencies because they reduce collaboration and increase data inconsistencies. In addition, they are a source of risk, including security and regulatory issues.

Data governance helps eliminate unnecessary data siloes and makes data discoverable and available whenever and wherever it adds value. Data catalogs, discussed in this chapter, as well as the responsibilities of data stewards (covered in Chapter 8), are two essential ways that data governance can help solve these limitations.

Unfortunately, most organizations don't automatically come with a universal search engine that can help locate and serve up any type of data or information stored in the enterprise. Being able to tame and explore *data sprawl* — a term for the myriad of data types and sources that most businesses grapple with today — is not easily achieved without investing specialized effort.

According to an IBM survey, business leaders who want to interact with data said they spend about 70 percent of the time trying to find what they need and only 30 percent of the time analyzing it.

The ease at which you access data from across the Internet via a browser is seldom the experience in a business. In a weird twist, it's often easier to find information about your organization by Googling it rather than using your own internal search systems. Of course, if the data is protected behind your organization's firewall, a public search engine won't help either.

REMEMBER

Knowing what data is available in an organization is a prerequisite to unleashing the data's value. After all, if you don't know what's available, where it is, and you can't discover or access it, the data is useless. Without data visibility, your options are limited. Worse yet, you may not know what you don't know. That is a business risk and it's a top concern of data governance.

Knowing what data is available is essential for the following reasons:

>> Better informed decision-making

>> Ensuring compliance and regulatory requirements

>> Lower costs by avoiding duplicate system and data efforts

>> Improved data analytics and reporting

>> Higher performing systems

>> More efficient operations

>> Reducing data inconsistencies across the enterprise

Fortunately, the vendor community is ready to help you build your internal search capabilities. It's taken some time, but solutions have come a long way. With investment and effort, finding data and information in the enterprise is possible.

Data catalogs

You can take a few approaches to assist your organization so that your team members can find data. One option involves the creation of an enterprise search engine. It's certainly possible, but not easy, and will face some limitations such as the discoverability of confidential data that is deliberately siloed. In addition, a search engine won't necessarily provide insights on whether data is available, current, accurate, or complete. Its common purpose is simply to provide you with the location of the data.

Another, increasingly popular, method of data discoverability is the creation of an enterprise data catalog. Like a store catalog that categorizes products and includes details such as availability and price, a data catalog lists the availability of data sets and includes a wide range of valuable details about that data.

The three essential benefits of data catalogs are:

>> **Finding data:** Helps users identify and locate data that may be useful

>> **Understanding data:** Answers a wide variety of data questions such as its purpose and who uses it

>> **Making data more useful:** Creates visibility, describes value, and provides access information

REMEMBER

Done right, a data catalog delivers a comprehensive inventory that provides an enterprise view of all data. This view provides essential insight that helps with leveraging data value and provides a robust tool to assist with data governance. Yippee!

Figure 4-1 illustrates the basic building blocks of a data catalog.

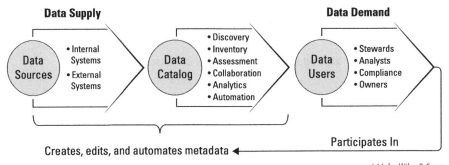

(c) John Wiley & Sons

FIGURE 4-1: A basic orientation of the components of a data catalog.

A data catalog is more than just a list of all data sets. Sure, for many organizations, this feature alone would add enormous value. What makes a data catalog particularly valuable is that it contains data about the data. It's called *metadata*. This content can be curated manually and also by automated processes which can acquire it from other sources. Artificial intelligence (AI) is now playing a growing role in the latter.

A data catalog can contain three types of metadata: technical, business, and operational.

>> **Technical metadata:** Data about the design of a data set such as its tables, columns, file names, and other documentation related to the source system.

>> **Business metadata:** Organizational data such as a business description, how it is used, its relevancy, an assessment of data quality, and users and their interactions.

>> **Operational metadata:** Data such as when the data was last accessed, who accessed it, and when was it last backed up.

Examples of metadata include the following:

>> Associated systems

>> File names

>> File locations

>> Data owners

>> Data descriptions

>> Dates created

>> Dates last modified

>> List of database tables and views

>> Data stewards

>> Size of data sets

>> Quality score

>> Comments

For a large number of stakeholders ranging from data analysts to data stewards, a data catalog presents many advantages. Primarily, the ability to find data tops the list. But it provides much more than that.

With a data catalog, an organization can:

>> Know what data it has (and by extension, know what data is missing)

>> Reduce data duplication

>> Increase operational efficiencies and innovation

>> Understand data quality

>> Manage compliance

>> Enjoy cost savings from improved operations

If you'd like to view and interact with a public data catalog, check out the U.S. federal government's open data portal data catalog at https://catalog.data. gov/dataset. While reviewing any of the data sets there, explore the metadata associated with each to get a sense of types and details.

REMEMBER

A well-managed data catalog can be transformational for an organization. The effort to create and maintain one should not be understated. But, without a doubt, a data catalog is often the basis for delivering on successful data governance and data management.

CASE STUDY: UNLOCKING DATA SILOES WITH A DATA CATALOG

Background

A European power company has embraced data governance in support of its mission of decarbonizing the production of electricity. The organization generates and distributes energy across multiple countries. Data is essential to every part of their business. For example, daily operations, like evaluating equipment performance, require deep data insights. Making data central to these tasks translates to considerable cost savings.

Protecting data from misuse is also important. Not only must the business adhere to the regulatory requirements in all countries where they operate — but they must also comply with Europe's General Data Protection Regulations (GDPR), which governs the use of personal data. Failure to do so can result in fines totaling millions of euros.

Problem Statement

The challenge facing the company was how to power their mission by enabling business units and partners to collaborate using the business and technical data locked away in siloed systems, while also ensuring a high degree of data compliance.

The Solution

They found a large part of the solution in the implementation of a data catalog with robust data governance functionality.

The data catalog facilitated collaboration and innovation by enabling vastly improved search and discovery of data across the organization. In addition, team members could share their expertise through articles in the catalog, speeding the transfer of knowledge throughout the company.

Compliance requirements were improved by the catalog interface guiding compliant behavior using workflows. In this way, the data catalog taught people how to use data compliantly and ensured they followed the relevant policies based on the data at hand.

From data to insights

In a business context, deriving insights is almost the entire point of collecting data.

In Chapter 2, I discussed that raw data has little value until it is given context. It then becomes information, which becomes the basis for taking an action. Eventually, through the addition of experiences, practicalities, values, and other dimensions, data becomes insight. Insight provides a deep understanding of something and is the ultimate positive manifestation of data. It has the highest value to an organization because it can support decisions and drive actions.

That last sentence is worth unpacking. Whether an organization uses insight to support decisions or drive actions is a choice. Most organizations will do some of both, but when insights are used primarily to drive action, the value of the underlying data is truly realized. Put another way, actionable data is the most valuable data to an organization.

 If you can't use your data to make better decisions and drive your organization forward, the data may just be worthless.

WARNING

Acquiring and applying insight from data means defining the following:

>> **Context:** Understanding the environment and objectives of the outcome

>> **Need:** Determining how insight will help to accomplish the objective

>> **Vision:** Having ideas about how insight will help and what that might look like in practice

>> **Outcome:** Specifying how insights will be adopted and success will be measured

These dimensions can be used to answer questions such as:

>> What data is required?

>> Does the data exist?

>> Is it current?

>> Is it easily available?

>> What format is the data in?

>> What kind of data analysis is required?

>> How will the data be presented?

WARNING

Converting data into insights is no easy task. It's complicated and skilled work and relies on good quality data that is accessible. Those tasked with delivering insights often cite data quality, data volume, work effort, and integrating data from various sources as the top reasons that make it difficult and create a deterrent to adoption.

The wrong actions taken in response to insights can have devastating business consequences. Trusting insights requires a high degree of confidence in both those producing the analytics and those receiving the results. While the vast majority of organizations want to rely on insights, recent surveys suggest that only a minority of leaders act on the insights provided.

REMEMBER

Quality insights can provide a competitive advantage and operational excellence, but organizations have work to do to fully realize their potential.

Data analytics

Intuitively, data can contain enormous business value, but it must be unleashed. Simply staring at pages of columns and rows of data is unlikely to reveal any notable insights. It may give you a headache or you might get lucky and discover a pattern in the data. More realistically, to realize the benefits of data and discover insights, you need analytics. Analytics unlocks the power embedded in good quality data.

Data analytics involves both specialized skills and software to explore data sets and extract insights that may be useful to an organization.

Sometimes the term is used interchangeably with data analysis. Data analysis is concerned with identifying a data set, examining it, and reporting on any findings. It's a subset of data analytics and it typically focuses on what data from the past tells us. On the other hand, data analytics is a complete science that involves collecting, cleaning, organizing, storing, administering, and analyzing data. In addition to informing you about the past, it is also used to help project possibilities into the future.

The similarity in terms and overall purpose should be noted, but understanding the difference is important.

The source of data for analytics is one or a combination of the following:

>> **First-party data:** Data that an organization collects.

>> **Second-party data:** Data that is obtained from another organization.

>> **Third-party data:** Aggregated data obtained from a provider.

Typical uses of contemporary data analytics tools and techniques include:

>> Vastly improved decision-making

>> Focused marketing campaigns

>> Understanding the competitive landscape

>> Designing more innovative products

>> Better customer service

>> Improved operations

>> Insights on customer behavior

In recent years, data analytics has matured considerably, and its value to businesses has skyrocketed. This is the result of all types of organizations recognizing and prioritizing the value of data, the advent of big data, the emergence of data science as a respected business competency, and the arrival of game-changing new analytics tools. These tools now regularly incorporate AI to help identify patterns and relationships in data. This AI can augment some of the traditional data analyst responsibilities to increase speed and accuracy.

REMEMBER

Any organization that is serious about increasing the use of data for a wide range of business purposes must be ready to govern its data analytics capabilities. This includes policies and procedures, experienced talent, and a suite of contemporary software tools.

Data monetization

In Chapter 3, I discussed the basis for data being considered an intangible asset of an organization. An asset is something owned that has the expectation of delivering value. Unlike tangible assets such as inventory and property, data falls into the same category as assets such as copyrights and software.

Data doesn't show up on the balance sheet. Those assets that are required to be included in the accounts are carefully assessed so that an accurate picture can be captured of an organization's financials. In addition to being a necessary mechanism for accountability, tax, and loan support, valuing provides a basis for understanding the importance and role of each asset.

REMEMBER

Intuitively, when something has high value, it's likely to be treated differently from things with little value.

Without a process to place a price on data set — called *data valuation* — the value of a given data set may be highly subjective and may differ considerably between the perspectives of team members. In fact, it's possible for an organization to not fully appreciate the value of specific data sets. Without this knowledge, it's much harder to take advantage of the opportunities that some data sets may provide, such as business growth and operational excellence.

When data provides an economic benefit to an organization, it's called *data monetization*. It's a succinct, albeit cruder, way to generally consider the ultimate role of data in a for-profit enterprise.

Data valuation, while generally recommended in larger enterprises, is a requirement for advanced data monetization such as selling or licensing data.

(It's very likely that some of your personal information is being traded often in an open marketplace. You probably agreed to it in the small print that none of us ever read when using a new online service. It means that data about you has a market price.)

Many ways exist to determine data valuation. Here's a brief summary of a few methods.

>> **Cost value method:** Value is calculated by determining how much it costs to produce, store, and replace lost data. It's a simple method and can be useful as a lightweight approach, but it is subjective and doesn't necessarily account for the economic value that the data can produce.

>> **Market value approach:** Value is calculated by researching how comparable data is being priced in the open market. It's a great approach if market-based comparable data exists but doesn't work for the vast number of data sets that are not traded.

>> **Economic value approach:** Value is calculated by measuring the impact a data set has on the business's bottom line. It's a difficult approach because it may be nearly impossible to identify the specific value of the data relative to other contributors of value.

>> **With-and-without method:** Value is calculated by quantifying the impact on cash flow if a data set needs to be replaced. Scenarios with and without the data are explored and the difference between cash flow is used to determine data value. Like others, this can be challenging to pinpoint the specific impact of a data set.

REMEMBER

What's clear from data valuation methods is that none of them are perfect. Above all, data valuation is really hard. Don't be discouraged. It's hard for every type of organization. Fortunately, a number of providers are ready to help if you want outside assistance.

Assuming your organization realizes that data is a strategic corporate asset, you must be intentional in how you manage that asset. Called *data asset management*, a business must know what data sets it has and understand their value. It must have a plan for utilization and a mechanism to measure return-on-investment.

TIP

Bottom line: For optimal data monetization, organizations must manage high-value data with the same priority and rigor (and maybe even more) that it treats its most important tangible assets.

Data-driven decision making

I recall a fable I heard a few years ago that I still find useful when considering data for decision-making. I'll paraphrase it here.

A long time ago, the Tsar of Russia was told by his advisors that many people were getting sick in Siberia. The tsar was aghast and asked questions to understand why this might be happening. Several reasons were given, but one stood out to him. An advisor told him that there appeared to be a higher number of doctors in Siberia at that moment relative to the rest of Russia. Immediately, the tsar understood the issue. He commanded his most skilled military men to go to Siberia and kill all the doctors.

Perhaps the most important value for most enterprises to derive from data is the ability to make better, more-informed decisions. It's a theme you'll notice again and again in this book. It's not that other uses aren't important. It's the fact that while some qualities of data contribute to specific functions such as targeted marketing, the decision-enabling function of data is open to every function.

REMEMBER

Simply stated, data-driven decision-making (DDDM) is the process of using data to drive business decisions.

Basic DDDM can be practiced by most team members. Think about it. Most of us are informed by data every day and make a variety of decisions based on it, at work and at home. It's fair to say that at some level, it's just a feature of being human. There's probably a decision or two you wish you'd made differently or perhaps would have benefited from better data. But for DDDM to be really effective and to contribute to high performance, an organization needs a data culture, and specific skills and tools.

Organizations that excel at DDDM achieve it through deliberate actions and investments. Critically, there must be leadership support for a culture that advocates decisions rooted in data appreciation and analytics. Executives who demonstrate DDDM are role models for the entire enterprise. In practical terms, it also means enabling team members to have access to data, tools, and training. Ensuring the right people can use the right data at the right time requires data-security and data-use policies, both core functions of data governance.

TIP

Quality DDDM is learned. Don't expect team members to ace it without training.

Consider this six-step process to data-driven decision-making:

1. **Define the objectives:** This step involves understanding the objectives relative to the effort and their alignment with organizational goals. This will help you scope the work and define the metrics. In fact, it can be useful to define success and then work backward. For example, if you're trying to increase sales in a particular region, you need to identify which metrics to capture in order to determine whether you achieved that objective.

2. **Identify the data:** In addition to using a data catalog, enterprise search, or similar, this step requires engaging with impacted stakeholders. Getting input from a diverse group of people and teams will help you scope the data. This

may generate the need to gather data that doesn't exist. You may need to consult with data stewards, data owners, and others with data governance responsibilities.

3. **Prepare the data:** After Step 2, you'll understand the degree of preparation you need. If the problem you're trying to solve is narrow and the data is easily accessible and high-quality, you'll be in pretty good shape. In most cases, your situation is unlikely to be this rosy. The data necessary to meet your decision-making objectives will likely come in a variety of formats and will be in need of some remediation (I'm being kind here). You may need some deep data science skills to prepare the data for use in a data analytics platform.

4. **Analyze the data:** Once you reach this point, the fun begins. The assumption is that you're using a useful analytics tool. For complex analysis and continuous efforts, several tools will be used. This could include support for an ETL architecture (Extract, Transform, and Load). This is when data is extracted from one system and made ready and available for use in another. To analyze this data, you will also need relevant representations such as visualizations. These could include graphs and charts. Your tool selection and how the data is presented will depend largely on the audience. For executives, a dashboard may be the right approach.

5. **Determine the findings:** Once you have data that you can display in a variety of ways, you can ask questions of it. For example, if you're trying to understand customer demographics relative to sales in a particular region, you may want to toggle between different age ranges. While all phases of DDDM have complexity, the tough work here is knowing which questions to ask. This skill is aided by training, but experience helps.

6. **Take action:** That's it. Make your decisions. If you've completed Steps 1-5 well, but no action is taken (assuming that's not the decision based on analyzing the data since concluding that no decision is necessary is, in fact, a decision), you've wasted a lot of time. DDDM is all about the decisions that result in *actions*.

While a first pass at a new problem will require most of these steps in sequence, it's common to iterate through some of the steps to get to a good place for analysis. For example, when analysis in underway, it may be obvious that you're missing some data. This may require you going back to Step 2.

Data-driven decision-making — done right — can be a game-changer for any organization. With the culture, skills, and tools, better decisions will be made, and they'll be made more quickly too. As a bonus, team members will feel more empowered, and the process will often lead to greater collaboration between business units.

Developing a Data Strategy for Improved Results

So much of this book is focused on communicating the deliberate actions that are required to deliver your data's potential. In my experience and through research, it becomes clear that many organizations take a more passive role relative to their data assets. Efforts are too often reactive. In addition, rather than having a plan and making strategic data-related investments, actions are either complementary to larger initiatives or responsive to some immediate challenge or opportunity.

Consider these reasons that organizations don't take a proactive approach to managing data:

>> It ain't broke, so why fix it?

>> It's too expensive and time-consuming to focus on data

>> It's far too complicated

>> Data management and governance — what's that?

Every one of these is valid. If your business is not open or able to recognize the potential upside of managing data as a high-value asset, it will be an uphill battle to convince them otherwise. (By the way, I discuss how to make the case for data governance in Chapter 5.)

That said, once you make the decision to manage data as the high-value asset it is, you're going to need a plan. That's when a data strategy becomes the starting point.

Why every organization needs a data strategy

REMEMBER

The purpose of any type of strategy is to agree on a set of guiding principles that inform decision-making in support of a desired outcome. In simple terms, it's the roadmap on how to reach your goals.

Businesses have visions that describe *why* they exist. They have missions that state *what* they do. To achieve their visions and missions, a strategy will answer *how* they will do it.

For a given end-state, people must agree on how decisions will be made and how resources will be allocated. A strategy must have clarity and make it easy for all leaders and team members to know what they need to do, what they need to avoid, and how actions should be prioritized.

Operating without an agreed and current strategy carries enormous risks. People may have different ideas of what the desired outcomes are and as a result conflicts emerge. For example, if one leader believes the strategy is to increase net profit over the next twelve months and another believes it is to grow market share during that same period, these different efforts can result in a whole lot of chaos.

Despite the obvious risks, many organizations don't have a current and well-communicated strategy. For one thing, it's hard to create and execute on a strategy. It's also often considered a bureaucratic effort when some leaders believe all the energy should be on execution every day.

TIP

The behavior and outcomes of organizations that have a clear and agreed-upon strategy is often evident. Research shows that they typically execute with efficiency, have higher profits, grow larger, and more frequently hit their other success targets.

Strategic plans aren't limited to the big picture goals like higher profit and market growth. While all strategies ultimately marry up to the vision and mission of the organization, guiding principles can also be used to drive change. For example, if the organization's goal is to grow profits by 20 percent in 18 months, the human resources department should have a strategy on how that growth will be supported by recruitment. The same goes for every other function, from marketing to information technology.

It doesn't stop there. Strategy can apply to processes and assets too. Seems like a strategy for strategies might be important too, right?

If I've been successful so far in this book, you should be somewhat, if not totally, convinced that today, data is one of the most important assets that a business can use in support of their performance goals. It's not a stretch to see that you must have a clear roadmap for managing this core asset.

REMEMBER

After all, the existence of data does not equate to ensuring it is usable, accessible, high-quality, secure, and compliant. Additionally, turning data into value requires skills, policies, tools, and processes.

You need a data strategy in order to elevate data to become a strategic resource. That strategy should reflect the size and complexity of your business and the industry in which you operate. Small businesses should have a data strategy, but they shouldn't look anything like those used at a multinational level.

A good data strategy will guide decision-making and resource allocation around data in support of the organization. It will demonstrate and communicate data as a priority and ensure that it is treated in a manner to optimize the success of the organization.

REMEMBER

If your organization doesn't have a data strategy, create one. If you have a data strategy, make sure it's current and effectively communicated.

Creating a data strategy

So, you've made the decision to create a data strategy. That's great. Before jumping in, consider the following characteristics as a guide to your approach:

>> **Data maturity:** This can be defined simply as the degree to which the organization already uses and optimizes data and has experience and skills, as well as the quality of the existing data. All organizations use data, but there's a big difference between those that have prioritized it for a long period and those just deciding to treat it as a strategic asset. For example, without some basic data standards, security policies, and a process to cleanse data, layering analytics on top of it will likely cause frustration and in the worst case, errors in the results.

>> **Industry and size:** You can think of data prioritization through two frameworks: defense and offence. Defense deals with fundamental areas such as data security and quality. Offence is using data for insight management and market-facing initiatives. Every organization does both, but most emphasize one over the other depending on the industry and its size. For example, a healthcare company may prioritize a defense framework for data given the highly regulated nature of the industry.

With data maturity, industry, and size considered, a commensurate data strategy should follow. If you run a small business, don't let the bureaucracy of a complex data strategy become a burden. Equally, you won't see positive results if you don't apply the right level of sophistication to a data strategy if you work for a large, complex, and highly regulated organization.

A data strategy should typically account for these five areas of data requirements:

>> **Identify:** To find and make data usable, it must be clearly defined and described. This includes a file name, a file format, and metadata.

>> **Store:** Design and develop the capabilities for supporting the place and process for hosting data and how it will be shared, accessed, and processed.

>> **Provision:** Determine the processes to share and reuse data and define the guidelines for access.

>> **Process:** Raw data must be transformed to become valuable. This includes processes for data cleansing, standardization, and integration with other data sets.

>> **Govern:** Institute processes to manage and communicate data policies for data use within the organization.

Data requirements should consider these four data strategy components:

>> **Alignment with the business:** A data strategy is a subset of the overall business strategy. This means the data strategy must support and advance the larger goals of the organization. When determining the goals of the data strategy, where possible, map them as clearly as possible to illustrate how they are in support of the business strategy. For example, the business may want to reduce customer acquisition costs. A data strategy will be a valuable way to identify potential customers with a higher likelihood of conversion to buyers. Keep in mind that the strategy of a business evolves constantly, sometimes slowly and other times quickly. Your data strategy has to evolve in sync, as appropriate.

>> **Identifying roles and responsibilities:** A strategy requires people to take specific actions. Without action, a strategy is a worthless document. In the data strategy, you'll want to document the different roles that team members will play. Most will be data consumers. These are the employees who access and use data. They will certainly have responsibilities. For example, there will be an expectation about how different classifications of data should be handled. If something is public, then that's entirely different than something that's confidential. However, the bulk of the responsibility for ensuring that a data strategy can be delivered and maintained will rest with team members such as the information technology staff, data scientists and analysts, data stewards and owners, and management. It will be quickly apparent that data strategy and data governance have overlapping and dependent goals. For this reason, the deeper discussion on data governance roles in Chapter 8 is highly relevant here.

>> **Data architecture:** This area relates to the processes, systems, and applications that support working with data. Basic areas include defining data storage needs and analysis tools. It also includes items such as a data catalog, a *data warehouse* where data can be stored and made ready for analysis, and the methods and tools for *data pipelines*, moving data from a data source to a destination, and related ETL (extract, transform, and load) functions. A data strategy should support the scalability of your data architecture as well as

have some flexibility as needs change. Note that data architecture is often the driver of choosing and designing data management processes and systems.

>> **Data management:** This area is the broad umbrella of activities that manage the full lifecycle of data in an organization. It recognizes that data is a strategic asset and must have the attendant processes, procedures, policies, skills, and tools to ensure it is treated in such a manner. This includes areas such as the management of data security and privacy, quality, metadata, integration, master data management, and analytics.

REMEMBER

Data governance establishes the rules for data use, and data management ensures that, in the act of realizing data value in the organization, these rules are followed. For example, a data governance policy may state that data with a certain confidentiality classification may only be accessible by a specific role level in the organization. Data management will be the processes, tools, and staff that ensure that this governance rule is followed.

Since you know that a data strategy may need to evolve, data management and data governance must be updated in parallel. If either of them becomes out of sync with the data strategy, you should expect some ugly problems to arise. I've summarized data strategy in Figure 4-2.

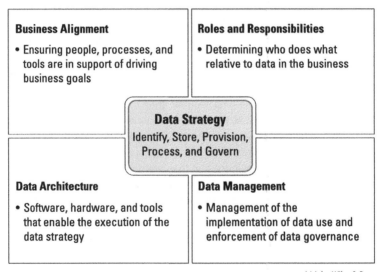

FIGURE 4-2:
The four components of a data strategy.

(c) John Wiley & Sons

Managing and monitoring your data strategy

You have a lot to celebrate if you successfully design, create, and implement a data strategy in your organization. You are ahead of a lot of businesses and your ability to leverage the value of data and increase organization performance has been enhanced. There are no guarantees of success yet, but you're positioned well.

The bigger picture is that you have buy-in, a roadmap, and execution is underway, but the accompanying data governance and data management functions must also be in place. Fortunately, you're reading this book, which means your data governance strategy will be first class!

TIP

All strategies must be open to periodic modification. It's not realistic to expect a strategy to be fixed for its duration in a fast-moving business world. Your evolving customer expectations, organizational needs, the economy, and more all play a role in forcing a strategy to adapt.

Few teams get their strategies right the first time too. You create a strategy with the information you have plus a whole lot of assumptions. As the strategy plays out, you'll find errors and gaps. It will also become apparent whether the objectives, goals, and metrics were correctly calibrated. It's a problem if any are way off the mark. These are all triggers to go back and review the plan and make any adjustments.

Course corrections that are made in a timely fashion reflect good leadership.

REMEMBER

The worst thing you can do is design a strategy, implement it, and place the plan on a shelf only to revisit it three to five years later.

Monitoring your data strategy means having the right metrics, getting feedback regularly from participants, and auditing related outcomes.

All strategies, including your data strategy, must be regularly reviewed and modified as necessary. This is a core characteristic of an agile organization in the 21st century.

2

Delivering Data Governance

Chapter **5**

Building the Business Case for Data Governance

I n all types of organizations, data governance is becoming more important and more pressing with every day that passes. A world being transformed by digi-talization requires us to have quality data that is managed well. More and more companies have data governance plans in place and there's more demand for implementations, skills, and tools than ever before.

Yet, despite all this, many business leaders still have not bought into the idea of data governance. Some even reject it all together. This rigidity can be an area of frustration for many stakeholders, including senior executives such as the CDO and the COO. Data scientists and analysts, auditors, and the legal staff are often the first to see the benefits and welcome data governance programs.

Many still see data governance as a defensive capability, meaning they believe it's only about managing risk. For them, it translates to higher costs with minimal returns. There's still work to do to convince leaders that a defensive capability can also mean lower costs and better operations. Of those who aren't ready to move forward with data governance, even fewer are thinking about the business growth opportunities it holds.

That said, many leaders do understand data governance and do recognize that it's a growing requirement for running their organizations well. They just don't know yet how to get from point A to point B. These leaders need to be presented with the right business cases and metrics to become convinced.

To get approval and move forward with your data governance program, you need to be able to convincingly communicate how data governance aligns with business outcomes.

This chapter provides a basic overview for creating a business case for data governance and discusses how to successfully present it to your decision-makers.

Identifying the Business Case for Data Governance

I suspect that you turned to this chapter because you already recognize the value of data governance and are ready to acquire some additional skills to design and implement a program, but your colleagues and management are not yet convinced. Surveys often reveal a lack of leadership interest and support as significant reasons that data governance is not adopted or is not successful after deployment.

WARNING

Let's be even more honest — many of the people you work with probably don't even know what data governance is. That's not a criticism, but more of a commentary on the education needed to elucidate this important area.

Another way of looking at this challenge is to recognize that many people have responsibilities and do data governance-type activities, but they don't realize that what they're doing is data governance. For example, you're performing data governance if you review data sets to ensure they're in compliance with laws and regulations.

Data-related responsibilities are getting done, but there's often a lack of formality and glaring weaknesses. Opportunities are being missed at every turn.

Organizations typically value the data they work with and try to ensure it is managed well. However, many don't do it with the necessary rigor. They don't audit their efforts or measure their outcomes. These businesses are doing what they think they need to do, but are likely falling well short of fully leveraging their data assets. They're also dealing with unnecessary levels of risk.

What you've likely recognized is that formalizing a data governance program has significant benefits to your organization. You need to educate your colleagues across business functions and build a case for leadership to approve the program and, if necessary, provide a budget.

The case for data governance typically involves one or more of these three core areas:

>> Protecting the business (risk focus)

>> Running the business (cost focus)

>> Growing the business (revenue focus)

Some organizations may be ready to move forward with data governance but need a little more convincing. Others may be starting from scratch and need to build a more elaborate proposal. Each business will fall somewhere on or between these two extremes. One of your first tasks is to assess your organization's position. My bet is that you already have an initial sense.

Drivers of change

Data governance has become one of the most important organizational competencies over the past few years and it continues to grow in demand. This is because the digital transformation is creating new possibilities and risks. The last 300 years has demonstrated that almost nothing stays the same. In fact, the rate of change, something we all acknowledge and often experience, is accelerating.

We're now in what looks like the early years of a fourth industrial revolution. In this revolution, digital technologies and data are at the center of every business. In addition, the digital and physical worlds are increasingly intersecting. For example, businesses, factories, cities, and homes are deploying billions of devices that are connected to the Internet.

The Internet of Things (IoT), which will likely exceed 75 billion devices by 2025, is made up of hardware, software, data, connectivity, services, and more. IoT is already introducing remarkable new capabilities into our lives.

In every macro area, from politics to demographics, from how we make things to consumer expectations, and from economics to healthcare to climate change and beyond, there's a beat of disruption that is impossible to ignore.

The absence of action is the risk of irrelevancy. No organization can rest while the planet marches onward.

There's an overwhelming amount of change at play, but digitalization appears to be a commonality that runs through it, either as a response or a driver. Every organization is now a technology business. Don't believe me? Consider the implications to your business, or any business, of turning off access to the Internet for a few days.

An increasingly hyperconnected, data-centric world — one that is experiencing a fourth industrial revolution — is creating remarkable new business opportunities, spinning up difficult challenges such as worker displacement through automation, and elevating a wide range of existing and new risks that include pervasive challenges to data privacy and security.

REMEMBER

If nothing was changing or the change was slow, this issue wouldn't be so urgent. But everything is changing, and that change has growing velocity. The nature and value of data and the relationship between organizations, people, and data is being profoundly impacted.

Formal data governance is a reasonable, deliberate, and mature response to change. It should be viewed as something an organization can control and that will help a business thrive, grow, and manage risks.

The absence of data governance may mean that, as time passes, there will be less control over circumstances, unmanaged risks will have painful consequences, and valuable data will be poorly utilized.

A world of data abundance driven by a digital transformation can be an opportunity rather than considered just another source of business risk that needs to be managed.

You now have a good starting point for building your business case for data governance. But it's just the start. Let's look at some specifics.

Supporting governance, compliance, and risk

The argument that data is a valuable asset that can be leveraged to improve your organization's performance may be enough to persuade many leaders and colleagues. However, you might need additional arguments. Meeting compliance and risk-management requirements and increasing the bottom line are compelling arguments.

Compliance and risk management aren't the most glamorous parts of running a business. The mere mention of either is a turn-off for those who want to focus on areas such as sales, marketing, or innovation. For quite a few though, professions and skills in these areas are highly attractive and provide a good career. As a reader of this book, you might fall into either category. That said, whether you're in love with compliance and risk or find the topics unexciting, they are essential disciplines.

Compliance is about ensuring you meet official requirements such as government regulations when conducting business activities. It includes ensuring the organization and the individuals are following rules, standards, and ethical guidelines.

WARNING

All organizations are subject to compliance requirements. If you want to run a business, you must understand those requirements. The penalties for non-compliance can include fines, lawsuits, loss of reputation, and more. The consequences are real.

Organizations must be compliant to protect themselves and those they serve. In the context of data, compliance means handling data in such a way that all formal obligations are met in a timely and appropriate manner. Data compliance requirements differ from industry to industry. Some are rigorous, such as those in healthcare, insurance, and banking.

These requirements come from federal, state, and local authorities, as well as supply-chain partners, professional organizations, and internally.

Today, the list of laws that have data compliance requirements has expanded greatly and includes rigorous obligations relative to privacy, handling, and disclosures. For example, the General Data Protection Regulation (GDPR) is a legal framework that describes how the personal information of individuals who live in a country within the European Union are collected and processed.

Examples of data compliance requirements include:

>> **Retention:** Ensuring that data is available for a certain period of time

>> **Access:** Determining and permitting who can view and access certain data

>> **Reporting:** Producing reports on a schedule that regulatory agencies require

>> **Handling:** Collecting, storing, and using data only in specific ways

>> **Protecting:** Implementing mechanisms to support privacy and cybersecurity

The degree to which data compliance is managed depends on the size of the organization, the volume of data it creates and manages, and the industry it belongs to. That said, given the elevated role of data in a growing number of organizations, it follows that data compliance is increasing for a much broader group of organizations.

TIP

The right question to ask *now* when making the case for formal data governance is whether your organization can risk not prioritizing data compliance.

Historically, the value of data governance has been most associated with reducing data compliance issues. It has been viewed, appropriately, as a risk-management discipline. Today, governing data is required for addressing a larger set of risk-related issues.

Risk is loosely defined as the probability of something bad happening. High risk means an increased probability that there will be an undesirable outcome. Low risk is the opposite.

TIP

Governance is a lever for probability. Good governance reduces the probability of risk. It doesn't eliminate it, but it goes a long way. Bad governance or no governance is a formula for high risk.

Let's look at data security and privacy compliance requirements as risk areas. Data governance provides a way to manage these areas. A data governance policy will document the minimum cybersecurity requirements for a specific data set. For instance, to ensure compliance with the Payment Card Industry (PCI) Security Council — a group of financial organizations including Visa and Mastercard — credit card numbers must follow a set of security standards to protect cardholders from theft and fraud.

Knowing what risks exist requires a risk assessment strategy. You have to know where your exposure is, then prioritize and address it. Being proactive helps you avoid violations. A general rule is to conduct risk assessments at least annually.

What we've been discussing here now falls into a recognized triad of governance, risk, and compliance or GRC. In the simplest terms, GRC is a broad set of processes and procedures that assist organizations in meeting their objectives, reducing uncertainty, and behaving with integrity. GRC helps with running a business well. While the concepts aren't new, they are much more important in today's interconnected world, as risks are more frequent, more complex, and have the potential to be far more damaging than in the past.

Of course, GRC is not limited to data. However, governing data compliance and risk is of particular significance in today's data-driven environment and must be considered part of an overall GRC program.

Data compliance and risk management are strong arguments to support the creation of a formal data governance program.

Improving the financial bottom line

While the arguments around managing risk and adapting to change are compelling alone for adopting a data governance program, sometimes you have to speak the language that just about every leader understands. That's the language of money. I'm not talking about reducing spending or avoiding costs. I'm talking about making money. It's the reason most organizations exist.

You already know that data is one of the most valuable assets an organization possesses (you know this because I keep repeating it in this book). It's certainly valuable because many products and services need it to exist. In addition, it is converted into timely insights that enable businesses to make better decisions.

Data, when managed well, can also contribute directly to creating new value.

While I'll acknowledge that identifying a direct line between raw data use and the bottom line is tough, it's not too much of a stretch to trace its contributions.

For example, in a highly competitive world, businesses are continually trying to innovate. They want to create and introduce new, successful products and services into the marketplace. Innovation devours data. In addition to insights on opportunity, data can be collected on prototypes, on results of experiments, and on pilot feedback. Data can help with comparisons and with A/B testing — this is where the same service is delivered to two groups, with each group having a slightly different experience and then measuring the results from both groups. Data can be used to drive new ideas that are dependent on novel uses of data. Artificial intelligence, for example, uses data to deliver new and surprising solutions.

Data can tell leaders a whole lot about how a business is being run and, in doing so, get products and services to market quicker.

Quantitative results from customer feedback, such as the popular net promoter score — a measure of how likely a person is to recommend your product or service — can lead to market course corrections.

Finally, data can drive your marketing efforts so that you are able to reach the right audience and convert promotions into sales. The entire field of marketing has been transformed because of the big data being produced via social media, other web interactions, and from the use of credit cards.

Other arguments for supporting a data governance program

At this point, I think you have enough for your business case. However, since this is such an important part of the data governance journey, here are a few more areas to consider when developing your business case. Data governance can:

>> Improve data quality

>> Reduce the time team members spend looking for data

>> Reveal smart uses for data

>> Save money

>> Encourage collaboration by reducing organizational silos

>> Show that data is fun and can support creativity

You can probably think of others, and you'll find more reasons scattered throughout this book. But hopefully they're not required. If the case for a data governance program can't be made with the reasons I've provided, then perhaps there are bigger challenges to be addressed in your organization.

Creating a Data Governance Strategy Proposal

Being clear on the business case and how you're going to sell the idea to decision-makers is an important milestone. But let's be candid; many initiatives don't move forward simply with an articulated business case. You have to bring the people and content together in a manner that increases the chances of approval. There's still some sticky work ahead.

Involving the right stakeholders

In the enterprise world, data is everyone's concern. I mean it. It's everyone's concern. Whether the person is a new intern or the CEO, how they handle and manage data is a priority of the business world.

You might ask, why is data the concern of somebody whose job is completely detached from matters related to data management?

Here's an example. If we assume that almost all team members have a business email account, imagine for a moment that they accidently receive a spreadsheet with confidential data. Of course, this situation is not supposed to happen. But it does happen. You're smiling because you've experienced incidents like this in your career.

What happens next matters. Does the team member open the file, explore the contents, and then forward it on to their colleagues or friends? Optimally, the team member has been trained and is aware of the process to follow. In addition, they will tell appropriate stakeholders about the issue so that it can be avoided in the future. You need an immediate process and a mitigation process.

With this simple example, you can see that governing data is the concern of all team members. So, who do you involve when creating the business case for a data governance program?

The responsibilities of this cross-functional team include:

>> Communicating the appropriate business case

>> Defining scope

>> Identifying desired outcomes and metrics

>> Surfacing costs

>> Outlining major deliverables

>> Suggesting training approaches

TIP

My recommendation is to involve a group of team members from different functions and at different levels. You need a diversity of perspectives. You want to get buy-in early in the game. People are more likely to support a major initiative if they've been involved from the start.

WARNING

Resistance to a new initiative can be the result of management swooping in and dictating a new process or system.

Spend time on this part of the work. Don't rush to develop a proposal at the cost of leaving supportive stakeholders behind. They might otherwise be your biggest advocates. If you're getting pressure to move quickly (this is rare and would be a good sign), remind management that it's in everyone's interest and the success of the data governance program to get it right.

Don't forget the educational component of this phase. To each potential collaborator, you need to explain what data governance is, why it matters, and how the program will benefit them, their team, their responsibilities, and the success of the entire organization. The first part of this chapter provides you with some starting points to consider.

While I encourage you to include a diverse set of collaborators from across your business, there are some essential members to enlist, including:

>> Chief Information Officer (CIO)

>> Chief Technology Officer (CTO)

>> Chief Data Officer (CDO)

>> An executive sponsor. This is a champion who likely sits in the C-suite. It could be one of the previously mentioned folks or even the CEO. Given the increasing value of data on revenue generation, it could be the CFO or Chief Revenue Officer (CRO). If the role of data is seen more in alignment with operational effectiveness, the COO could be a good option.

>> An auditor

>> Someone from legal

>> Someone from analytics

>> Someone from reporting

>> Data owners

These participants will help you craft and deliver the proposal. But it goes further than that. In all likelihood, these team members should also be part of the design and implementation phases. Don't surprise them with that invitation after the fact. They need to know that their participation is valuable throughout the implementation and even into the operationalization of the program.

REMEMBER

Data governance is not simply implemented and then everyone gets to wash their hands of it. You're building an ongoing program that includes specific responsibilities for team members across the organization. It's worth saying it again. Data is everyone's concern.

Documenting and delivering the business case

Building a business case for a new organizational program isn't easy. These programs face considerable headwinds. Few organizations have abundant budgets and excess time. The emphasis is typically on revenue generation and anything that distracts from that core goal or siphons profit is minimized.

In addition, explaining the benefits of data governance is difficult. You might be starting from scratch with many leaders in explaining what it is and how it is essential and brings value to your organization.

In addition to the support of stakeholders across the organization and an executive sponsor, you need a high-quality proposal and presentation that aligns data governance with your business's goals and mission.

The document described here can either be in the form of a business case document or a presentation. The former may have more depth and details, but both generally contain the same content and structure.

Let's look at the proposed document structure:

>> **Executive summary:** In a few paragraphs, but no more than a single page, provide a brief overview of the proposal. Think of this as the page that someone with little time will read to get an overview of the main value of the proposal.

>> **Proposal objective:** In this section, briefly outline the purpose of the proposal. Specifically, your goal is to get approval to move forward with designing and implementing the program. Decision-makers like to know what expectations you have of them at the beginning of a meeting.

>> **Definition:** Provide a succinct definition of data governance and its value. Provide two-three examples.

>> **Vision statement:** This is a short but meaningful paragraph that describes the future of a successful data governance program. It must align with business goals.

>> **The business case:** This is the substance of the proposal. Describe why a data governance program is essential to the business and the value it will bring specifically to your organization. State all your assumptions. Describe the organizational impact.

Whether or not you intend to make the case in all three of the following areas, you should describe the value and where you and your team believe the emphasis will be. Of course, it may be equally distributed among all three areas. Provide examples for each. I've provided a few as guidance.

>> Protecting the business (risk focus)

  Avoid fines and penalties for non-compliance

  Increase privacy

>> Running the business (cost focus)

　　Reduce data duplication

　　Increase speed to find data

>> Growing the business (revenue focus)

　　Identify new markets and customers

　　Accelerate innovation

Back to the document structure:

>> **The plan:** Provide a high-level overview of what it will take in terms of time and milestones. Include items such as training, tools, and communications needs.

>> **Challenges and risks:** Be candid when assessing the journey ahead. Briefly document the potential obstacles.

>> **The cost:** Assuming you are winning the business case argument, it's going to come down to cost. Make sure the cost isn't a surprise. I recommend sharing the proposal in advance of the meeting, so decision-makers have a chance to review it. It's not uncommon to include the cost in the executive summary. I discuss cost in more detail in the section later in this chapter entitled, "Considering and presenting costs."

Avoid having the cost section be an area of contention. One way to address this is to understand, perhaps from the executive sponsor, the range of budget that would be generally accepted.

>> **Summary:** Your last page should be an overview of the proposal. Be clear about what you're requesting and the business value. Spend a little time reminding them what success will look like.

TIP

Finally, remind the decision-makers what is now required of them. You want a decision from them, right? Ask them!

Leave time for a robust discussion. Be prepared to be tasked with follow-up questions and modifications. This just means you have to do some extra work with your team and present again.

Considering and presenting costs

So, how do you determine the cost needed to design and implement a data governance program? Don't forget that you also need to determine the ongoing costs to keep the program running. Many cost variables are specific to the business in question. To get started, consider the following:

>> What size is your organization?

>> How complex are its functions?

>> Does the business operate in a highly regulated industry?

>> To what degree is data used?

>> How mature are the data management processes?

>> What level of data governance effort is desired?

>> What outcomes are expected?

>> What is the cost of not implementing data governance?

These are just a few of the considerations that you need to evaluate when putting together a budget.

TIP

Consider presenting costs relative to benefits. For example, while the budget for a project might be $500,000, the revenue it generates is $10,000,000. You can see how this presents a different and essential perspective.

Begin with a projection of benefits. Work with your team on these areas. This is a collaborative effort. Since this will be a cross-functional team, they will bring the potential financial benefits from their perspectives. These will be estimates and you can present them as ranges too. For example, at a minimum you'll want to consider these major categories:

>> Revenue growth

>> Cost avoidance

>> Increased performance

No doubt, providing dollar values to expected benefits can often be tricky. For example, if you had to make the business case for buying insurance today, how might you do that?

REMEMBER

Always state your assumptions. At a minimum this will create a basis for under-standing, but it will also drive healthy discussion.

One way to approach costs is to provide three values for each cost area. You deter-mine a cost for a low, medium, and high implementation. Low is the equivalent of minimal effort and high is for the best case where there are few budget or techni-cal limitations.

You can also present a budget that is incremental over a few years. It's not necessary to implement an entire data governance program is one shot. It may make sense to prioritize elements and deploy them over a longer time. This way, design and implementation costs are expended in smaller blocks, and benefits can be assessed along the way, thus providing either support or caution and course corrections to further efforts.

Typical costs to consider:

>> **Staff:** Full-time and part-time (where an existing employee spends a proportion of their time on data governance). In Chapter 8, I discuss different roles and their efforts in data governance.

>> **Consultants:** For example, you may need outside assistance in developing and documenting policies and procedures. External expertise can be useful across the program requirements.

>> **Tools:** You'll want to explore software for analytics, a data catalog, other data management needs including storage, data warehousing, customizations and configurations, and application programming interfaces (APIs).

REMEMBER

You'll need to distinguish between one-off implementation costs and ongoing costs. Keep in mind that many data governance tools are cloud-based, so while there is some initial implementation cost, running these systems is an ongoing operational expense.

TIP

You might be curious about how your numbers stack up against other organizations. In a study from 2020, one analyst firm concluded the average cost of running a data governance program was in the range of 2.5 to 7.5 percent of the budget of the information technology (IT) department. However, you should also do research on organizations that compare more directly to yours.

There's also a third perspective you may consider in your cost proposal. This is the price of *not* implementing data governance. For example, an analysis conducted recently suggested that bad data management in the United States may be costing businesses around $4 trillion per year.

After collecting and documenting all the benefits and costs, you're ready to present the information in a financial template that tries to clearly demonstrate value versus cost.

Chapter **6**

Focusing on the Fundamentals of Data Governance

I t's a reasonable observation that data governance can seem overwhelming at first. Like most new programs with a substantial agenda, the topic can be seen at the outset as complex and difficult to implement. That's not wrong. Data governance can be complex and difficult to implement.

While the deployment of a comprehensive data governance program for a sophisticated organization requires long-term support and investment, all organizations begin the journey from the same place: the beginning.

In the course of rolling out the program, small and large businesses will quickly diverge. Smaller organizations will have found the right level of rigor and effort to ensure their needs are met. Larger, more complex organizations will continue to build a program with additional hiring, acquiring more tools, and developing a higher volume of policies and processes.

In either case, all organizations must begin their journey with some fundamental approaches and understandings. This chapter covers the basics of approaching your data governance development effort and it focuses on the fundamental areas that data governance serves. Revisiting these basics often will serve as a healthy reminder.

Establishing Basic Approaches to Data Governance

It's a good bet that you and your organization want your data governance program to succeed. If the deliberations are over and the decision has been made to move forward with the development of a program, now's the time to ensure you leverage every advantage to increase the chances of success.

You know data governance is hard to implement. It's also tough to maintain over the long term. At some point, your data governance program will just be part of how your organization operates. Until that time, there are a few basic approaches that must be considered. If adopted, these approaches will go a long way to helping with the success of the program.

While not an exhaustive list, I've compiled some of the most important approaches. They are:

>> Transparency

>> Accountability

>> Standardization

>> Change management

The following sections briefly explore each one.

Transparency

Outside of the core team that is involved in the decisions and the development of the data governance program, the rest of the organization will be curious and probably quite anxious about what is being deployed. Many will make the wrong assumptions about the program. They may believe it's more bureaucracy with few benefits. Others will not understand why they are being asked to do certain tasks.

You'll need to accept that no matter what you do, these sentiments may persist. The challenge is to keep these reactions as the minority.

If pushback is excessive, the program may be at risk.

Being transparent about the program from the start and continuing to be so for the duration is a recommended approach. Don't be secretive about the effort. There's no reason to be. This is a chance to be collaborative and engage team members in processes that add value and improve the organization. Create opportunities for everyone to learn about data governance — why it's important to the organization, what is being created, and importantly, what it may mean to everyone. If you think it will create additional workload for some team members, then be candid. But ensure that you communicate that these new processes will bring about a range of noteworthy benefits.

Transparency as a basic approach to the program is about being clear on *why* and *what* is being done, as well as *who* is responsible at every step of the way.

To measure your success, when data governance is implemented, all team members should know what their responsibilities are at any point during the lifecycle of data and why those responsibilities exist. For example, certain data should never be posted on a public website. The process to ensure this policy is communicated and how it is enforced must be clear to those that have rights over the organization's public-facing website.

Accountability

You'll see a pattern with my proposed basic approaches. Many of them are related. With transparency, you must ensure that data governance processes are clear, communicated, understood, and executed by those responsible for them. This is where accountability comes in.

In a data governance program, specific team members have roles they are expected to perform. In other words, they are accountable for outcomes. They should understand and buy-in to whatever is expected in the documented and enforced data policies and processes.

The data governance team must engage impacted team members early, fully describe expectations, and optimally achieve consensus on what will be done, how it will be measured, and how it will be enforced. The absence of clarity here may result in confusion over who is accountable. When that happens, nothing might happen. It could also result in duplication of effort. Neither of these scenarios are a good thing.

Accountability means that the right people know what is required and who specifically is responsible.

Data is a cross-functional asset and involves many different types of stakeholders. You'll want to be clear about when something is a technology responsibility versus one that belongs to the business teams. In addition, accountability means knowing whether process and policy requirements apply to those who create and collect data, those who manage it, those who use it, or team members who are part of the data governance core team.

Standardization

While somewhat of an outlier in this list, building a data governance program with a data standardization mindset and a commitment to standardize is exactly the right approach.

Making data standardization a priority program aspiration, despite the ambitious nature of the undertaking, is a statement of the seriousness of the effort.

Data standardization improves the quality of data and makes it easier for a business to use. By having data standards, it's easier for data to be shared, exchanged, combined, and understood.

Imagine the difficulty of consolidating data from different sources that are in a variety of formats or contain similar data but are organized another way. Data professionals regularly face this daunting challenge.

Data standardization can be thought of as a workflow that converts the structure of different data sets into a common format. It also helps with internal and external communications. Think of standards like a protocol that can create smoother engagement between stakeholders. It avoids the metaphorical awkwardness of reaching out to shake someone's hand and they try to fist bump you.

A simple example is how an organization treats the format of a calendar date in a database. Here are just a few of the ways a date could be recorded:

>> January 1, 1970

>> Jan 1, 1970

>> 1/1/70

>> 1/1/1970

>> 1st January 1970

And on and on. You get the idea. Having no date standardization is the stuff of nightmares for people who work with data. Identify a standard format, agree on it, and then start using it. Do that as a team with that mindset, and you're well on your way to having good data governance.

TIP

Hey, and one more thing. Not all data can or should be standardized. Unstructured data, for example, must often be managed in a non-standard format. Recognize the limits of what is possible and move forward accordingly.

CASE STUDY: STANDARDIZATION SOLVES SEVERAL GLOBAL OPERATING CHALLENGES

Background and Problem Statement

A large, international food and beverage company recognized that their lack of a unified and standard approach to data governance across all their territories was resulting in a number of significant challenges and limitations. For example, without agreement on data definitions, teams struggled to provide leadership with a view of consolidated global reports. At a regional level, operational examples such as inventory databases with poor quality data were resulting in excess inventory carrying costs and ordering parts already in stock. Their ongoing, rapid expansion, which entailed both mergers and acquisitions, was exacerbating the issue.

To their credit, the organization had created a high-quality data governance program, but it hadn't been implemented consistently across all their businesses.

The Solution

The solution was to get their global leadership team to champion the deployment of the program in a standard manner across the entire enterprise. Existing business divisions and those being on-boarded were required to adhere to the executive-sponsored mandate. The global model was required, but some localization such as language, was also supported.

The effort included the deployment of agreed-upon data processes and policies, and the assignment of regional team members to specific data-related responsibilities. These team members were given local authority and required to report up to a number of centralized data leadership roles.

(continued)

(continued)

Several previously independent database systems were configured, using new fit-for-purpose tools, to interface with each other and to leverage a single source of master data. In addition, a wide range of data tools were eliminated in favor of a global standard data toolkit.

Results and Lessons Learned

While the end-state was a success with most goals being met, everyone involved agreed that it was a highly complex and difficult effort. They learned that the best approach was to implement the standardization process in a progressive manner, hitting measurable milestones along the way.

Data governance achieves its most valuable results when a standard framework is deployed and enforced consistently across the enterprise.

Case study insights provided courtesy of Sahil Naqvi (www.linkedin.com/in/ sahil-naqvi-86104a7).

Change management

Once a data governance plan is designed and deployed, it never changes.

Nope.

That's not correct at all.

You must enter into a data governance effort with the understanding that it needs the capability to be responsive to business needs as they evolve.

REMEMBER

Your policies and processes may need to quickly change in response to new laws and regulations.

For example, the introduction of specific health data handling requirements as part of the U.S. federal law, the Health Insurance Portability and Accountability Act of 1996 (HIPAA), meant that all health organizations and those that interfaced with them needed to incorporate a number of complex data standards.

TIP

Your data governance program must have a documented and agreed process for managing change. In the spirit of a transparent program, all team members should know how to access the change management process and exercise it.

Change management may be required at the program level, but it could also be a requirement at a project level.

Data governance is a change management mechanism for data. For example, consider the following requirements:

>> Changes to data models

>> Changes to values in reference tables

>> Changes to data structures

>> Changes to data movement

>> Changes to data steward responsibilities

REMEMBER

There's another important way to think about change management in the context of data governance and vice versa.

Change management involves the methods that an organization uses to implement change in support of its objectives and goals. It results in new or amended processes and procedures.

With the implementation of a data governance program, you're focused on positive change. The environment prior to the introduction of data governance will be different from that after it is implemented. Data governance requires change management methods to be implemented.

TIP

Data governance achieves positive changes to outcomes at the organization. Framing your efforts through this lens can help maintain the program as a strategic initiative and as a candidate for the change management processes within the organization.

Examining Where Data Governance Brings Value

This chapter is designed to present some of the fundamentals of data governance. While variations of this content pop up throughout the book, this section succinctly lists the core areas where a data governance program brings value to your data strategy and organizational requirements and goals.

I've identified the following nine areas as central to data governance. There are probably others, but this list will serve you well in describing the value of any program. They aren't in any particular order. You can decide for your purposes, which are the most important.

>> Privacy

>> Availability

>> Usability

>> Consistency

>> Compliance

>> Security

>> Integrity

>> Business intelligence (BI)

>> Quality

Privacy

Data privacy is concerned with the protection of personal data, often referred to as personal information (PI) or personal identifiable information (PII), from those who shouldn't have access to it. It includes the ability for an individual or organization to control and determine who can access that data. Examples include names, addresses, birth dates, marital status, location, and well, just about anything you consider to be private.

WARNING

In many countries around the world, data privacy for specific types of personal data is a matter of strict laws and regulations. These legal obligations include how data is protected, who can access and give permission to data, and how it can be shared. Failure to comply can result in significant penalties such as legal action, financial penalties, and damage to brand.

Perhaps among the most important functions of data governance is ensuring data privacy. With data governance, compliance is enforced through documented and understood policies and procedures for ensuring that different data sets are clearly identified, stored, processed, and used appropriately.

Availability

When considering the topic of data security, it is easy to assume it's about limiting access to certain data sets. Certainly, if data is sensitive and only a few people with special designations are supposed to access it, then it needs to be secured. But data security is also about ensuring that people and applications that need access to specific data sets can access them at the right time and at the right place. This is the opposite side of the same coin.

REMEMBER

Data governance is concerned with data availability in the sense that ensuring that those who are approved to access data can and those who don't have permission can't. It includes the people, processes, and technologies required to make data available and usable, manage access, respond to issues such as system outages, and ensure it is discoverable.

Usability

The existence of data doesn't equate to the usability of data. While we are living in a period of big data, where there is more data being generated than can even be managed, its volume isn't necessarily an indicator of value. Usability is concerned with the degree in which a person or application can make sense of data and derive meaningful outcomes.

For example, unstructured data may be collected on customer opinions. If the intent is to understand how people feel about something, a large volume of big blocks of text may not be that valuable either to an analyst or an analytics application. Instead, the data may need to be parsed — broken into parts — to extract, say, relevant adjectives. Processing the data in this way may now make it more usable for the intended purpose.

Similarly, data presented in summary on a management dashboard or via visualizations can quickly elevate its meaning and thus its usability.

Usability can be improved by:

>> **Relevance:** Data must be aligned with business need.

>> **Quality:** Data must be fit for use. See my comments on data quality later in this section.

>> **Structure:** Data must be organized in a meaningful manner.

>> **Metadata:** Data must include documented guidance such as what the data represents.

>> **Tools:** Team members need access to the right tools to manipulate data.

Consistency

When similar data is used across an organization but not necessarily derived from the same repository, each occurrence of the data must be the same; otherwise, significant issues may arise.

REMEMBER

Data consistency involves the processes and technologies to ensure different sources of the same data have the same values.

For example, if an organization has a data set with customer names and addresses, but this data set is duplicated in multiple systems (it's not optimal, but often happens for a variety of reasons), when an address changes, that change should be reflected in all duplicates. Without updates to all the duplicates, data inconsistencies will emerge quickly. You can imagine the issues that will cause for marketing and other departments.

A broader definition of data consistency means that team members all get the same view of data, regardless of the method in which they access data and where and when it is accessed.

Compliance

See Chapter 5, which explores compliance in detail.

Security

WARNING

Many people confuse the terms privacy and security. So let me clear that up right away.

Privacy, as discussed earlier in this section, refers to the protection of personal information (PI) and personal identifiable information (PII) and the ability to control who has access to it. *Security* is concerned with how protections are implemented. For example, you might enter your credit card number in a system with the expectation that it is kept private. This is your expectation of privacy. The provider would be required to enforce that privacy by, say, encrypting the part of the database that contained the credit card information. That's security.

Broadly, data security is concerned with protecting data from unauthorized access, loss of integrity, or theft at any time in the life of the data. It involves the entire ecosystem of data, from the physical security of a building to the hardware and storage devices, to the software and administrative controls. It also includes policies and procedures.

REMEMBER

Data governance works in concert with cybersecurity — the combination of data and systems security — to provide a foundation for data security. A mature data governance environment ensures that those concerned in protecting data know what data is available, where it is, who has access to it, who owns it, and how it is managed and used. The figure in the sidebar shows an overview of one of the most popular cybersecurity frameworks.

NIST'S CYBERSECURITY FRAMEWORK

The National Institute of Standards and Technology (NIST) provides a framework to help organizations manage their cybersecurity risks. It enables team members throughout an organization to develop a shared understanding of data and systems risks.

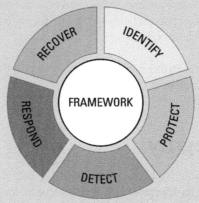

Image courtesy of National Institute of Standards and Technology (NIST)

Identify

The Identify function assists in developing an organizational understanding to managing cybersecurity risk to systems, people, assets, data, and capabilities. Understanding the business context, the resources that support critical functions, and the related cybersecurity risks enables an organization to focus and prioritize its efforts, consistent with its risk-management strategy and business needs.

Protect

The Protect function outlines appropriate safeguards to ensure delivery of critical infrastructure services. It supports the ability to limit or contain the impact of a potential cybersecurity event.

(continued)

(continued)

Detect

The Detect function defines the appropriate activities to identify the occurrence of a cybersecurity event. It enables timely discovery of cybersecurity events.

Respond

The Respond function includes appropriate activities to take action regarding a detected cybersecurity incident. It supports the ability to contain the impact of a potential cyber-security incident.

Recover

The Recover function identifies appropriate activities to maintain plans for resilience and to restore any capabilities or services that were impaired due to a cybersecurity incident. It supports timely recovery to normal operations to reduce the impact from a cybersecurity incident.

You can learn more about NIST's cybersecurity framework here: www.nist.gov/cyberframework/framework.

Integrity

REMEMBER

Data integrity is concerned with the completeness, accuracy, and quality of data during its lifecycle. Problems can occur in data sets from a simple human error such as the accidental deletion of a record. But it can also be as complex as a mali-cious employee or hacker deliberately changing data to cause downstream issues.

Data integrity can occur when one system references another that no longer sup-ports the reference. You know this experience, for example, when you click on a website link that is not active anymore. While a non-working web link can be a nuisance, a database reference can cause an entire application to fail.

This topic also spans to include incomplete data sets, sources with errors and missing values, and a whole range of cybersecurity attack strategies.

WARNING

When there are data integrity issues, confidence can fall in the data, and that has its own set of complications for system users and owners.

Avoiding and lowering the risks associated with data integrity is a component of data governance since it includes support for processes in data security, inconsis-tencies, availability, and other aspects of data management.

Business intelligence

Business intelligence, often referred to simply as BI, refers to data tools, applications, and best practices that use data from a variety of sources to create insights for organizations.

REMEMBER

BI supports the notion of the data-driven business. With data presented in a usable manner, it can help to drive change, reduce inefficiencies, and respond to evolving market conditions.

BI includes related activities such as data mining (discovering insights in large data sets), online analytical processing — OLAP (analysis of data from multiple systems simultaneously), data visualization, querying, and reporting.

In a recent survey, executives maintained that breakthrough performance with BI is only possible through the use of data governance. This is because BI requires teams to understand what data is available, where it is, and to have access to it at the right time.

Quality

This is a big one. If an organization is going to rely on the enormous value that data can bring to the table, it must be high-quality data.

TIP

Subsequently, if data governance is going to succeed in supporting that organizational aspiration, data must be high quality. In Chapter 2, I also explore why quality data matters.

REMEMBER

Data quality is concerned with the techniques and activities used to ensure that data is fit for the purpose in which it is being used. When data is well suited for a specific business need, this is considered high-quality data.

WARNING

Data is subject to all manner of quality challenges. These can include data that is duplicated in the same data set, incomplete and erroneous data, and poorly defined and unorganized data.

Assessing data quality can be determined by judging its condition based on these six dimensions:

>> **Accuracy:** Data should reflect the reality of what it represents.

>> **Completeness:** Data should include the entire relevant set of content.

>> **Consistency:** Similar data values used across systems should not be in conflict (see the previous section called "Consistency").

- >> **Validity:** Data should be collected according to parameters, a defined range, and in the correct format.

- >> **Uniqueness:** Data should have no duplicates.

- >> **Timeliness:** Relevant data should be available and used when it is required.

Achieving consistent data quality is one of the most important outcomes of good data governance. It's often said that you can't have data quality without some form of data governance. These six dimensions, for example, can form the basis for data governance policies and procedures.

TIP

When data has owners, when standards are required and policies and procedures are followed, data quality can be the outcome.

3
Developing Data Governance

Chapter **7**

Establishing Data Governance Objectives

Your data governance program must reflect the needs of your organization. This means that what you design, build, and then maintain, must be aligned to the business.

Fortunately, if you're at this stage of considering the scope of the data governance program, it means your organization understands the value and importance of managing data. Yippee! They also recognize that data must be managed for compliance purposes and to reduce risks that come with handling all types of data.

These basics are a vital foundation, but now the work begins to determine what additional objectives should be within the scope of the data governance program. You and your team need to fully immerse itself in understanding the vision and purpose of the organization. Becoming familiar with the business strategy and conducting inclusive interviews with a wide range of stakeholders is a priority. In addition to appreciating how data governance can support the organization's vision, you need to identify where the data gaps and risks are today.

Once the hard work of aligning the data governance program with the business vision has been drafted and validated, you need to shift your attention to determining how success can be achieved and measured. Certainly, metrics are central, but other factors need to be considered too.

Finally, as you establish the program, it may be useful for you and the organization to identify a level of maturity in data governance that best reflects your performance goals. It's not essential, but can be useful in tracking your progress and for benchmarking.

This chapter explores these areas and provides specific guidance to help you on your journey.

Defining an Organization's Priorities

TIP

Starting your data governance work doesn't begin with understanding your data. It begins with understanding your business. This insight must drive your early efforts to design the data governance program. There will be plenty of time and opportunity later to go deep into the data.

In an organization, everyone and everything must be aligned to its vision and purpose. If you run a business function that isn't 100 percent contributing toward the goals of the organization, that function's days are likely numbered. It does happen. Sometimes a function is no longer required. Businesses and their needs change all the time. Data governance, already a function that will have skeptics and some reluctant adoption, needs all the advantages it can take right from the start.

REMEMBER

Optimally, data governance must be seamlessly plugged into existing functions and tightly aligned with the objectives of the business. Anything less will cause unnecessary distraction and at worst, failure of the program.

Alignment with organizational needs

Open almost any business textbook and you'll read about business alignment. You've probably heard your organization's leaders speak about it too. Let's be honest; it's a pretty buzzy term. Actually, buzzy and fuzzy. In other words, it's preached a lot these days but is it actually understood? Candidly, business alignment is important for everyone in an organization to understand and to participate in.

To understand business alignment, I like to use the metaphor of an orchestra. A conductor stands in front of 90 or more musicians and helps guide them through a beautiful piece of music. The conductor ensures everyone is playing together at the same pace, in sync, and are unified in conveying the joy of the music. Success is everyone literally on the same page of music, communicating as appropriate, listening to messages, moving in the same direction, and arriving at a perfect well-received conclusion.

Conversely, if any of the musicians are not in rhythm or are out of tune, it will be immediately noticed. It will result in a bad experience for the orchestra, the conductor, and the audience. It will also be a bad day for the musician.

You can think of the orchestra members as the staff and functions of a business and the conductor as the CEO and leadership team.

A business that runs well and is aligned means that all staff and functions are working tightly together and playing the same tune. Business functions understand the purpose of their work and how it integrates into the larger mission and vision of the organization.

They are being guided by the CEO and other leaders with clarity and skill. To quote the late Jack Welsh, former CEO of General Electric and considered one of the great American industrialists, "Good business leaders create a vision, articulate the vision, passionately own the vision, and relentlessly drive it to completion."

REMEMBER

Research data supports the benefits of business alignment. For example, organizations that combine excellent execution with strategic alignment achieve 90 percent of their project objectives. Those that are misaligned hit the mark only 34 percent of the time.

Running a business as tightly and expertly as a world-class orchestra is highly aspirational. Few organizations achieve that kind of success. That said, many do get close, but it requires considerable effort and distinguished leadership.

You could assume that business alignment is obvious. After all, why wouldn't all business functions be aligned with the broader purpose of the organization? To understand the answer to this question, let's explore data governance alignment with the business and the challenges it may face.

To continue the orchestra metaphor, introducing data governance is like adding a new musician. If the musician is unskilled, out of tune, not communicating with the conductor, and out of rhythm with the rest of the orchestra, that person is not going to be successful.

WARNING

Data governance must understand its role, be responsive to leadership, and add clear value. Equally, leadership must see the value, invite its participation, and support its involvement. If any of these areas are out of alignment, you've got a problem.

Issues can occur and business alignment disrupted when leaders and team members don't see value in a function or understand its role and their role in it. They can resist support when something seems abstract or creates more unnecessary work. A function can also fail if it doesn't communicate its purpose and alignment with the business, it imposes a burden on others without explanation, and it fails to demonstrate continuous value.

Data governance can also become misaligned with the business if its deployment and uses create more risks than benefits. For example, if implemented poorly, data governance may not reduce compliance risks or increase data quality. It may impose a disproportionate burden on team members in how they handle data and result in resistance and pushback that delivers bad data management.

REMEMBER

Traditionally in business, when a new function is introduced, there is an expectation of almost immediate, tangible, and measurable results. These include areas such as increased revenue and profit, headcount reductions, and larger market share. Data governance will bring value, but it can take time and often it's harder to directly measure. For example, reducing risk is a core function of data governance and that quality can be invisible when it does its job and is successful. In other words, since risk is being reduced, an issue to measure doesn't occur.

Business alignment, including ensuring that data governance is plugged in appropriately to the organization's purpose, requires at a minimum:

>> Fully understanding the organization's requirements

>> Continuous leadership support

>> Integration with mission and vision

>> Defined and communicated value and purpose

>> Regular reporting and metrics

Each organization has its own needs and the motivation for data governance will be driven by those. There isn't a one-size-fits-them-all approach. As discussed in Chapter 5, data governance will serve one, two, or all three of these areas: a risk focus, a cost focus, or a revenue focus. Aligning data governance with the business requires fully understanding the focus areas to incorporate.

You'll document and get initial agreement on business alignment during the business case and strategy development phases.

TIP

Remaining business aligned is a continuous responsibility. Confirm it often and evolve the program as the organization requires.

Ensuring inclusiveness

Fortunately, the topic of inclusiveness has been significantly elevated in just the last few years. Leaders and recruiters are making a greater effort to hire people who represent all types of diversity in their organizations. They realize that increasing the variety of perspectives and voices at the table is, in fact, a really good business decision.

Beyond inclusiveness as just being the right thing to do, the research is pretty conclusive that inclusive business cultures generate more revenue and greater profit. One study showed 2.3 times higher profits per employee.

REMEMBER

Inclusiveness is about doing the right thing and doing well. But inclusiveness extends beyond hiring. It's about making it possible for team members to have more input on decisions and have greater opportunity to help shape the business. It's about lowering barriers so that access to opportunity in an organization is more equal and fairer.

It shouldn't be a surprise that team members want to share their ideas and skills. However, they need the culture and often the invitation to make that happen. Too many organizations still aren't inclusive in many of their activities and, not only is this unfair, but it is a missed business advantage.

Data governance often manifests for day-to-day team members in the form of new responsibilities and obligations. They get made aware of new processes, top-down mandates, policies, new tools such as a data catalog, and if they are lucky, some training. Sure, this gets the program out, understood, and underway, but it doesn't necessarily light the fire for those whose central daily concern isn't data.

TIP

There is a ton of innovation and knowledge sitting in the heads of team members. Just look at how much all of us share publicly online through a wide variety of platforms. Collaboration and knowledge sharing happens all the time outside the enterprise. The trick for business leaders is to unleash that same enthusiasm inside the organization.

One of the simplest ways to create inclusiveness in the formation of your data governance program is to invite participation. I recommend making inclusiveness central to your efforts.

I discuss different and diverse roles in the data governance program in Chapter 8. While discussing inclusiveness here, I'm including these roles but also suggesting the engagement of a much broader set of team members at every level in every part of the organization.

Across the organization, team members observe the role of data, they have tacit knowledge, they are closest to issues, and they often have ideas on solutions. Nobody understands data and its role more than those who operate in the context of its use.

By inviting participation in whatever form is most effective, you can help to liberate insights that build a better data governance program and one that has a greater likelihood of support from across the organization. You will also get more ownership for processes and data. Data governance by definition is a shared and enterprise-wide responsibility, so you want to emphasize distributed responsibilities and management.

Adopting an inclusiveness approach to your data governance program will help to better define objectives, design the program, and then implement and maintain it. Learn from the mistakes of an exclusively top-down leadership approach and give yourself the best opportunity for your data governance program to succeed right from the start.

Determining the Desired Outcomes

Designing a successful data governance program means aligning with business objectives and consistently delivering value. But what exactly does success look like? How can you measure success? Identifying and managing specific data metrics is central, but there are other factors too, such as acceptance of the program and the development of a data culture.

You need to define your success criteria before the program launches and then continuously as the program is maintained for the long term. Spend time in this process, as it will pay dividends. Articulating what success will look like is an excellent way to set expectations.

Understanding and achieving program success

Being able to communicate the value and success of a data governance program may be required not only as the program is operating — this requirement is essential — but also prior to and during the implementation stage.

As a complex program, data governance often requires significant time and money to maintain. To be sustained and even further matured, value must be continuously demonstrated and communicated.

You'll likely spend extensive time building the business case and getting buy-in from decision-makers about the need for a data governance program. This is time well spent. As some point, someone is probably going to ask what a successful program will look like. It's a good question to be able to answer well, because it forces you to articulate the vision and strategic benefits of a future state, even if you're not sure what tactical metrics will be achieved.

In addition, making a promise on what is expected in terms of success is also a way to shape expectations. You might also discover that your idea of success is not in alignment with expectations. If this is going to happen, this is exactly the right time to learn that insight.

Prior to the creation of the program is the right time to get all stakeholders on the same page. You have to make success relevant to stakeholders. It will add more time to this phase of the effort, but every moment spent building alignment, relevance, and agreement on expectations is absolutely worth it.

With the assumption that the data governance program is executed well and assimilated into the organization, be clear on what success will look like before you build the program. You'll also report on those successes when the program is operating. The tools to communicate success include data-related metrics and other information.

If you're looking for specific data governance metrics and key performance indicators (KPIs), you can skip to Chapter 12. In this section, I describe the bigger picture relative to measuring success.

REMEMBER

Metrics matter, but success has measurements beyond specific qualitative targets.

It's worth reminding that, in business, achieving targets can take many forms. For example, it's always possible to take a variety of approaches that get the same result, but the cost of getting there may be quite different. Specifically, you could reach a target by issuing a series of threats or you could create an environment where individuals are motivated and excited to achieve results.

Same outcome, very different approach.

TIP

I encourage you to articulate data governance success in terms of the raw metrics and the positive and rewarding data culture that can be created. A broad quantitative and qualitative approach is optimal.

A way to look at communicating success is through the following five dimensions. I've included brief examples of scope for each. These dimensions are also the building blocks to data governance success.

>> **Strategic alignment:** Do the data governance outcomes support and align with the goals and objectives of the organization?

>> **Data culture:** Is the data governance program improving areas such as data quality, data standardization, data democratization, and improved data-driven decision-making?

>> **People:** Relative to data governance and value, do team members have training, do they understand their role, and are the governance requirements communicated clearly?

>> **Process:** To what degree are the data governance processes supporting privacy, risk, compliance, addressing data issues, and other data requirements?

>> **Technology:** Are the right technology solutions available to team members and effective in supporting each of these dimensions?

Figure 7-1 illustrates how these five dimensions become building blocks to success.

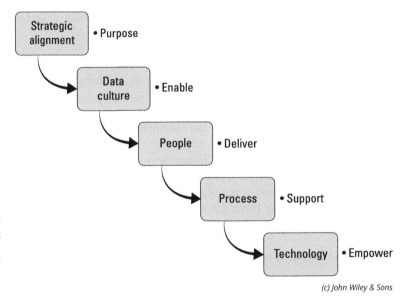

FIGURE 7-1:
The building blocks of data governance success.

You want data governance to succeed. That's obvious. If you and your team have done your job, the organization will also want the program to succeed. You won't convert everyone but getting almost everyone to see the value and support the effort is an acceptable goal.

TIP

Don't move forward if there isn't an acceptable level of support.

There are a few things you can do to increase the likelihood of data governance success:

>> **Measure success:** This first item seems strange. Why would measuring success increase the likelihood of success? The fact is that many organizations that deploy data governance programs don't put mechanisms in place to report on metrics and success. Without this data, there's no way to know if success is being achieved. You also can't make course corrections when things aren't going well, which is to be expected. If something isn't working well, you want to know about it so that you can remedy it.

>> **Run as a program:** Some organizations approach data governance as a project. They do many of the right things such as creating standards, policies, and deploying tools. They may even provide training. Then the project ends, the team disperses, and it's not clear what the business is left with. This is problematic. The right way to approach data governance is as a program. Of course, at first, it begins as a project. You have to sell the program, get budgeting, and there is plenty to build. But as the project aspects wind down, the operational parts ramp up.

>> **Engage raving fans:** Not everyone is going to be a fan of the data governance program. Let's be really clear about that. In fact, you may experience blatant political hostility to the notion of such a program. I'm not an organizational psychologist, so I'll avoid any deeper commentary on that for now. Just know that, unlike many of the other projects and programs you work on, you'll need to work even harder to convert some leaders and team members. What you want to do early is to find those people who totally get the value of data governance and are, in fact, excited by the prospect of the value it can bring to their role, function, and the organization. Find these people early, keep them close as your allies, and tap into their passion.

>> **Grow incrementally:** You're reading this book, so I already know that you are an over-achiever. You want to build a data governance program that crushes it. As this book outlines, data governance can be an expansive program. As the upper end, data governance can be baked into almost every aspect of an organization's function. It can be a central operating philosophy that touches everything and everybody. But equally, data governance may be deployed to have a narrower focus. Perhaps its goal in the organization is to ensure privacy when handling personal data. There will be a wide spectrum of ambition for the program by each business. Success can be increased by developing the program in smaller blocks starting with the minimum measurable activities. Quick wins can also build credibility and rapidly demonstrate value. Then as time passes and confidence increases, the program can be matured, and more capabilities can be added. The next section in this chapter

on maturity models illustrates how different levels of maturity can be quantified and targeted.

>> **Amplify roles:** In Chapter 8, you discover many of the essential roles within data governance. Some roles, depending on the size of the organization, will be full-time. Many others, particularly in smaller businesses, will be part-time. Either way, these roles are how data governance is achieved. When data governance is deployed, the business may learn about data stewards and owners for the first time. They may not understand their roles and how to work with them. Successful data governance programs ensure that these roles and their responsibilities are communicated clearly and often, and their value is amplified. These are your data governance champions. Make sure those in these roles know that and all their stakeholders.

>> **Embrace cross-functional engagement:** Okay, fair enough, many of the responsibilities in data governance do involve your information technology (IT) staff. They'll be on the hook for systems, many data management tasks, cybersecurity, and a whole bunch more. It would be too easy to point to IT as the responsible party for data governance. When pointing at someone else, you're pointing away from yourself. It's a way of saying it's someone else's responsibility. If the organization believes data governance belongs to IT, it will wash its hands of accountability and the program will flounder and even fail. I can't say this any louder: data governance is everyone's responsibility. Roles and responsibilities will differ for sure, but each role has value and is important at its time and place.

>> **Communicate often:** Here's a piece of advice that I've incorporated into my life and work for many years with a great deal of success: *Tell people what you're going to do, tell them you're doing it, and then tell them what you did.* Even if you think people know what's going on, there's a good chance they don't or if they do, they don't have enough information. In any project or program, communication plays a large role. You must communicate clearly and often. There's a chance of over-communication but that's a more acceptable criticism than under-communication, which will cause many more problems. This is such an important topic that I explore it in detail in Chapter 9.

Agreeing on a desired maturity level

Organizations constantly make choices about their desired level of performance. These choices may be based on criteria such as strategy, need, capability, and cost. For example, in developing software, a business may decide that it's important for them to have defined, repeatable processes to ensure quality outcomes. However, they may also have little interest in being an organization that sets the standard for others. Being a follower may just be fine for them to meet their needs.

Striving for a certain performance goal is often represented as a level within a maturity model. These models, which explicitly document ascending levels of performance maturity, have been developed for many industries by a wide variety of bodies.

For example, in software development, the Software Engineering Institute Capability Maturity Model (SEICMM) has five levels. Level one represents a basic and weak level of software development with significant room for improvement, whereas level five is the optimal level of performance in building software. Organizations that create software may decide on a desired level that best aligns with their needs and goals. The maturity model provides them with a roadmap and performance benchmarks. For example, if they are currently assessed at level two, but want to be level four, they have a way to manage the improvement process and know when they reach their goal.

Just like in software development and many other domains, data governance also has maturity models. Several respected models exist from organizations such as IBM, Gartner, and Oracle. Fortunately, they all follow a relatively similar pattern and, just like many other maturity models, there are typically five levels.

I've taken the best aspects of several data governance maturity models and created one that captures the core qualities of each. Figure 7-2 is a visual representation of this model.

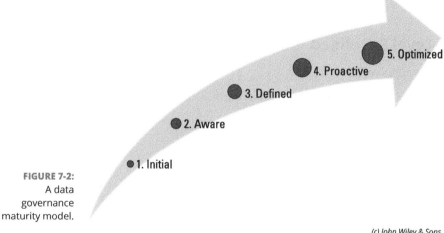

FIGURE 7-2: A data governance maturity model.

(c) John Wiley & Sons

As you review each level, consider the following:

>> If you have an existing data governance program, what level best aligns with its performance?

>> If you are creating a data governance program, what level would you like to achieve?

Level 1: Initial

>> Data governance is not implemented

>> The value of data is not well understood

>> Managing data needs is generally chaotic

>> Data compliance and risk issues are reactive

Level 2: Aware

>> The value of data is recognized

>> Data management processes exist

>> A form of data inventory is available

>> The challenges of poor data quality are understood

Level 3: Defined

>> Data policies exist

>> Many data owners and stewards are in place

>> A data catalog is available

>> Master data management is implemented

Level 4: Proactive

>> Data policies are enforced

>> Data quality standards are established and monitored

>> Enterprise data governance is implemented

>> Data models are available for the enterprise

Level 5: Optimized

>> Data governance automation is implemented

>> A data culture has been established

>> Data management is enterprise-wide

>> Data is being used for competitive advantage

REMEMBER

A data governance maturity model is something that you use for the purposes of creating a performance roadmap. It's not set in stone. You should feel free to modify the model based on discussions in your organization. At the end of the day, the maturity model is a tool to serve your needs.

As you embark on your data governance journey, a maturity model will be your travelling friend. Use it in conjunction with your organization's data governance objectives. It will help you to find your destination and determine how you'll get there.

Chapter **8**

Identifying Data Governance Roles and Responsibilities

I n the process of designing and developing data governance for your organization, you need to identify the roles and responsibilities necessary for delivering and maintaining the program. Tools, systems, procedures, and policies are all essential, but won't achieve success alone. Data governance remains a highly human-dependent subject. You need the right people, in the right roles, doing the right thing.

Data governance is an enterprise-wide and centrally-managed ongoing effort. It's not a series of projects that start and end. To be successful, you need to work with your colleagues to identify and assign responsibilities to a wide range of business stakeholders.

In this chapter, I identify and explore the typical roles and responsibilities found in organizations that have successfully deployed data governance programs. In addition to permanent governance councils, I also discuss the roles of executives and others across the organization and explain how their efforts can make or break the goals of the program.

Exploring Roles and Responsibilities in Data Governance

Despite some excellent tools and even with a growing number of automation solutions, you need to rely on people with a variety of skills to drive a successful data governance program.

As early as the proposal stage, you need to decide and document the high-level roles and responsibilities that you anticipate will be required to support a successful program. You need this information in order to help decision-makers understand the scope and commitment of the program, as well as the potential costs. Later, during the design phase, you'll develop more detail on specific responsibilities and how roles will work together across the organization.

TIP

The supporting organization you need will reflect the objectives of the program, the industry, and the size and complexity of the organization:

>> Depending on the organization and its needs, managing data governance can be as simple as the lead role being part of just one person's existing job or as elaborate as a large team that is centralized and decentralized across functions.

>> I recommend creating data governance programs that start small and grow over time. This also applies to the team that will be formed in support of the program. Start small and add more people and responsibilities as time passes and benefits are validated.

>> Most people in an organization will have some responsibilities for data governance. Any user who handles data in their role, from data entry to data analysis will be in scope.

>> Also included are most C-suite leaders, managers, supervisors, technical staff, legal, sales, marketing, accounting, and auditors. Vendors and other external partners may have important responsibilities too.

This chapter explores common roles with elevated and substantive data governance tasks and accountabilities.

WARNING

Determining the roles you'll need and who will fill them requires careful consideration. Each has challenges. If you don't identify the right roles, there will be gaps in operating the program. Depending on the size of these gaps, issues will quickly escalate. Similarly, appointing the wrong people — something that can happen in any recruitment process — can result in dysfunction that can unravel the basics of a data governance program.

Identify the right roles and make some smart personnel appointments and your chances of getting off to a strong start are improved. In other words, the pressure is on to appropriately design and staff data governance.

In considering the roles and responsibilities in the organization, you can think about team members in three levels of participation.

>> **Strategic:** Decision-makers and those with oversight for the program. Examples: Data Governance Board (DGB) and C-level staff such as the Chief Executive Officer, Chief Information Officer, and Chief Data Officer.

>> **Tactical:** Team members with specific data governance responsibilities across the organization. Examples: Data steward, data owner, cybersecurity analyst, data architect, and compliance officer.

>> **Operational:** Team members in specific functions that handle and use data in their work.

If there is a dedicated data governance team or even just a data governance manager, these individuals' work will span across all three layers. Figure 8-1 illustrates this organizational structure.

Data governance manager

Someone needs to lead and manage the enterprise-wide data governance program. This is the role of the data governance manager. Depending on the size of the organization and degree of responsibilities, this could certainly be a senior manager or director level too. Sometimes it is fulfilled by the role of the Chief Data Officer. In smaller businesses, it might be just part of someone's main role.

REMEMBER

A data governance manager leads and often has hands-on responsibilities for establishing and maintaining the data governance program across the enterprise. This person is a data champion who helps to create a vision for data in the organization. This includes developing a roadmap and executing an implementation plan.

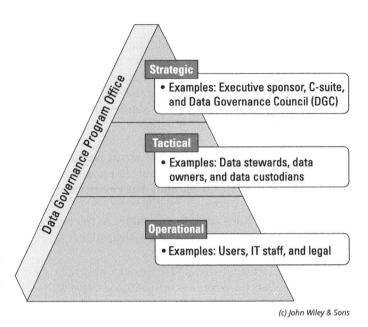

FIGURE 8-1:
Comprehensive view of a data governance organization.

Data Governance Program Office

Strategic
- Examples: Executive sponsor, C-suite, and Data Governance Council (DGC)

Tactical
- Examples: Data stewards, data owners, and data custodians

Operational
- Examples: Users, IT staff, and legal

(c) John Wiley & Sons

Within scope is oversight for policies, standards, and practices related to data management. It should focus on data quality, consistency, and security across organizational functions.

This person is the central point of contact for data governance and works closely with all levels of staff across the organization.

Other responsibilities may include:

>> Identifying data governance roles, responsibilities, accountabilities across the enterprise.

>> Facilitating the creation of data standards.

>> Defining data governance metrics.

>> Leading teams, committees, and projects relative to data priorities.

>> Overseeing and providing input into regular data governance reports for leadership and other teams.

>> Coordinating activities between the business and technology to ensure data priorities.

>> Assisting with the identification and acquisition of data management tools.

>> Championing data as an enterprise asset and sustaining an innovative vision on behalf and with leadership.

Data owner

When working on a project, I often ask who owns a particular data set. This question often results in blank stares. I'm trying to determine who is the one leader who really cares about this data I'm working with and knows if it is, for example, accurate, current, compliant, and complete. The blank stares are a result of the organization putting little to no emphasis on data ownership. It's not necessarily deliberate. The absence of data ownership can be simply the result of it being an unfamiliar competency.

TIP

Each data set requires an owner. Simple as that.

Data owners have responsibilities relative to data that falls within their purview. For example, sales data likely falls under the head of sales. Perhaps customer data too. Prospective customer data might belong to marketing. In a city organization, permit data likely belongs to the planning director. Some data is widely shared and as a result may roll up to the Chief Information Officer as a custodian of shared enterprise data. You're probably getting the idea now.

Some organizations use the term *data trustee* when referring to the typical responsibilities of a data owner. These terms are interchangeable to a degree, although some will point out that a data trustee is usually a senior executive, and the role is a small part of what they do.

REMEMBER

Data owners need to care about the data most important to them, because, frankly, no one else will. For example, if you are the head of legal and the systems you use store legal data, that data is your concern. It doesn't mean it belongs to you — although that might be semantics — it means that you care about its quality, integrity, availability, and more. You also have authority for who can access the data.

WARNING

I've shared a lot in this book about data governance being the source of some disruption. The act of assigning data to owners is one of the challenges you will face. Stakeholders who never thought about data ownership previously will be stunned by the notion that they now have responsibilities vis-à-vis their data!

Other responsibilities may include:

>> Ensuring data accuracy.

>> Improving data quality.

>> Resolving data issues.

>> Reviewing relevant master data management.

>> Providing input on regulatory and compliance issues.

>> Enforcing data policies and standards.

Data steward

The role of the data steward is at the heart of data governance. In my view, this role is essential for making the whole program work. A data steward has account-ability for the day-to-day management of data in the organization. They are sub-ject matter experts for data sets within their purview, which could span from a workgroup to a department to an entire business function.

Data stewards work with other data stewards who represent different parts of the organization to make data use decisions, focus on enterprise data quality, and resolve data issues. Importantly, a data steward is the expert representative who acts on behalf of one or more data owners in a business unit.

Data stewards aren't technology staff, and they may not be full-time positions but rather part of an existing role in a business function. Technical knowledge is valuable, but not necessary.

REMEMBER

However, they are data specialists, and they have data-related skills. They deeply understand the data within their scope. Of course, some data stewards are tech-nology team members who come to the table with technical expertise.

The role is an individual contributor, but it is highly collaborative with other stakeholders. Data stewards are typically members of the Data Governance Board (DGB), discussed later in this chapter, and they may also convene their own Data Steward Council (DSC).

Other responsibilities may include:

>> Identifying and defining data assets within the area of responsibility.

>> Working collaboratively to create processes, procedures, policies, standards, and controls.

>> Focusing on ensuring data quality.

>> Communicating data value and issues with other data stewards and data owners.

>> Optimizing the use and flow of data across the organization.

>> Ensuring compliance and security of data.

>> Resolving data issues in the data lifecycle.

>> Reporting activities, issues, and decisions to data owners.

>> Representing the interests of data owners and their business function on the DGB.

Data custodian

There can be some confusion about the differences between data owners, stewards, and custodians. A data owner is usually a senior leader within a business function with ultimate responsibility for the strategy, quality, value, and access approvals for data in their domain. The data steward is the day-to-day action-oriented representative for the data owner to ensure data responsibilities are carried out and data quality is maintained. A data custodian is a technology role and typically lives in the IT organization. This person ensures the protection, safe transport, and appropriate storage of business data. I've summarized these focus areas in Figure 8-2.

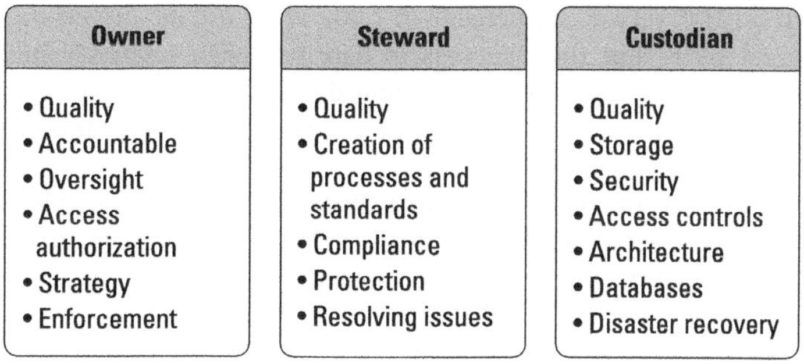

FIGURE 8-2:
How each of
these data roles
differs in their
areas of focus.

Owner	Steward	Custodian
• Quality • Accountable • Oversight • Access authorization • Strategy • Enforcement	• Quality • Creation of processes and standards • Compliance • Protection • Resolving issues	• Quality • Storage • Security • Access controls • Architecture • Databases • Disaster recovery

(c) John Wiley & Sons

Sometimes a data steward and data custodian are the same role. You can decide this for your organization.

Often, a data custodian is a database administrator. They focus on how data should be protected, stored, and transported based on business requirements. Data custodians also manage the servers, backups, networks, and now the cloud architecture where data increasingly resides. They are knowledgeable in *data lineage*, meaning they understand where data has come from, what it is subjected to, and how it moves. Data custodians also have visibility to and can manage the *data schema*, which is the architecture of how a database is designed and constructed.

Unlike data owners and stewards, a data custodian knows the technical details of data and how it's stored, but not about its value and use in the organization.

Other responsibilities may include:

>> Implementing user access requirements.

>> Managing system-level data rules.

>> Ensuring data quality during data processing such as extract-transport-load (ETL) functions.

>> Collaborating with data stewards to resolve data issues.

>> Maintaining data redundancy and disaster recovery.

>> Providing audit reports on data.

Roles of the chiefs in data governance

Today, a growing number of leaders recognize the value of data. In fact, according to an IDC survey, 83 percent of CEOs want a data-driven organization. That's great news, but their success to date has been relatively limited. Specifically, despite their aspiration to become data-driven, 63 percent of executives in a recent Deloitte survey said they don't believe their companies are data-driven.

There are a number of reasons for the lack of progress, but a lot of research points to weaknesses in leadership, creating the conditions for a thriving data culture. Only five percent of executives cite technology as the source of the issues.

A data culture is present in an organization that exhibits behaviors consistent with valuing data as a contributor toward success. These organizations have deeply integrated data into their operations and identity. They provide the skills and tools for team members to be data-driven in how they conduct their work. A data culture can be recognized as one where people, processes, and technology are aligned to support timely data-driven decision-making. These cultures solve all manner of challenges, from the simplest to the most complex, using data where it makes sense.

In organizations of all types, culture is often the result of the actions and orientation of leadership. The Chief Executive Officer (CEO), in particular, is cited as the central source of shaping culture. But it doesn't stop at the CEO. Responsibility lies with all members of the C-suite, that is, the executive positions in a company with the word *Chief* in their job title. When it comes to data, how these chiefs access and use data, speak about data, and drive decisions from a data perspective speaks volumes.

If these chiefs expect their teams to be data-driven, but don't demonstrate the behaviors themselves, it sends a mixed message. It has the potential to create the conditions for an organization that may only humor the notion of a data culture.

Clearly, for data governance to have any likelihood of success, a modicum of a data culture is a prerequisite. In the following section, I discuss how several of the C-suite members can support both a data culture and the behaviors necessary to govern data.

Chief Executive Officer (CEO)

An organization's most senior leader is the CEO. Some other entities may have a different title, such as a partnership calling its highest role a managing partner. Whatever the role is called, the person tasked with running the business from day-to-day and who all other C-suite leaders report to, has the most influence on its culture.

REMEMBER

How the CEO behaves, what they believe, and the values they champion will trickle down through their direct reports and into the entire organization. If a CEO comes to the role with a data-driven posture and preaches the importance of data to the organization, this presents an advantage. The CEO reports will get this message quickly and the organization will be on its way to beginning or elevating a data culture.

However, in the event that they don't immediately present with a data-driven mindset, all is not lost. CEOs, just like any team member, can be educated. The absence or resistance to a data-centric orientation may not be the result of some deliberate choice. It may just be that they aren't aware of the ultimate value of data, how it can be used, and how it can be governed.

TIP

In this situation, other leaders, perhaps the Chief Data Officer (CDO) or equivalent, can view this as an opportunity to coach the CEO. Demonstrating value perhaps through presenting the high risks of non-compliance or with data to support reaching new customers will all go a long way. Converting the CEO to be the biggest advocate of data won't happen overnight and will be measured on a case-by-case basis.

Over a period of time, if there's no progress in converting the CEO into being a passionate data-driven leader, I fear this may be a red flag.

Assuming the CEO is on the same page relative to the value and priority of data, here's a summary of actions they can take to support a data culture:

>> **Lead by example:** Model behavior in the use of data in areas such as decision-making, risk management, and business growth.

- >> **Education:** Provide support and funds for data training and tools.

- >> **Rewards:** Create incentives for leaders and team members that encourage data-driven behaviors.

- >> **Recognition:** Bring attention and highlight individual and team data successes.

- >> **Marketing:** Provide forums such as open houses and communities of practice for team members to learn about the potential for data, including demonstrating real solutions.

The CEO could be the data governance sponsor, an executive who serves as a conduit between the C-suite and the data governance leadership groups. It's more likely the CEO will appoint an executive sponsor who they trust and believe is best qualified.

TIP

The executive sponsor for data governance must be given the authority to make strategic decisions, including funding approval authority.

Chief Data Officer (CDO)

The Chief Data Officer (CDO), as the name suggests, is the most senior executive responsible for overseeing and governing data in the organization. In the last few years, as more enterprises have recognized the importance of data and the growing risk, compliance, and regulatory requirements, many have appointed a CDO.

REMEMBER

In fact, in a lot of organizations, the CDO is the data governance leader. This will be a decision unique to your business. But regardless of whether it's their role or someone else's, the CDO is ultimately accountable for the operations of data governance.

The CDO is centrally concerned with ensuring that data is treated as a valuable asset, and it's diligently managed and governed. This role is a champion of data in all its aspects and works to break down data silos and maximize its enterprise value. They may work alone or, depending on the size of the organization, they may have sizable teams that include data managers, analysts, scientists, and technologists.

Many in the C-suite look to the CDO to help find opportunities to create value from data. This requires collaboration and helping other leaders to ask the right questions about data. The CDO must partner with all leaders, as the role is cross-functional in its oversight and impact. It provides a voice for a data vision on behalf of its C-suite peers.

The CDO is second only to the CEO in being most likely to shape a data culture. The CDO must be a role model in how data can be used, managed, and governed. This role will provide opportunities for team members and groups to shine in their use of data, including making investments in data skills, literacy, and tools. Similar to all C-suite executives, the CDO must provide a vision and a roadmap for what is possible. Related to this, they lead the creation of a data strategy. Refer to data strategy creation in Chapter 4.

While many roles related to data are concerned with a specific aspect such as access, the CDO must have a 360-degree view of data across the organization. This includes the role of data as a business asset, but also in the technologies that support and manage data. The CDO works closely with information technology (IT) leadership on a variety of data aspects, including some of the IT-specific data governance responsibilities — hosting, processing, and security.

Finally, an important part of the CDO's role is to help to improve data quality — a core dimension of data governance. While data quality is increasingly part of everyone's role, the CDO has a leadership obligation to focus on data factors such as accuracy, completeness, consistency, reliability, and currency.

Chief Compliance Officer (CCO)

The Chief Compliance Officer (CCO) is the executive tasked with the primary responsibility for overseeing — no surprise — compliance areas in the organization. Compliance areas for organizations include laws, regulations, policies, and procedures related to their industry and responsibilities.

The CCO leads, guides, or works alongside those who create compliance-related programs that enable the identification, prevention, detection, and correction of non-compliance issues. The role continuously improves processes and evolves them as conditions require.

This role is required to provide confidence to the C-suite and other reporting authorities that the organization has appropriate controls, processes, and procedures in place. The CCO has responsibility to ensure that the business is equipped to comply with its obligations. This includes making sure that compliance items are understood by leaders and team members across the organization. The CCO must identify training needs and communicate updates to requirements.

In the event of a material non-compliance issue, the CCO must bring the issue to the attention of the CEO and other leaders.

As you can imagine, the CCO works closely with the Chief Data Officer and the data governance leader. While the CCO has responsibility for all compliance issues, the role will intersect in matters of data. Increasingly, many of the CCO compliance areas have a data component, so you can expect frequent interaction between these different roles. The data governance leader must view the CCO as an ally. After all, the goals of both roles are highly aligned. A CCO can provide timely updates to the data leaders as well as being someone who can identify and alert them to risks.

Chief Information Officer (CIO)

The Chief Information Officer (CIO) is the executive responsible for all technology that supports the goals of the organization. By the way, this is a role I've filled twice in my career, once in the private sector and once in the public sector. Data was a priority focus of my work in both instances.

A CIO creates the information technology (IT) strategy that identifies, aligns, and supports the software, hardware, data, and networks with the needs of the business. The CIO is part technologist, part business leader. In recent years, there's been greater emphasis on the latter given the role that technology now has in driving almost every organization. As a result, the CIO must deeply understand the needs of the business and know how current and emerging technologies can help run operations and support success in the marketplace. They often act as a liaison between the business and the technology teams.

REMEMBER

Under the purview of the CIO are the data custodian responsibilities. These include areas such as supporting how data is processed, stored, moved, searchable, secured, and backed up. In addition, in the absence of a Chief Data Officer, a CIO often has that role.

CIOs are often data owners too. This is because many data sets don't belong to a specific function but rather are shared among the organization. In these instances, the CIO is an obvious choice as they manage a shared function. As a simple example, the data that enables an email system would be an obvious data ownership responsibility for a CIO.

TIP

The CIO and CDO work closely as executive-level partners. Each depends on each other to be successful. The better the collaboration and relationship, the greater it is for data governance and ultimately, the business.

At the risk of over-simplifying the relationship, the CDO focuses on driving the value of data, while the CIO must empower and support that value through providing the underlying technology architecture and infrastructure. Where a CDO or data governance manager drives data governance, the implementation and support of data governance is enabled by data management systems. Those are the purview of the CIO.

Of course, in reality, the demarcation is much less clear. For one thing, the CIO has a strategic role and can provide advisory services to the C-suite and other leaders in the use of data.

Today, CIOs have accepted these essential and priority responsibilities relative to data governance. The CIO is part of the team.

Chief Information Security Officer (CISO)

The Chief Information Security Officer (CISO) is the most senior executive responsible for establishing the security of technology systems and ensuring that data is protected. Collectively this field has become commonly known as *cybersecurity*. The CISO works closely with the CIO to ensure that systems, networks, and data are appropriately protected.

The protection of data falls into three categories: Confidentiality, Integrity, and Availability, known as the *CIA triad*:

>> **Confidentiality:** Ensuring only authorized users have access to data within a system.

>> **Integrity:** Ensuring that data is trustworthy and free of tampering.

>> **Availability:** Ensuring that data is available where and when users require it.

REMEMBER

A CISO creates and maintains an information security strategy that includes policies, architecture, processes, and systems to reduce risks. Both compliance responsibilities and risk management are top concerns of this role.

CISOs constantly review the threat landscape to understand the threats to the organization. They must be constantly vigilant as cybersecurity risks evolve quickly. In addition to implementing and supporting solutions to protect the organization, the CISO is tasked with a leadership role in responding to security incidents that inevitably occur. Solving the issue, reducing the impact, and then working with the CIO to reduce its reoccurrence are central to the role.

WARNING

Unfortunately, cybersecurity continues to be a major risk for every type of organization. The possibility of data breaches is exceptionally high. According to the 2021 Cyberthreat Defense Report (CDR), 86 percent of organizations were compromised by a cyberattack.

Ensuring the protection of data — the CIA triad — is core to data governance. For this reason, the CISO is a central leader in supporting data governance objectives, working alongside the CDO and CIO.

CDOs aren't necessarily technologists. Some are, and that's a real asset to an organization. Most CDOs must rely on the CIO and CISO to provide relevant technology support. CISOs will help implement the security policies of data governance by identifying appropriate controls and then working with the CIO to deploy them.

Through understanding data governance needs, the CISO can also make determinations regarding enterprise-wide cybersecurity solutions, such as *multi-factor authentication*. This is when more than one method, say, beyond a login name and password, is required to gain access to a system. As an example, thumbprints are often used.

REMEMBER

The CDO, CIO, and CISO are the primary executives that oversee and enable data governance. These roles require superior collaboration and communication skills. If these three can work well together, understand their roles, have CEO support and a budget, well, maybe, just maybe, a solid foundation will be set for data governance success.

Creating Data Governance Leadership Groups

On any given day, at any given moment, data responsibility is in the hands of data users. These are team members who handle data in the course of their work. Consider anyone who enters data, creates a report, submits a query, or builds an application. It could be anyone from an intern right through to a senior executive. It's almost everyone. Each has relevant responsibilities. With data governance, those responsibilities take on additional importance and urgency.

These obligations are the result of groups that are formally created to deliver and support data governance. These groups have responsibilities that include deploying and overseeing a strategy, creating standards, enforcing rules, and operating and maintaining the program.

In this section, I explore the most common formal groups that bring leaders and team members together to ensure that data governance runs smoothly and is itself governed.

Data Stewardship Council (DSC)

Earlier in this chapter, I summarized the role of the data steward and emphasized that this is the central role in making data governance a successful reality.

Depending on the size and complexity of the organization, each data steward usually represents a business function, such as sales or marketing, and they carry the major responsibilities for data governance.

REMEMBER

It wouldn't be efficient if each data steward carried out their responsibilities independently and without coordination and collaboration across the enterprise. After all, with data governance, you're focused on maximizing the value of data and reducing its risks as an enterprise asset. Data stewards working alone and without coordination would be insufficient to achieve the aspirations of good data governance.

TIP

What's needed is a forum for data stewards to guide and standardize their cross-organizational activities. Called the Data Stewardship Council (DSC), this is the formal group that brings the data stewards together on a regular basis for the purposes of coordinating and ensuring consistency in efforts.

The DSC is led by the enterprise data steward and is tasked with providing leadership, program management, and metrics for the council. An enterprise data steward can simply be a nominated data steward among the group, but it can also be the data governance manager and even the chief data officer.

Regular meetings are held and are the forum for making enterprise-wide decisions on data governance operations and reaching agreement on consistent approaches. In implementation, data stewards will localize the guidance to the needs of their business function. For example, the group may agree on the use of metadata, but the terms relevant to a specific domain will be at the discretion of the function.

The actions in scope of the DSC are usually tactical. Higher-level strategic guidance is usually provided by the Data Governance Council, which I discuss later.

The DSC advances the data governance program by the following:

>> Aligning data efforts with business goals.

>> Seeking ways to explore data value.

>> Advising on new standards and modifications to existing standards.

>> Resolving enterprise-wide data issues.

>> Creating and communicating data recommendations to stakeholders.

>> Providing data metrics.

>> Evaluating and providing feedback on the effectiveness of data governance.

Data Governance Council (DGC)

While the Data Stewardship Council (DSC) is a tactically-focused group, the organization requires another data governance group that provides executive-level strategic guidance and oversight.

A Data Governance Council (DGC), also referred to as a Data Governance Board or Data Governance Committee, is the organization's overall governing body for data governance strategy and support. Its priorities include approving policies and standards, prioritizing data efforts, enforcement efforts, and communicating value up and down the organization. The DGC empowers the entire organization to create value with data while also ensuring compliance with security, privacy, and other regulations.

REMEMBER

The DGC is comprised of a variety of participants that appropriately represent the organization. Again, its composition will be a reflection of the size and complexity of the organization. Remember to design these groups commensurate with available resources, capacity, and need. If they are overstaffed, people will criticize them as overkill. Understaff them and you won't have sufficient governance in place to run an effective program. Also note that in some organizations, the Data Governance Council is combined with the Data Stewardship Council. It's just one group.

The board can be run by a nominated executive, although if that is the approach, data skills and experience should be a consideration. More often, the Chief Information Officer, Chief Data Officer, or data governance manager is assigned to lead the group.

Members of the DGC, sometimes referred to as *data governors*, may include one or more of the following:

>> Representatives from each major business function

>> Enterprise data steward

>> IT manager

>> Security analyst

>> Legal analyst

>> Auditor

>> Representative for data users

>> Depending on who is running the council, the CIO, CDO, CISO, and data governance manager

Additional responsibilities of the DGC include:

>> Approving standards, procedures, and policies. Smaller organizations may require the DGC to create these too.

>> Approving funds for data governance efforts.

>> Reviewing and approving data tools.

>> Establishing data governance goals and overseeing progress.

>> Prioritizing data projects.

>> Providing guidance and actions to the Data Stewardship Council (DSC).

>> Resolving enterprise-wide data issues that can't be resolved by the DSC.

>> Communicating and promoting the value of data governance across the organization.

>> Enforcing the data governance program.

>> Evaluating the effectiveness of data governance and initiating course corrections as necessary.

>> Overseeing the ethical use of data.

Data Governance Program Office (DGPO)

I've discussed the Data Stewardship Council (tactical focus) and the Data Governance Council (strategic focus), two of the central governing bodies for your organization's data governance program. However, a group must be tasked with coordinating day-to-day operations of the program. The DSC and DGC are both formal teams that meet on a periodic basis. For example, the DSC may meet monthly and the DGC quarterly. An operational team needs to be active and engaged potentially daily. This is the Data Governance Program Office (DGPO), or sometimes simply referred to as the Data Governance Office (DGO).

REMEMBER

The DGPO may just be a collection of staff who spend a small part of their role engaged in operational activities. It could also be an office of one, with just the data governance manager as the only full-time employee. Large and complex organizations will have several full-time employees with the data governance manager as the official lead.

Team members, full- and part-time, may include one or more of the following:

>> Data analyst

>> Data governance specialist

>> Project manager

>> Compliance analyst

>> Security analyst

>> Technical writers

>> Reporting analyst

You need to determine what makes sense for your business.

The primary purpose of the DGPO is to be a support team to formally coordinate the activities of the DSC, DGC, and data stewards, owners, custodians, and users.

Additional responsibilities of the DGC include:

>> Overseeing the development and maintenance of the data governance program.

>> Administration, including scheduling and facilitating agendas for the DSC and DGC.

>> Creating and delivering data governance training.

>> Developing reports for leadership and the DGC.

>> Evaluating and providing feedback on the effectiveness the data governance program.

Chapter **9**

Designing a Data Governance Program

N o two data governance programs are alike. They have similarities, but your program will reflect your organization's unique needs. The size of the business matters, as does its complexity and the industry. But perhaps the most defining quality is the focus of the efforts. For some organizations, lowering risk is the main priority. Others want less risk but seek to have data a source of innovation.

A data governance program doesn't really exist — and shouldn't — if the goals are not clear and defined. There can be some notional aspect to initiating a program, say, to ensure that data privacy is enforced. But an argument like that doesn't need a data governance program. It just needs some policies and leadership support.

By embarking on a program, you're sending a message that the organization has some important data-related goals and the only way to achieve them is through an investment in the people, processes, and technology of an ongoing initiative.

To get the program underway requires defining the problem and analyzing it and then designing the solution. You and your team need to identify the right stakeholders. You need to work closely with them to design the program. A thorough understanding of stakeholder needs, as well as their explicit approval, are prerequisites.

Once the stakeholders' needs are established, the central instruments in the operations of the data governance program involves the creation of supporting policies and procedures. These artifacts become a sort of guidebook to steer the most essential components of the program.

This chapter covers the basics of the analysis phase of the data governance program and the beginning of the build phase.

Analyzing Stakeholder Needs

Increasingly, almost all leaders and team members of an organization interact with data at some level. For some, engagement with data is a big part of their daily work; for others it's occasional and incidental.

REMEMBER

With the assumption that new processes, policies, and expectations regarding data are going to impact some team members, various degrees of interest and concern are to be expected. Individuals who consider these changes to be impactful to their work and have an interest in the consequences are your data governance stakeholders.

The nature of data means that stakeholders can be found in almost every part of an organization. They work in different functions and have diverse requirements and objectives. I worked in local government for almost a decade, and I can attest that the functions of the libraries were different from the fire service, even though they were part of the same organization.

Identifying data governance stakeholders

In developing the data governance program, you want to meet and talk to many stakeholders. It's impossible to speak to everyone, of course, unless the business is small. You need to identity some people who can speak to and represent the overall needs of a function.

TIP

For many stakeholders, you just need to add them to the program's communication plan. They don't need to be involved in development; they just need to be informed.

Chapter 8 discussed the many roles and groups required for a high-performing data governance program to succeed. These are stakeholders too. Since they will be formally engaged in the program and many will have significant responsibilities, the assumption is that they will make their voices heard and will have direct input on the design and development of the program.

Once you have the core program stakeholders covered, the challenge is to find the others. These are the users across the organization who perform data-related tasks and others who are engaged in areas such as analytics, compliance, and cybersecurity. Another type of stakeholder is called a *data consumer*. This is a large category of user who uses data to make decisions. They appreciate quality data, access, searchability, and ease of use.

In my career of over 30 years, I've found that projects and initiatives are more successful when you engage stakeholders right from the beginning. From the start right through to operating the program, you want allies and champions. Empowered stakeholders provide quality input, different perspectives, and honest feedback.

Take your time to identify who should be involved in your data governance program. Those you invite depend on the size and complexity of your organization as well as on the scope of the program.

The success of the data governance program will depend less on team members adhering to another management mandated initiative, and more on stakeholders who are engaged in the process and understand how it adds significant value to the organization.

Analysis techniques for data governance programs

Unquestionably, the central driver in developing a data governance program are the needs of your organization. The program must be aligned with the goals of the business and it has to solve core issues. It must have value and achieve certain outcomes. After all, it can be a sizable and expensive program to build, deploy, and maintain. It shouldn't be pursued lightly.

Beyond the high-level goals of increasing the value and lowering the risks associated with data, you need to elicit specifics that will inform the overall data governance plan and help in the development of policies and processes.

Identifying, analyzing, and documenting the needs of the program is often called *requirements gathering*. It's a discovery process and is typically the first major phase of developing a solution.

Analysis of data governance needs falls into four categories, each covered in the following sections.

Understand the business strategy

Those tasked with developing the data governance program need to become exceptionally well-informed on the strategy of the business.

WARNING

In my experience, most team members in an organization have a fairly superficial understanding of the details of an organization's strategy. If you want to test this, ask a colleague to describe the vision, mission, and goals of the organization. Perhaps begin by asking yourself the same.

While you and your colleague may not be able to answer this question with clarity and depth, the data governance team must dive deep into these details. This requires reading and becoming familiar with the organization's strategy documentation. It also includes interviews with many senior executives. Outcomes from this work should answer how the role of data will evolve. For example, if a business goal is to grow into new markets, what might be needed to ensure that the right data is available to the right people to make this happen?

REMEMBER

Understanding the business strategy helps ensure that when the proposal for the data governance program is pitched, it will be aligned and in support of organizational goals.

Here's a summary of such analysis techniques:

>> Reading documentation such as strategic plans and relevant public disclosures

>> Interviewing executives

>> Conducting a questionnaire or survey for leaders

>> Researching the external website and intranet

Identify data assets

Data governance is about your data assets, so it makes sense that identifying and analyzing what data assets exist internally and are interfaced with externally is an essential task at the start of your journey.

You're at an incredible advantage if a quality inventory of data sets exists, but my guess is that this will be unlikely. After all, data governance programs are often the reason that data inventories and catalogs are created.

An inventory needn't be perfect or include absolutely everything at this time. For sure, it should have the data that matters most to the organization. At this stage, this inventory is to help you define the data governance program and determine scope. Once the program is up and running, the work to refine and mature the inventory will get underway.

With the inventory established, you, your team, and the data owners and stewards will assess the quality and risk levels for each data set. The marketplace has a number of data quality tools that can be utilized here. These tools can find and flag issues in data. I discuss data governance tools in Chapter 11.

Finally, you can categorize and prioritize based on the outcomes of the analysis.

Here's a summary of such analysis techniques:

>> Identify, catalog, and categorize data assets

>> Interviews with data owners, stewards, and other stakeholders

>> Use of data quality tools

>> Data modeling (see the next section in this chapter)

Conduct a risk analysis

In Chapter 5, I explored the role of data governance in data risk management. Many argue that lowering the risk of data use is the primary purpose of data governance. It's an important driver and should generally be front and center among a small set of priority concerns. As data governance has matured and the role of data has been elevated, the value of a governance program has expanded greatly.

Data risk management must be understood early and will form the basis of both your program proposal and the associated policies and processes.

Communicating and educating your organization about the consequences of poor data management, such as fines, bad publicity, and loss of customer trust, can be powerful motivators.

Understanding and mitigating the risks of data must be viewed as a subset of the obligations organizations have toward overall risk management. You and I might be focused on the risks of data, but a business has to worry about many more risks. A good way to position data risk in training and communications is to frame it in this context. Data risk isn't something novel and abstract; rather, it's an extension of risk efforts already underway.

A large part of understanding the risk to certain data sets will be answered by interviews with relevant stakeholders. For example, if you speak to a human resources manager, they will likely know the basic laws and regulations governing how personal information is handled. Subject matter experts are going to be at the center of understanding risk. However, what you may discover too is that many team members are not even aware of their obligations toward certain data sets. In order words, they may not know the risks.

REMEMBER

Whether the risks are known or not, eliciting and documenting data risks will initially be a collaborative effort between the data governance project team and the relevant stakeholders.

An essential source of insight will be identifying the laws and regulations specific to functions and industries. If your stakeholders are bringing these to the table, the data governance team can help. Fortunately, the compliance responsibilities for organizations can quickly be found online.

Summary of analysis techniques:

>> Interviews with data owners, stewards, and other stakeholders

>> High-level review of laws, regulations, and similar obligations

>> An internal or third-party risk assessment

Collect stakeholder requirements

TIP

Make it a priority to include as many individuals and teams as possible in the analysis and requirements gathering phase of the data governance program. In addition to getting diverse insights and good coverage of the issues and opportunities, involving people early and often creates more buy-in to the program.

You're going to meet with a lot of team members to elicit their input. But you're also going to use this opportunity to educate them on the benefits of data governance. Many people will get engaged out of curiosity since the topic will be new to them. Educating team members at this point will get them motivated too and will have the added benefit of driving the analysis process.

REMEMBER

While the fear of mismanaged data is persuasive to gain attention and support for the program, the real value comes from inspiring people to think of the possibilities that data can bring to their function and to the business.

The primary analysis methods you'll conduct with individuals and teams are presentations, discussions, and interviews. These can take the form of a multi-hour workshop. You or your designee should use this opportunity to present the case for data governance and then facilitate a discussion about data needs.

TIP

During these sessions, you can use case studies that illustrate how utilizing data governance is a positive force and also where its absence can create a lot of issues for organizations. Use examples that are well aligned to your business. If you are in the automotive industry and all your case studies are about healthcare, participants will find it harder to connect the dots.

Here's a summary of such analysis techniques:

>> Interviews with a broad variety of team members from across the organization

>> Workshops with the same, but in a group setting

>> Data modeling

In most of these analysis processes, particularly those that directly interface with team members, there's an opportunity to sell the benefits of the program. It's also a chance for team members to learn from each other, to identify collaboration possibilities, and to determine who may make great candidates as data owners, stewards, or those who will help create policies and procedures.

REMEMBER

Good outcomes from this analysis are identifying the needs for the data governance program and creating data champions in the organization.

Tips for requirements gathering

Ensuring that stakeholder's data needs are captured accurately is an important component of a data governance program. This phase, called *requirements gathering,* is part of both on-boarding and ongoing data governance operations. It's often an area that doesn't get sufficient attention. Research suggests that almost 50 percent of unmet needs in a project are a result of poor requirements management.

Here are a few brief tips for improving your requirements game:

>> Ensure you are eliciting requirements from the right stakeholders.

>> Establish purpose and scope right at the start.

>> Avoid jargon when engaging with a stakeholder. Data science topics and technology in general have a lot of terms that may not be familiar to the audience.

- **>>** Choose from one or more requirements techniques depending on what's more suitable. These include one-on-one interviews, surveys, questionnaires, and brainstorming.

- **>>** Use open and closed questioning. In open questions, the interviewee can elaborate their answers as they see fit with few limitations. In closed questions, the interviewer guides the discussion with specific and constrained questions.

- **>>** Document requirements through written notes, audio and video recording (get permission first!), and even automated transcription software.

- **>>** Confirm the requirements with the stakeholder soon after they are captured.

- **>>** Iterate the documentation if more sessions with a stakeholder are required.

- **>>** Provide the requirements to an independent stakeholder for review.

- **>>** Get the stakeholders to approve the requirements. (Special tip: I always like to have them sign their name in agreement in a small ceremony. They pay more attention to the details this way!).

The role of data modeling

In order to build a data governance program and operate it well, knowledge about how data flows and is processed within and across systems, called the *data pipeline,* is a highly desirable requirement. With this visibility, you can understand characteristics such as who has data access and their access levels, and how data is managed, secured, integrated, and stored. In addition, understanding and participating in the planning and designing of new systems will help ensure that data governance is baked in right from the start.

REMEMBER

Analyzing the data architecture of existing systems and designing it for new systems can be achieved through the use of data modeling.

Data modeling is the process of defining and documenting the requirements and structure of data for a specific solution. These models take the form of graphical representations of a specification, and text and symbols, in the same way that a plumbing engineer might illustrate the flow of water on an overhead drawing of a building.

Data modelers, those with the analytical and technical skills for this specialized work, collaborate with a variety of stakeholders, including those with responsibility for data management and analytics teams, to translate business needs into the technical specifications for data. These data modelers can create the models for new solutions, and they can also analyze and reverse-engineer the models from existing solutions. A wide range of effective software tools are at the disposal of data modelers to support this work.

Data models can take several forms and are determined by preference and needs. Here are three of the most popular:

>> **Conceptual:** High-level requirements that define business needs and rules

>> **Logical:** Detailed definition of how the data will meet the needs

>> **Physical:** The design of the technical implementation of the solution

Data models use specific industry terms and graphical representations. They can also contain data descriptions, rules, constraints, default values, and security parameters.

A popular data model is called an entity-relationship diagram or ERD. This model documents entities (things), attributes (parts of things), relationships, and constraints. Figure 9-1 is a simple illustration of the relationship between three entities: a college, student, and course. The entities have attributes listed beneath them. College, for example, includes its name and address. The lines between each entity have symbols with specific meanings. In this instance, a college has many students, but a student only has one college. A student can take one or more courses and a course can have one or more students.

FIGURE 9-1:
Simple entity-
relationship
diagram (ERD) of
college data and
relationships.

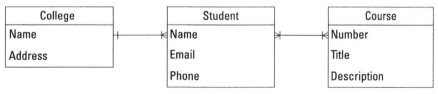

(c) John Wiley & Sons

REMEMBER

As you can see, a data model, even a simple one, can communicate a lot about data in an existing or proposed system. These models can quickly surface issues such as missing entities and attributes, relationship errors, security issues, standards, integration, and access problems.

When data governance is involved in the design of data models, this is an opportunity to enforce, for example, standards, common data definitions — characteristics that assist with data sharing — and security requirements.

Every organization should aspire to have an enterprise data model (EDM), a complete view of the data that is managed across an entire organization. Acknowledging that an EDM will not be at the fingertips of most organizations, an EDM which, at least, contains all the most important data processes should be on the early to-do list of a maturing data culture. *Data warehouse* (a repository of enterprise data ready to be used for specific purposes) and *data lake* (a repository of raw data without a specific purpose) projects will likely demand a fairly advanced EDM.

Data modeling enables and supports both the creation of data governance and its ongoing operations.

Knowledge graphs

While knowledge graphs have been around since the late 1980s, for many organizations their value for data governance and data management has only begun to surface recently.

A knowledge graph records and stores data entities, their relationships, and associated events. This information is contained in a graph database and can be queried or visualized as a graph structure. Unlike other, more traditional, data stores such as a flat database, a knowledge graph provides substantial detail about the context and meaning of data, and data flow across a process or the enterprise. Organizations are discovering that knowledge graphs are a more useful way of understanding data.

REMEMBER

Since knowledge graphs present the possibility of visualizing and producing output that contains data meaning, context, and its relationships to other data and events, it offers value in data analysis, analytics, data-driven insights, sharing, and more.

For data governance, knowledge graphs offer unparalleled visibility into the nature of data in the enterprise. For example, the relationships between data and its flow are particularly valuable for identifying points of weakness and risk. In addition, it can surface areas where data quality must be prioritized, where untapped data value can be gleaned, and identify patterns of data use.

In a knowledge graph, insight is much deeper than simply the connection between two entities such as a student and a student's grades. A knowledge graph brings meaning and context to connections. When we describe data in this way, it's called an *ontology*. Knowledge graphs are the technical implementation of an ontology.

An example of an ontology is shown in the knowledge graph in Figure 9-2. You can see that the company has three employees identified here. Two employees, Neha and Monica, report directly to the CEO. You can also see that Melina reports to Neha. Also, Monica is working on a project called Policy Dev. With this graph, you can also say that there is only one project right now and only one staff member, apart from the CEO, has a direct report. It's true that it may be possible to derive this information in different ways, including querying a traditional database. However, isn't this so much easier?

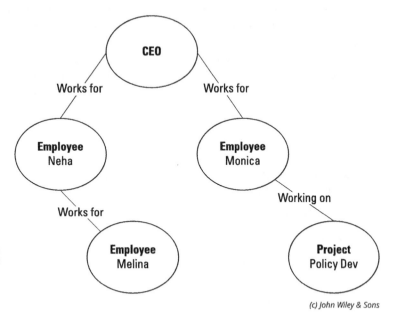

(c) John Wiley & Sons

FIGURE 9-2:
Example of knowledge graph visualization.

REMEMBER

Knowledge graphs help you learn about data and its insights, but it's also used for building data-centric solutions. Facebook uses them to make connection recommendations. Search engines use them to provide more accurate results.

Knowledge graphs create a data model from data extracted from one or more sources. They can be created manually by subject matter experts, but increasingly there are software-based solutions that utilize artificial intelligence to build the model.

The source of a knowledge graph is a graph database. This is where the graph data is stored, managed, and queried. Knowledge graphs support an array of capabilities including data extractors, graph mappers, data validators, visualization capabilities, and search tools.

Top uses of a knowledge graph:

>> Provides a meaningful view of data across the enterprise, its relationships, and uses.

RESOURCE DESCRIPTION FRAMEWORK STANDARD

The most popular framework for describing knowledge graph models is the RDF, or Resource Description Framework Standard. It was developed and approved by the World Wide Web Consortium, the W3C. The relationships stored in RDF are known as triples and take the form subject-predicate-object. This means one object (the subject) is linked to another one (the object), via a word that connects them (the predicate). For example, Melina works for Neha. Melina is the subject, works for is the predicate, and Neha is the object.

>> More easily connects structured and unstructured data sources to provide richer insights.

>> Enables superior data discovery across the enterprise.

>> Improves data standardization.

>> Supports the needs of many data governance requirements such as identifying risks.

>> Enables a wide range of software innovation.

While knowledge graphs are still rare, they are a growing tool for all types of organizations and may be a real advantage for your data governance program.

Developing Policies and Procedures

Policies and procedures implement the external and internal requirements of data governance. These are the tools to ensure compliance and support for laws, regulations, best practices, and standards. Done right, they are the central instruments for helping to reduce risk. In addition, as organization's grow, managing consistency and reducing chaos becomes more urgent. Policies and procedures bring desirable clarity and order.

However, all of these positive outcomes are only achievable if leaders act as champions and team members follow them. They also must be current, and this requires regular reviews. Out-of-date policies and procedures increase risk, stifle innovation, and can create more harm than good.

Policies and procedures are a central component of a data governance program. They guide your organization's decisions and behaviors about data assets.

Designing policies and procedures

Your organization has decided to implement data governance. A strategy has been approved. The team is taking shape. Extensive analysis has been completed. Now it's time to create and deploy the first policies and procedures that are going to govern and guide data value and compliance.

WARNING

Policies and procedures are often terms that are used interchangeably. That would be incorrect. While they are highly complementary, they are different and it's essential to understand the difference right up front.

A *policy* is an agreed approach for guiding decisions in order to reach certain outcomes. They steer day-to-day actions in support of an organization's philosophy, strategy, and the conditions of the marketplace including laws and regulations. Policies are more than just rules; they communicate an organization's values and culture. Examples of policies include managing employee sick time, social media use, and of course, how data must be handled.

The implementation of a policy is a procedure. A *procedure* describes the step-by-step actions that should be followed to comply with a policy. They have a clear start and finish. While a policy primarily describes what is required, a procedure documents how it must be carried out. As an example, a vacation policy will describe the number of years an employee must work to be entitled to a certain number of paid days off. The accompanying procedure will describe the steps required to get time off approved.

You might wonder whether a procedure is the same as a process. A *process* is a high-level description and flow of how to get a desired outcome. This means it's likely a sequence of multiple tasks. An example would be the hiring process, which includes advertising a role right through to on-boarding a new hire. A *procedure* is the steps within one task. So, in my example, a procedure is advertising for a new role. Then another procedure is making an offer. A series of procedures can ultimately result in the new hire starting work.

Table 9-1 summarizes the differences between policies and procedures.

TABLE 9-1

Differences between Policies and Procedures

Policy	Procedure
Doesn't change often	Continuously evolving
Addresses who, what, when, and why	Addresses who, what, when, and how
Relatively broad in scope	Narrow and detailed in scope
Rules	Steps
Enterprise-wide	Limited to a specific activity
Not dependent on procedures	Dependent on policies

Creating policies and procedures

Data governance policies and procedures can be created by different stakeholders. The decision whether to centralize their creation, say, to the Data Governance Office (DGO) or the Data Governance Council (DGC), which is common, depends on each organization. For certain, data owners and stewards must be integral here.

REMEMBER

Regardless of who takes the lead to generate them, there must be consistent creation, review, and approval processes. Include the input of many stakeholders in these areas. These activities are all valuable building blocks of a data culture.

Some basic data governance policies may include:

>> **Data access policy:** This policy may describe the organization's approach to managing data security and the conditions in which a team member will be granted access to data. It could include areas such as approval and security requirements.

>> **Data usage policy:** This policy may describe the manner in which the organization expects data to be managed. It could include areas such as descriptions of what it considers data mishandling, unethical use, and the requirement to adhere to privacy laws and regulations.

>> **Data provenance policy:** This policy may describe the expectation that certain data, such as that used in clinical trials, can be traced back to its original source and creation (a process called *data lineage*). It could include what business functions and data types are in scope, documentation requirements, and the necessity to record access information since data creation.

>> **Data retention and archival policy:** This policy may describe the details of how long data should be retained and be accessible per requirements such as regulations. It may also include when the data should be archived and how long the archive should be kept.

The seven-step process to develop a policy and procedure is as follows:

1. **Understand**

   - Fully analyze and document the drivers and goals of the policy.

   - Seek approval of requirements by the right stakeholders before proceeding.

2. **Research**

   - Explore what other organizations are doing.

   - Determine if a similar policy exists in your organization.

3. **Create**

   - Draft the policy and procedures.

   - Collaborate with others to ensure diverse and detailed input.

   - Be clear and concise. Avoid jargon.

4. **Review**

   - Circulate the policy widely for review and validation.

   - Incorporate feedback.

5. **Approve**

   - Seek appropriate approval.

6. **Implement**

   - Communicate the policy.

   - Offer training on the policy.

7. **Review**

   - Perform regular reviews and updates of the policy and procedures.

Figure 9-3 summarizes these essential seven steps.

Designing a policy document

Once a policy has been identified for creation, you need to produce the actual policy (Step 3 in Figure 9-3) with its attendant procedures. I suggest that the Data Governance Office agree on a standard template working in collaboration with other stakeholders. Consistency in documentation elevates predictability and as a result reduces the burden on policy stakeholders to have to decipher different policy formats.

FIGURE 9-3:
Seven-step
process to create
data governance
policies and
procedures.

(c) John Wiley & Sons

Here are the minimum suggested items to include in a data governance policy and procedures template.

>> **Document ID:** Using a unique identifier supports search and referencing.

>> **Policy Name:** Use a name that is meaningful. For example, Data Quality and Integrity.

>> **Date Created:** Knowing when the policy was created is useful for historical and reference purposes.

>> **Last Updated:** This date lets the user know how current the policy is.

>> **Owner:** This could be the data owner, the business function, Chief Data Officer (CDO), or other. Don't use an actual name. Instead refer to a role. For example, with data owner, use Head of Marketing.

>> **Purpose:** This is where the reason for the policy is briefly described. It should include how the policy supports the goals of the organization.

>> **Scope:** Here you include who and what is impacted by the policy.

>> **Rules:** This is a description or list of the rules that guide the policy.

>> **Roles and Responsibilities:** This section lists specific stakeholders and their obligations.

>> **Procedure:** If appropriate, here's where you list the specific steps that must be taken in support of the policy.

>> **Definitions (optional):** I suggest including this as a way to explain any jargon that's unfamiliar to the user.

>> **Resources:** This section lists resources such as the laws or regulations that are driving the policy. It can also be links and citations to resources where a user can learn more about the broader context of the policy. For example, it could include a link to understand the penalties of non-compliance.

>> **Review Process (optional):** This section outlines details on the review process, such as how often and by whom it is updated.

Figure 9-4 provides an example of a data governance policy and procedure document.

Document ID	DG-031-22-SEC
Policy Name	Data Retention Policy
Date Created	August 14, 2003
Last Updated	February 18, 2020
Owner	Chief Data Officer
Purpose	The organization is required by laws, regulations, and other business requirements to preserve certain electronic data and information for the purposes of activities such as litigation, audits, and investigations. In addition, some data must be disposed of under certain conditions and time periods. This policy guides our support and behaviors relative to our data retention obligations.
Scope	All electronically stored information and its data sources are subject to this policy to varying degrees dependent on functional domain, and data and information classification.
Rules	If data and information have been determined to fall within this policy, relevant team members are obligated to follow specific procedures identified in this policy.
Roles and Responsibilities	All staff are subject to the obligations in this policy if applicable.
Procedure	For a given dataset or information asset: • Determine classification by referencing the data and information classification policy ref: DG-031-23-SEC • If classification if DC0 or DC1, there are no data retention requirements. • For DC2 and above, strictly adhere to the retention requirements as described in policy ref: DG-031-24-SEC • When uncertain, do not delete any data or information. Consult with your supervisor or a member of the Data Governance Office.
Definitions	Dataset: A collection of related data. Information asset: A body of information, defined and managed as a single unit Data and Information Classification: Data and information organized into related categories.
Resources	General Data Protection Regulations California Privacy Rights Act Internal Revenue Service (IRS)
Review Process	This policy is reviewed every two-years by the Chief Data Officer.

FIGURE 9-4: An example data governance policy and procedure document.

IN THIS CHAPTER

» **Managing the change requirements of data governance**

» **Designing a communications campaign**

» **Developing a data governance training plan**

» **Understanding the value of data governance in business functions**

» **Exploring data governance in the context of emerging technologies**

Chapter **10**

Deploying a Data Governance Program

As with most major projects, there is typically a series of milestones that will need to be met along the way. Projects move through a series of notable gates that takes them from an idea to design, development, and testing, and then onward to prepare for and deliver the solution.

Each project milestone requires planning and preparation, and no step should be underestimated. Failure to prepare adequately can bring you challenges that can range from those that are simply a nuisance to ones that can result in a significant derailing of your efforts.

Data governance is much more than a one-time project because you are designing and developing a program that will be ongoing once it is deployed. It will also be a solution that is in constant evolution, changing as conditions and needs dictate, and operating in a state of continuous improvement.

That said, in the absence of any previous efforts, you'll (hopefully) only formally introduce data governance once to the organization. At that moment, the intent is to have the program run perpetually for the life of the business. When data governance is implemented well, it becomes core to how the organization operates. It shouldn't be considered or deployed as a set of standalone processes that require frequent detours from the flow of everyday tasks. You want it to be as non-invasive as possible.

Setting the right tone, achieving as much acceptance as soon as possible from teams across the organization, and ensuring a well-planned deployment requires a focus on change management, communications, and training. This chapter provides ideas and some guidance on achieving a successful deployment.

As a bonus, I also cover how the deployment of data governance brings value to core business units in organizations. Finally, I share some thoughts on the role of data governance relative to emerging technologies in your organization.

Implementing a Data Governance Program

In my 30-year career, I've had the opportunity to work on hundreds of projects of all shapes and sizes. Some were quick and easy; others were long and complex. Many projects were highly successful, but admittedly, some had a range of complex challenges. The projects that go well are often forgotten over a short period, but those that provided unanticipated heartache linger much longer in memory. Those are the projects where some of the best learning occurs. One area of project management that I've learned much about is getting the deployment phase right.

Project teams love to build things — products and services — and get them into the hands of users. The joy of the work is seeing the positive results of everyone's effort. Sometimes in the momentum toward delivery, some details are overlooked that can have devastating effects on the outcome.

For me, change management, communications, and training are some of the areas that are essential to success and yet are not sufficiently addressed. These areas aren't necessarily the most glamorous part of the project, but they are vital and can be the difference between a project that crushes it and one that falls flat on its face.

Change management

The hard work of getting the data governance program approved, then designed, and finally developed, has resulted in a program that's ready to be rolled out. You're ready to move the organization from one state to another. Let's go, right? Just wait one moment. Not so fast. We're talking about humans here.

WARNING

Unfortunately, just like with so many projects and initiatives, you can't just press a button, cross your fingers, and watch as your work gets smoothly adopted by your target audience. That would be nice, but you already know it's wishful thinking.

REMEMBER

Introducing a data governance program is the act of introducing change and if there's one thing that defines organizational resistance, it's the introduction of change.

For many, there's comfort in predictability. People get used to how things are being done and they aren't particularly keen on learning new things. New tools and processes are stressful. For many, disrupting work routines can make people uncomfortable and trigger pushback. Change creates frustration, confusion, anger, and even feelings of loss. Of course, change can also be a source of excitement, renewed commitment, and even relief. There are any number of reasons why organizations struggle with change. It's why there are volumes of research and literature on the topic.

Accepting that there will be resistance to change, that change will be hard, but that you want the change to succeed, means you and your team need a plan. Preparing for the consequences that the new data governance processes will introduce and being ready to support and help during the change, is collectively known as change management.

TIP

Change management is an area that, when prioritized and properly executed, can result in significantly better results than efforts that get deployed without a formal plan and adopt a more reactive approach.

Stakeholders will often point to poor change management as the culprit for an initiative rollout that doesn't go well or outright bombs. As the old adage says, failing to plan is planning to fail.

At its core, change management is about developing a thoughtful and structured plan to manage organizational change. It considers the challenges of deployment and adoption and has prepared contingencies and responses to challenges that may be faced, particularly those related to the human aspects.

The value of change management in deploying a data management program can achieve the following:

>> Ensures that the program is aligned with leadership expectations

>> Prepares stakeholders for the changes ahead

>> Creates opportunities to communicate value

>> Reduces business disruption

>> Engages stakeholders before, during, and after the change

>> Anticipates and plans for the impact of data governance on the organization

Change management has three distinct phases:

1. **Preparing for change:** In this early phase, you make the case for data governance and get leadership buy-in. You'll want leaders to support the program and be vocal and visible advocates. You will gain an approved strategy and engage stakeholders in the design and build-out of it. There will be a project plan and checklist for deployment. The positive consequences of the anticipated change should be communicated often.

2. **Managing change:** In this phase, you and your team are executing the project plan. Communication is paramount. Impacted stakeholders must know, for example, what is happening, when they should expect it, and their role in the change.

3. **Reinforcing change:** In this final phase, the change is underway or has been implemented. The team responsible for the change must be listening for feedback from stakeholders. This feedback can be used for scheduling improvements. The change management team must also address issues of resistance.

Figure 10-1 illustrates the three phases of change management at a high level.

An effort can certainly fail if the technical aspects are not correctly constructed. Quality testing and piloting, for example, can help to reduce these risks. More difficult to control and anticipate are the behaviors of people during a change process. Change management is about planning and being prepared for all types of eventualities, but with a great emphasis on the human challenges.

Individuals and teams are better able to manage change when they:

>> Understand the change and their role in it

>> Have access to clear communications and instructions

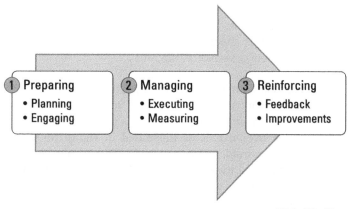

(c) John Wiley & Sons

FIGURE 10-1:
The three phases
of change
management.

>> Are provided with training

>> Receive motivation and incentives to support the change

>> Feel supported and valued for their roles in the change

Organizations are better able to manage change when they:

>> Have committed leaders who champion the change

>> Document and prepare for the changes and their impacts

>> Understand who is involved and impacted

>> Have clear plans for the implementation of change across the organization

>> Clearly understand the roles, responsibilities, and processes

It will be clear relatively quickly whether the data governance program is functioning as anticipated. If you've prepared and executed your change management plan in a thoughtful and deliberate manner, data governance will begin to produce results. After all, the whole purpose of organizational change is to arrive at a place that is better than where you came from. Change management has transitioned the business from one state to another and the benefits are tangible.

Change management for data changes

So far in this chapter, I've addressed the change management required when introducing the data governance program to your organization. But change management must also be considered in the context of data changes that occur when your program is operational.

Data value is dynamic, and your organizational needs will be continually evolving. Managing this change in a deliberate manner should be considered within scope of your data governance program.

I worked for some time as a software engineering manager. In this role, my team and I were introducing new or modified software on a regular basis. We didn't just write the code and deploy it. We had a rigorous change management process. Following the overall process illustrated in Figure 10-1, we ensured that the software was approved, tested, and ready. We worked with stakeholders to schedule the change, and then we monitored the performance of the software post-deployment. With this care and attention, risk is kept low and the potential for success is elevated.

An important quality of change management is that it typically includes a communications process of alerting stakeholders in advance, during, and after a change. In this way, you can try to preempt questions, manage expectations, and provide confidence to stakeholders.

It's entirely possible and highly encouraged to adopt a change management process when making changes to your data environment. Instances where a change management process may make sense include:

>> Changes to data access

>> Changes to data ownership

>> Changes to data definitions and metadata

>> Modifications to values in reference tables

>> Updates to data governance policies

>> Introduction of new data sources

>> Any material changes to the organization's data architecture

>> Major changes to the data governance program

When I was a Chief Information Officer, members of my leadership team and I would host a regular technology-focused change management meeting. At this meeting, those who wanted to implement a change, either from the technology organization or business side, presented their change request. The requestor needed to complete all the change prerequisites and be prepared to discuss their objectives. If everything looked good, the request was approved. If not, the requestor had to do some additional work and then return to the change management meeting.

Data change requests can certainly be incorporated into an existing change management meeting, but depending on scale and your specific needs, you may also want to discuss the creation of a similar function within the data governance organization.

Figure 10-2 illustrates the common steps in an ongoing change management request and approval process.

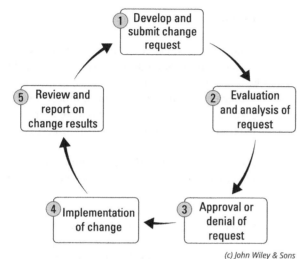

FIGURE 10-2: Typical ongoing change management request and approval process.

Announcing the program

For you and your team, creating and distributing high-quality communications will play a critical role in the success of your data governance program. For technically-oriented individuals — many of those folks play central roles in data — the notion of spending time and effort on communications can seem like a painful and distracting exercise. Communications can seem peripheral to the core mission; something necessary but not a priority.

It can be sobering to recognize that building a well-constructed product or service that people reject, ignore altogether, or are not aware of, is close to the equivalent of having not built anything at all. Ergo, high quality communications are vital.

All your efforts to create a powerful data governance program for the organization will be for nothing if the organization doesn't buy into it. To get team members convinced and engaged means building a high-quality product that produces results and by educating and communicating in the right manner.

In data governance, communications show up in a variety of contexts:

>> Selling the idea to decision-makers

>> Designing and building the program

>> Announcing the program

>> Ongoing operational needs throughout the life of the program

In this section, I focus on announcing the program to the organization.

REMEMBER

To help the introduction of new internal services and processes succeed, communicating enterprise-wide initiatives must be a priority responsibility for organizations. Fortunately, today, research tells us that leaders get this. They understand the power and importance of quality internal communications for achieving buy-in. Given the complexity and somewhat abstract nature of data governance for so many, introducing it requires even more specific attention than most projects.

TIP

You need to communicate information about data governance, but you also need to sell it. In this way, announcing the program is both basic communications and marketing.

Team members need to know what it is, why it matters, and the value it has to the organization and to each of them. I'll be candid; deploying data governance for the first time in an organization is a steep hill to climb. You need all the advantages you can get, and a good communications plan is one of those.

TIP

Consider the deployment of the data governance program the same way you might think about introducing a new service into the marketplace. You have to understand the market, construct a message, choose the right channels, reach your targets, and then make the sale.

The communication plan will need to answer the common Five W questions: Who, what, when, where, and why. I'd throw a How into the mix too.

The core messages you want to communicate over the course of weeks and even months include:

>> What is data governance?

>> Why has the organization decided to implement it now?

>> What is the value of data governance to the organization?

>> Who is impacted?

>> Who has responsibilities?

>> When is it happening?

>> What training and support assistance will be provided?

>> What tools will be available?

>> How will results be monitored, measured, and communicated?

The following sections explain some suggested approaches to introducing the data governance program.

Formalize the communications function

A good practice for all large efforts is to establish a formal communications plan. Figure 10-3 illustrates the core components of a communication plan. Designing, building, and running a plan means identifying a qualified communications leader and team, creating a strategy, providing it with funding, and executing an agreed project plan. If you're lucky, your organization may have an internal corporate communications function, or it might be outsourced to a qualified external provider. If not, you work with the resources you have. This team is responsible for creating a communications plan that is comprehensive and multichannel. If your budget allows and it's culturally agreeable, you might consider an entire brand for the data governance program. Here I'm referring to items such as a program logo, design templates and stylesheets, and taglines.

FIGURE 10-3:
The basic components of a data governance communications strategy.

(c) John Wiley & Sons

Preview the program

Months before the deployment, begin the communications plan. Word will be spreading anyway because team members from across the organization will already be engaged in the design and development of the program. Having a formal communications plan begin at this point can help manage the message and keep you and your team in control of facts. In the absence of official communications, organizations are notoriously good at fostering internal gossip that may be entirely incorrect. Bad or false information will only generate additional resistance to adoption. In previewing the program, you want to be abundantly clear about its value.

Use a variety of channels

Today, it's both a blessing and a curse that there are so many communication channels. My father who ran a factory in the 1970s and 1980s told me that when he wanted to communicate something, he'd have a poster pinned to a notice board near the entrance. As workers arrived, they were expected to read the poster. That was it. Ah, so much for simpler times! These days the options available to organizations include:

>> In-person and online town halls

>> Brownbag lunches

>> Conference calls and videos

>> Emails and instant messages

>> Broadcast voicemails

>> Team meetings

>> Websites and online collaboration platforms

The bad news? You're going to need most of them, and you'll need to customize the message for each channel and for different audiences as necessary.

TIP

The trick to superior 21st century communications is to meet your audience where they live.

Utilize many voices

The obvious choices for who the communications should come from will include the Chief Executive Officer, Chief Data Officer, Data Governance Sponsor, and Data Governance Manager. However, it's not necessary to limit it to those people. In fact, if you can get communications to come from people at a variety of levels in the organization representing all main functions such as sales, IT, operations, legal, compliance, security, and marketing, it may enable more team members to see its relevance. To help with a consistent message, the communications team must provide approved materials, such as slide decks, marketing videos, and talking points.

Provide examples of benefits

In announcing the data governance program, you're dealing with a mix of team members who, for example, are open and ready to embrace it, those that don't know what it is, those who know something, those who might be resistant but open-minded, and those that are ready to reject it no matter what. The journey to acceptance and adoption will have a variety of timetables for certain individuals and teams. Ideally you should identify the most difficult people to convert as part of your change management plan. Use the communications plan to provide ample opportunities to demonstrate value and to show how data governance aligns with the strategic objectives of the business. This should include relatable examples.

Use clear language

This book is proof that data governance is replete with new and largely unfamiliar terms, particularly if you don't have a data or technology background. While it's tempting to use words that the core data governance team understands and are entirely appropriate to explain a concept, to the extent possible, use words that are understandable to the broadest possible audience. Using terms, acronyms, and technical language only further alienates your intended audience and makes the topic less accessible.

Quick communication tips

When executing the communications plan, consider the following qualities. Each of these have been demonstrated to help elevate being heard and understood.

WARNING

Keep in mind, while you may pat yourself on the back for communicating to an intended audience, this doesn't necessarily equate to the recipients listening and accepting what is being communicated.

Clarity and simplicity

Explain it so that anyone without any prerequisite knowledge can understand. Avoid jargon, acronyms, and assumptions. Use clear messaging to connect with the audience. Depending on the channel, make it personal. For example, when sending an email or letter, ensure that it uses their name in the salutation.

Positivity and relevancy

Your messages should champion the benefits of data governance to the organiza-tion, teams, and individuals. Make it relatable. Imagine for a moment that you're explaining to a colleague that you're leading an effort to deploy data governance and they will be expected to participate. Sure, they're interested in what you're doing and what the program is all about, but you can be sure they're thinking, "What's in it for me?" You'll do yourself a favor if you prioritize the answer to this question early in any communications.

Consistency and repetition

Communicating before, during, and after deployment must have uniformity. To use a common expression: Tell them what you're going to do, tell them what you're doing, and then tell them what you've done. In addition, keep telling them. Frequency is essential. For data governance to take hold and become part of the organizational culture requires execution of a long-term communications campaign.

Creativity and playfulness

Team members receive communications all the time. Let's face it, most are dull and use corporate speak, and as a result, many are never read, listened to, or viewed. Data governance doesn't exactly excite most, so it will be even harder to attract attention. Consider a campaign that engages in joyful and surprising ways. There are amazing ideas that you can learn from others with a quick search online.

Communicating the launch of your data governance program, while only one aspect of what is required for success, is nevertheless a critical and priority focus. While not always the strength of people closest to deploying projects, and partic-ularly technically-focused ones, it requires attention if you're going to have great results for the program. The experience of organizations that have succeeded with data governance point to a thoughtful and comprehensive communication plan to launch the program. The outcomes have been greater acceptance early in the deployment, a sustained program, and better achievement of data goals and objectives.

Providing training

As a technology leader and educator for over 30 years, this section is a particular passion area of mine. Let me be perfectly blunt right from the start: Providing timely, customized, and ongoing training for internal organizational tools and processes is way too often poorly executed. For whatever reason, training often doesn't receive the prioritization it requires. If there's one consistent message

I've heard from teams in all types and sizes of businesses, it's that they don't get sufficiently trained to use the tools and do their jobs successfully.

One way that lack of training shows up is when team members make requests for system functions that would help them in their work, only to learn that the tools they already have provide those very functions.

More damaging when training is poorly supported is that team members are less effective and confident in their work, morale is low, turnover is high, and their ability to deliver good results are stifled.

Proving good quality training often results in increased productivity and performance, adherence to standards and alignment with objectives, reduced supervision and increased compliance, higher morale, and a more attractive place to work for existing and future employees.

Research on the importance of training, particularly in the deployment of new tools and processes, is clear: Without training, the chances of success with those tools and processes both in the short and long term are materially diminished.

Coupled with communications, data governance training is another essential component of your deployment requirements. Data governance practices and policies will be abstract for many. Even the notion of data value, quality, and handling will all be novel concepts. Even those with data skills and experience may not be familiar with or competent in the objectives and practices of data governance. For everyone, there's going to be a learning curve. For some, it will be steeper than for others.

Given that you're introducing something new and relatively complicated, the need for quality training couldn't be any stronger.

Training your organization in data governance cannot be overlooked or an afterthought or lightly addressed. Training must be taken seriously and made a priority at the deployment stage and then as an ongoing offering to the organization.

You'll need to consider the training requirements for the initial data governance launch and then the training requirements for ongoing needs. Use the following techniques to create an effective data governance training program:

>> **Determine the approach:** While it may be tempting to provide a one-size-fits-all training, data governance training needs to have different offerings depending on existing knowledge and skills, a trainee's role in the organization, and their learning style. Similar to communications, your training plan needs a strategy. Figure 10-4 shows the typical components for developing a

training plan. Your approach needs to also consider your budget and the ways in which it will be delivered. A first step in determining the approach is to understand the training needs of team members. A *gap analysis* — where you compare what they know with what they need to know — may be a good first step. This analysis can be completed using a questionnaire, survey, or through selective interviews.

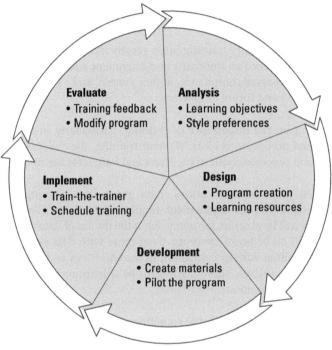

FIGURE 10-4:
The basic building blocks of a training plan.

(c) John Wiley & Sons

>> **Explore learning delivery methods:** Just like communications, you have more choices today than ever for delivering training to team members. It's likely you'll choose more than one as it will depend on role, preference, budget, and appropriateness. For example, some training may be suitable for a one-hour online e-learning module, while a more hands-on and detailed training would be better in a classroom setting. Methods include:

- Physical classroom

- Virtual classroom

- One-on-one instructions

- On-demand e-learning

- Reading materials

- Role-playing and simulations (online and in-person)

>> **Evaluate outcomes:** Some training will be effective, and some will fail to deliver. In order to ensure that the best training is delivered over the medium-to long-term, you must evaluate the training from the perspective of the student, but also in terms of whether the student understood and can implement what has been learned. Don't waste any time or money delivering training that is ineffective. It will also reduce confidence from team members if the training fails to deliver. Use the evaluation and feedback from training to constantly improve your offerings.

Based on results, stop doing what isn't working, continue doing what is working, and start doing the things you should be doing.

Using Data Governance Across the Enterprise

With or without a formal program, some form of data governance is already practiced in most business units. It's reasonable to assume that most teams today care about whether they have access to quality data, that it's secure, and that there's some modicum of effort to manage associated risks. They also use tools — whether improvised or formally deployed — to search for and analyze data. For example, for many individuals, a spreadsheet is the killer app for data management. Nothing wrong with that, especially if it gets them results. However, even though you can take a bus to a destination that's eight-hours away, if you can afford it and expeditiousness is a priority, a flight may be a better option.

When enterprise data governance is formally introduced to departments and teams, it can have a significant positive impact. While there are some universal upsides, departments get specific benefits that are aligned with their mission. In the following section, I share some ways that data governance brings specific value to the core functions of an organization.

The role of data governance in organizational functions

While this is not an exhaustive list, the departments mentioned in the following sections represent the main functions of most organizations.

Executive suite and general management

The executive suite is the top level of leaders — "the chiefs" — who run an organization. It's typically a small group of people who manage core functions and guide the direction of the organization. Titles include the chief executive officer (CEO) — the highest ranked person, the chief financial officer (CFO) — responsible for all finances, and the chief information officer (CIO) — responsible for information technology and systems.

All leaders, and the executive suite in particular, are increasingly recognizing the remarkable value of data. They know many of the ways that data can help them, for example, through data insights, analysis, and analytics. They understand data risks if not managed well, and they also feel the frustration of not being able to leverage data in areas such as competitive advantage and innovation.

Fundamentally, executives need quality data at the right time to make better decisions. That's a central requirement. Data governance, when executed well, is the mechanism that can ensure this happens.

Secondarily, but highly important to executives, is ensuring that organizational risk from data is managed well, and that departments and team members who need data can access it and leverage its value.

Data governance is the tool for executives to create a high-performing data culture and a data-driven enterprise.

Sales

The sales department led by the Head of Sales or the Sales Manager, intuitively, is responsible for selling products and services. Data has always been central to the operations of a sales team. It informs the basics of tracking products being sold, their revenue, and to whom, to the more sophisticated use in detecting where high-value opportunities can be pursued. Fundamentally, data is used by sales teams to increase volume and profit margins.

Sales has appreciated data governance longer than most, whether it has been informally or formally adopted. Given data's core role in sales, these teams have valued and welcomed high quality and timely data. Introducing formal data governance can provide them with exactly that.

For sales, the right data delivered to the right people with the right access at the right time provides insights on, for example:

>> Sales by time period

>> Sales by source

- » Revenue per sale

- » Revenue by customer

- » Market penetration

- » Year-over-year (YoY) growth

- » Sales lost to competitors

- » Net promoter score (the likelihood that a customer will recommend a product or service)

We've entered a period now where salespeople have more data available to them than ever before. It's leading to a more data-driven sales discipline where data informs all aspects of sales decision-making. This includes identifying prospects, increasing sales productivity and avoiding wasted efforts, reducing lost sales, and informing pricing.

TIP

One study revealed that a data-driven approach to sales can result in almost 6 percent more profit than competitors.

While sales teams can inform their decision-making through using the data they generate each day, data governance provides them with the framework and data management mechanisms to tap into historical data by providing the right access and the ability to find, connect, and analyze it. This older data can be a goldmine of insights for sales professionals.

Marketing

Much like sales, marketing today, led by a Chief Marketing Officer (CMO), is a deeply data-centric profession. But unlike sales, it hasn't had a long history of access to timely and accurate data. A famous quote from over 100 years ago, usually attributed to John Wanamaker, an American department store mogul, sums up the historical challenge of marketing, "Half the money I spend on advertising is wasted; the trouble is I don't know which half."

Fortunately, those days are now largely over.

Today, marketing professionals, whose focus is to promote and help sell products and services, have remarkable insight into the world in which they operate. The emergence of online business, smartphones, and in particular, social media, provides hundreds and sometimes thousands of data points about current customers, future customers, and any market they want to compete in.

Marketing has moved from casting a wide net and crossing fingers in the hope of catching a viable customer to hyper-personalized targeting. Marketers can find you and deliver a relevant message that has a high chance of closing a sale.

Data is enabling a golden age of marketing.

Today's marketing tools are data-driven and provide timely access to a multitude of sources. Marketers know the power that quality and timely data can bring, and they want to leverage it. For them, data governance isn't a nice-to-have; it's everything.

You may find that the marketing department are some of your biggest advocates. Make sure you take advantage of their support and advocacy for data governance.

Human resources

Coined in the 1960s, the term human resources (HR), led by the Chief HR Officer (CHRO) or Chief People Officer (CPO), relates to both the people and department who are focused on all matters related to an organization's employees. Today, HR is highly dependent on good data to make informed, people-related decisions.

Historically a challenge because of the availability of data and priority given to their needs, HR is beginning to get the quality data they need in a timely fashion. More than most departments though, there are a lot of laws and regulations in place for handling people-centric data and this elevates the need for data governance.

Like many departments, while they don't necessarily consider it in these terms, most HR departments have informal data governance processes in place. They are concerned with data dimensions such as availability, quality, security, and privacy. Some of this work is driven by business needs and some by the regulatory context in which they operate. They understand the need to protect personnel information (PI) such as date of birth, home address, and health attributes. HR must manage data carefully while also ensuring they can get their work done and their services delivered.

The motivation for many HR departments to move from an informal data governance posture to one that embraces the formality of a program is driven by increasing compliance requirements, elevated risks, increasing volumes of data, and a response to a more data-driven business environment. There is also a need to share personnel data more widely both internally and externally. For example, HR must provide data to outside providers in order to conduct background checks or validate credentials.

HR departments now benefit from access to a wide variety of data sources and all the features of a new generation of data analytics solutions. These tools help HR with recruitment, performance reviews, disciplinary issues, retirement processes, and workplace morale.

For HR, data governance provides them with the management processes to lower their inherent risks and increase the value of data in support of their needs.

Information technology

The Information Technology (IT) department, led by the Chief Information Officer (CIO), is tasked with the responsibility to design, develop, operate, and support the technology needs of the organization. Their purview includes hardware such as laptops and smartphones, software such as desktop applications and other device apps, networks, and data.

The role of IT relative to data is both as a provider of data services but also as a large consumer of data for operational purposes.

REMEMBER

IT plays a significant role in every organization in functions such as storing, managing, securing, and administering data. This department's role is so closely tied to the success or failure of data management, that it is assumed as the lead for data governance. As this book discusses in detail, IT does play an essential role, but data governance is a cross-organizational discipline, and associating responsibility solely to IT has been a source of many issues.

WARNING

The idea that, "don't worry, IT governs and manages our data" may be the reason that data initiatives and building a data culture are constrained in many organizations.

It's best to think of IT as a provider of essential data services such as storage, standards, security, application development and support, and account administration — many of the mechanics of data management — but not as those centrally accountable for the success of the processes, policies, and behaviors, of delivering a high-quality data governance program. IT has accountability, of course, but it is shared across the entire organization.

TIP

The CIO must work closely with other C-suite leaders, and in particular the Chief Data Officer (CDO), in ensuring the business has the data tools and capabilities to succeed.

IT is also a major consumer of data. The team needs data to run an increasingly complex technology environment. Answers are constantly required that help to maintain systems, ensure security, support customers, develop solutions, troubleshoot issues, and manage overall performance.

In both the internal needs of IT and in support of organizational requirements, managing data is a priority. Ensuring data availability, accessibility, quality, security, and more results from a well-managed data and enterprise architecture. This success is becoming increasingly dependent on a formal data governance program.

Finance

Who loves data more than our colleagues in the Finance department? This team, led by the Chief Financial Officer (CFO), is responsible for handling all aspects of money including income and expenditures. In addition, payroll, expense management, reporting, and economic analysis are all often in scope.

The finance team consumes and produces a high volume of data in their daily operations. In the short history of information technology, the finance team was one of the first and largest users of computer applications and systems. They recognized early the benefits of managing, *crunching* (the process of cleaning, reformatting, and structuring raw data), and analyzing financial data. Using information technology (IT) enabled their core tasks, for example, to be performed quicker, with greater accuracy, and against growing volumes of data.

The finance team typically owns and operates a core, data-intensive information system: The enterprise resource planning (ERP) application. This software is used to manage a variety of essential day-to-day business tasks with a particular emphasis on finance, accounting, budgeting, and procurement. ERPs are often highly integrated with other processes and systems in the enterprise. There's a priority requirement to ensure that data flows appropriately between these systems and that there is agreement on data standards.

Today, it's no surprise that the finance department is a major participant and advocate, working closely with all departments including IT, in quality data management. For example, finance leads in producing insightful reports that can help an organization's leaders manage the direction of the business.

REMEMBER

Finance departments derive value from data governance because they benefit from, for example, data standards, data quality, access to and integration with disparate data sources, risk management, master and reference data, and data analytics tools.

With the support of contemporary tools, in many enterprises, the finance team has become the analytics and reporting experts. They are central drivers of data-driven businesses.

Other departments

Of course, in organizations and particularly large enterprises, there are often many more departments and functions. Those described already, considered the central departments, are a representation of the need and advantages of a formal data governance program in an organization. As you can imagine, other departments and business functions — such as production, legal, compliance, auditors, and operations — are all dependent on well-managed data. Many of them have their own laws, regulations, and policies with regard to data. In addition, they each have specific needs related to managing risk.

For your organization, you need to interview, research, and understand each department's needs and how they may benefit from the data governance program. It's my assessment that many already exercise informal data governance and that bringing additional rigor will be welcomed, provided you and your team can make a compelling case.

Data governance in emerging technologies

It appears that the world is in the opening years of yet another industrial revolution. This one, like the three before it, is disrupting and transforming how so many of us work, live, and play.

Beginning in the 1700s, the industrial revolutions introduced new technologies and behaviors and each one left the world in a different state than the way they found it. Whether it was the use of steam to move machines and vehicles, electricity to light up darkness and power the infrastructure that has given us megacities, or the digital revolution that brought us computers and hyper-connectivity, these multi-decade transitions have each defined the world in which we live today.

Now, a fourth industrial revolution appears to be under way. It is being driven by a series of groundbreaking and maturing technologies that include digitalization, big data, artificial intelligence, the Internet of Things (IoT), digital twins, blockchain, and more. These technologies are being coupled with macro changes underway, such as shifting demographics, increasing urbanization, realigned geopolitics, an energy transition, and the perils of climate change. Together, this potent mix is a recipe for shaping a new future for humanity.

REMEMBER

With data being the engine, product, and by-product of the fourth industrial revolution and its emerging technologies, the need for data governance becomes a factor too important to ignore.

The following areas represent just a small selection of technologies that provide a glimpse of change underway and what each may mean to how you think about data governance.

Digital transformation

Supporting much of the technological change is increasing levels of digitalization, global connectivity, and greater volume, variety, and velocity of data creation.

These three factors are powering a digital transformation that is creating completely new innovation and business models, and redefining marketplace opportunities. How you and I do things from consuming information, to booking travel, getting healthcare, communicating with friends, watching videos, and so much more is being redefined almost on a daily basis. The physical world is being crushed and reimagined by a transition to digital at an astonishing rate.

This digital transformation is being powered by the fuel of data. It's also producing massive volumes of data. In this transformation's accelerated drive forward, leveraging this big data has flourished, but at the cost of outpacing many of the basic data management needs to protect against the negative consequences.

WARNING

Digital transformation is bringing value and positive change, but it's also creating a whole new array of challenges that include severe cybersecurity issues, frequent privacy breaches, online bullying and intimidation, massive proliferation of misinformation, and system dependencies that increase outage vulnerabilities to essential services.

The data challenges of digital transformation will be handled often at the enterprise level. But we also need increased levels of data governance at the regional, national, and international levels. Progress is being made, albeit at a relatively slow rate. For example, the General Data Protection Regulation (GDPR) enacted by the members of the European Union (EU) in 2016, provides data protection and privacy rules for citizens of EU member states.

The introduction of international data standards, by organizations such as the International Organization for Standardization (ISO), are also accelerating to support rapid cross-border payments, international trade, scientific research, public safety, and more.

REMEMBER

It's becoming clear that the digital transformation, a central phenomenon of the fourth industrial revolution, will drive further adoption of data governance across industries and economies.

Artificial intelligence

Artificial Intelligence (AI), the capability of a machine to imitate intelligent human behavior, is emerging as a powerful tool in all types of contexts and organizations. For example, it's helping you and I easily find information online, filter spam from email, and detect credit card fraud.

While it can feel like AI just emerged suddenly, it has been an area of research and development since the 1950s. It's only in the last few years that the necessary algorithms, processing power, big data tools, and other computing services have reached a level where AI is producing real value.

Most of the AI that's used today relies heavily on lots of data. In fact, larger and higher quality data sets are most often responsible for the best results. The bigger, the better. Those that build and support AI solutions are advocates for good data governance and management because it can facilitate the sourcing, identification, crunching, and channeling of quality data necessary for powering their solutions.

That said, it's the role of AI in helping to govern and manage data that is most relevant here.

Imagine the volume of data today that is already flowing within, and in and out of, an organization (it's only going to grow exponentially in the years ahead). The volume and velocity of this movement is not practical for human monitoring. The ability to enforce data rules or identify patterns of data behavior can now be achieved with AI. For example, if an employee, fearing they are about to be terminated, tries to harvest digital intellectual property (IP) and send it out of the organization, AI will detect and enforce rules that would prohibit such behavior. In another example, AI can detect if regulated data such as healthcare information has been copied and stored erroneously. An alert to the offending employee may be enough to have the data deleted or moved to avoid issues.

Strengths of today's state-of-the-art AI is its abilities to identify patterns, repeat routine processes quickly and without errors, and make predictions. These qualities are showing up in spreadsheets, ERPs, analytics solutions, and many other business applications. AI has become a partner in data value extraction and management. You've experienced it yourself. For example, type a few entries into adjoining spreadsheet cells, then move to the next cell, and if AI sees an entry pattern, it will suggest it for you.

As AI expands its use within the enterprise, data governance will be important to ensure, for example, that AI has the right quality data it needs at the right time. In addition, AI will be a popular way that data governance tools can deliver even higher value support to a data governance program.

The symbiotic relationship between AI and data governance will grow and prosper in the months and years ahead.

Internet of Things (IoT)

Today there are almost 5 billion people connected to the Internet. This still leaves a few billion to connect. Eventually, in the not-too-distant future, almost all those who want to be connected will have that option. There will be an upper limit to the number of human connections because there is a finite amount of people. The same can't be said for devices. By the middle of the 2020s, it's anticipated that over 75 billion things, such as industrial machines and home monitoring systems, will be connected to the Internet, and it will only continue to grow from there. There is no upper limit to the number of things we can connect.

These connected objects, what are being called collectively the Internet of Things (IoT), are being designed and developed to deliver a wide range of innovation. Devices in homes, factories, cities, offices, and just about everywhere else are connecting with the Internet and exchanging data with other devices, and with central and distributed control systems. In the early years of the 2020s, IoT devices were responsible for creating over four zettabytes of data annually. A number that will be left in the dust in just a few years as data volume explodes.

REMEMBER

The IoT ecosystem is a massive and rapidly growing data system.

Among many requirements, the scale of data being handled by IoT systems necessitates the management of network performance, processing capabilities, data storage facilities, cybersecurity, and privacy. The volume and velocity of data being created, processed, and moved is quickly overwhelming infrastructures that have been ill-prepared.

The IoT represents an increasingly important new channel of data for organizations. Not all the data will have value, and one role of data governance is to determine just that. Monitored and captured data needs to be evaluated to determine whether it should be stored and analyzed.

Some of the data produced during IoT activities will be *dark data*. That's the extraneous data that's created in processes as a by-product. It may not have value immediately, but could have in the future. Once again, data governance tools, policies, and procedures play a role in handling this dark data.

Applying data governance oversight to IoT technologies will include processes and tools for data management, including image compression, filtering, analytics, visualizations, quality control, compliance, security, and privacy.

Any organization that produces IoT solutions or utilizes them or data from IoT sources is well advised to implement the attendant data governance processes and tools as part of its data governance program.

Blockchain

Blockchain technology emerged in 2008 as the underlying system for enabling the Bitcoin cryptocurrency. Subsequently, while still remaining the dominant enabler of thousands of other cryptocurrencies, blockchain technology has also become the data processing solution for a wide range of applications. Industries that now use this technology for solving a wide variety of business problems include financial, government, entertainment, healthcare, and manufacturing.

FOUR LAYERS OF IOT ARCHITECTURE

An IoT environment receives data and delivers it to business processes in one direction. Additionally, users can push data, instructions, and code back in the opposite direction. Although designing an IoT architecture can quickly get complicated, the following are the basic four layers of any IoT platform.

- **Connected things:** This is the perception layer and is made up of the hardware and software endpoints that collect data.

- **Networks:** This is the transport layer and is responsible for moving the data from the source to the destination.

- **Middleware:** This is the processing layer and has many functions including data storage, data management, processing, and device management.

- **Applications:** This is the applications layer and provides the interface for business processes. This includes analytics software, control systems for IoT devices, visualization, and software development.

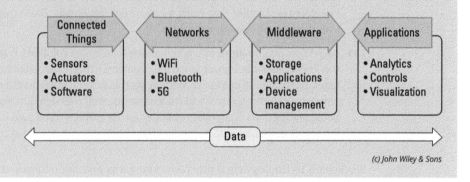

(c) John Wiley & Sons

At its most basic, blockchain technology is analogous to a traditional ledger or in contemporary terms, a database, in that it stores and manages data. However, the way it handles data is rather novel. Unlike traditional databases that reside on a central server and are accessed by client computers, a blockchain database has no centralized body, and instead a copy of the complete set of records resides on client computers. In addition, management of transactions in the system is handled by a mix of software code and the consensus of participant users.

REMEMBER

Blockchain databases have no delete function, meaning all transactions are stored and auditable indefinitely. This quality alone is typically a revelation for anyone who understands how data has historically been managed.

Principally, with blockchain technology, there is no central administration and no hierarchy of users. The technology removes the necessity to trust people, but rather trust is enabled by code. This notion is borderline revolutionary in the context of decades of technology architecture.

This unique design enables a high degree of data integrity and eliminates the traditional limitations of centralized database systems such as access management, processing delays, and a single point of failure.

Blockchain technology intersects data governance in at least two important ways:

>> First, a blockchain database is a self-contained data governance system. For example, it supports data integrity in its core design. In addition, it is a source of truth for transactions given the details captured, data lineage is inherent and fully auditable, and data management can be executed through the use of smart contracts — code that is executed on a blockchain system according to rules. Blockchains databases are transparent, ensure compliance rules, provide seamless access, and create transactions with elevated levels of credibility. They can also protect privacy through the use of private and public keys for access rather than centrally managed credentials. These qualities lend themselves to lower data risks.

>> Second, as organizations implement blockchain-based solutions, how might this impact their data governance requirements? There are certainly advantages, but there will be new challenges such as interoperability with other data-based systems. Also, blockchain systems need oversight just like others because they don't guarantee results when, for example, bad data is used. As the saying goes, bad data in, bad data out.

WARNING

Blockchain technology currently lacks standards and regulations, and it may not meet archiving and deletion requirements. As well, the skills to design, maintain, and support blockchain solutions, both from a technical and data governance perspective within an existing enterprise environment, may be in short supply.

Given the rate of blockchain technology growth and adoption and the distinctive advantages it has in the context of data governance and management, considering it in your data governance program will likely be an eventuality.

In the emerging technologies I discussed in this section, you'll notice that each is highly dependent on data *and* a producer of data. What becomes obvious is that the need to govern and manage data isn't going away as these remarkable technologies are adopted. On the contrary, each of them demonstrates that formal data governance programs are becoming even more important. That's good news for practitioners and vendors, but it's also another wake-up call for leaders to develop their programs as soon as possible.

4

Democratizing Data

Understand the ongoing requirements and methods for maintaining your data governance program

Identify data governance metrics and techniques for measuring the performance of your program

Explore ways to increase program success and manage common challenges

Chapter **11**

Running a Successful Data Governance Program

M aking sure that your newly minted data governance program has any chance of success after day one means paying attention to the requirements of day-to-day operations. For example, without a plan for ongoing communications, it's possible that team members will lose sight of the program's value, or they may not recall their obligations. Either of these two possibilities alone could be enough to create weaknesses that make the program vulnerable to failure.

In the chapter, I explore a few of the areas that a data governance team must consider in running the day-to-day of a successful data governance program.

I explore and discuss the importance of ongoing communications in addition to the need for regular status updates to relevant stakeholders. Of course, in the regular course of operations, data disputes emerge. The data governance team is well-positioned to facilitate these to a conclusion. I share my thoughts on how to go about this.

I also discuss how you can build a culture of continuous improvement in data governance that will result in an increasingly better performing program.

The regular operational responsibility for ensuring the authority and integrity of data through master and reference data management is also unpacked for you. Whether or not it becomes your responsibility, managing this data is at the heart of good data governance.

In the second part of this chapter, I discuss the role that software tools can play in managing a data governance program. This is also coupled with exploring the emergent practices of DataOps and DataGovOps, which incorporate a mix of contemporary techniques and technologies that can improve data governance outcomes.

Finally, I mention how the increasing use of data in the cloud by most organizations may require special attention, policies, and software tools.

Managing the Day-to-Day of a Data Governance Program

So much of the effort of data governance goes into planning, designing, developing, and deploying a program. The initial reward is having built a solution that can be used by the organization to help manage data, leverage its value, and reduce risks.

In reality, the real reward is managing a successful data governance program that is now operational. After all the initial work has been completed, the posture must change from one of design and building to an operational mode.

For this transition, some team members will melt away and return to their former jobs, but others will now assume completely new responsibilities. In addition, you and your data governance team will need to help maintain the program through such areas as ongoing communications, dispute resolution, a variety of data management areas, and foster a culture of continuous improvement.

In this section, I share my thoughts on many of the areas that need close attention to ensure the smooth operations of your data governance program on a day-to-day basis.

Ongoing program communications

My career is long enough that I've seen my share of projects and initiatives that have both succeeded and failed. I've always paid close attention to the factors that contribute to success and failure. The goal is to learn from both and maximize the successes.

WARNING

I've seen some of the best designed and built internal efforts fail after launch much to the dismay of project leaders and members. Even in the open marketplace, I've seen startups build a great product or service only to see it splutter and implode a few months after release.

Project members and startup employees are often dumbfounded. How is it possible that a well-executed project ends in a flop?

Out of a list of top issues, the source of failure often points to poor communications. In Chapter 10, I share a lot of guidance on the communications and change management necessary for launching your data governance program. Now I turn your attention to ongoing communications.

WARNING

For internal project teams and startups of all types, failure to maintain ongoing communications and marketing program can bring the best efforts to a grinding halt.

I'm serious about this. Ensure you have an ongoing communications plan and dedicate resources to it. The main objectives, called out in Figure 11-1, of an ongoing data governance communications program include:

>> Ensuring that impacted participants have awareness of the program, their responsibilities, ongoing efforts, and changes

>> Educating and training data governance participants in their role and obligations

>> Supporting data governance updates and changes

>> Creating a collaborative and transparent operating environment for data governance

To realize these objectives, your ongoing data governance program communications must cover areas such as:

>> Education for current employees

>> Education for on-boarding new employees

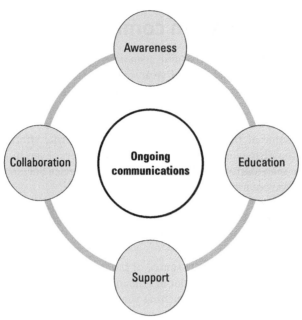

FIGURE 11-1:
Ongoing
communications
serves four main
objectives.

(c) John Wiley & Sons

>> Refreshing stakeholders on the value of data governance

>> Reminders about data governance obligations, enforcement, and consequences

>> Availability of existing and new tools and resources, and relevant training

>> Metrics, such as data governance performance, developed for different audiences

>> Meeting notifications and minutes for various audiences

>> New compliance and regulatory requirements

>> New business requirements for data governance

Working with your data governance team and members of the communications team (if your organization has one), you will identify the different communication channels that are available. It's likely you'll also use multiple channels for the same message. Finding ways to reach your audience where they are (rather than where you wish they were) is simply the nature of communications in the 21st century.

When communicating data governance, every interaction is an opportunity to remind participants of the value it brings.

TIP

Communications should avoid giving the impression that requests or new requirements feel like busy work that is adding little value. Data governance exists because it brings enormous value to the organization, but this fact can often be hidden from many team members. Communication interactions give you a chance to elevate and create clarity about its benefits. Don't lose the opportunity.

Table 11-1 presents a template you can use to develop your ongoing communications plan. I've populated the first two rows as an example.

TABLE 11-1   **Ongoing Data Governance Communication Plan Template**

#	Message	Purpose	Author	Audience	Frequency	Channels
1	Program updates	Information on progress and achievements of the program	Data Governance Manager	C-Suite, Data Governance Team, Data Stewards, Data Governance Council	Quarterly	Email, intranet
2	New data compliance requirement	Timely information on requirements of a new compliance requirement	Data Governance Council	Data Owners, Data Stewards	As required	Email, intranet, meetings
3						
4						
5						
6						
7						

Reporting on status

While I dive deep into identifying, capturing, and reporting on the specific metrics of data governance performance in Chapter 12, it's essential to point out the need for reporting as a positive ongoing responsibility.

REMEMBER

Creating and distributing data governance performance reports is an extension of your ongoing communication responsibilities.

Management will be particularly interested in how the program is progressing, the value and results it is delivering, and early warnings of any potential issues. It's not all going to be roses along the way.

In the first few months after deployment, many issues and challenges will emerge such as gaps in processes, complaints from staff, and non-conformity. Candid reports will surface items like these and also deliver the plan on how they are being resolved.

A good quality report gives an audience what they need when they need it. For leadership, for example, a regular report with meaningful outcomes identified will reassure them that the investment in data governance was worth it. It will provide the status of compliance requirements in the organization, and it can raise potential opportunities for their engagement in a decision.

Reports are generally created for a specific audience in mind. This has to do with relevancy and being within their purview and ability to make decisions. Some reports might be interesting to certain people, but not essential to their role and ability to affect change. They can be added as interested parties if they request but be careful of creating unnecessary noise. What I mean by this is that while some people may want a report, if they don't have decision authority and they don't understand the context of what they are receiving, it can be more disruptive than helpful to receive their input. To address an issue like this, consider providing them with a different report. Perhaps a report that is for a more general audience.

There will be multiple reports for different audiences. You'll work with your team and stakeholders to identify these reports.

On a regular frequency, review the reports that are being created and ensure that they are reaching the right people and providing important, actionable insights. If a report isn't doing that consistently, that's a clue that it might be time to stop producing a specific report.

Don't produce reports that are unnecessary. Just don't.

I've been in many organizations that keep creating reports that nobody reads. I recall one executive telling me they didn't know why they were receiving certain reports. That's a big clue right there.

Table 11-1 is a simple guide to identifying, gaining approval, and creating communication actions for the data governance program. This same table can be used for identifying what reports are necessary, their purpose, the audience, and the responsibility for creation, frequency, and channel of distribution.

Continuous improvement

You've designed, developed, and now deployed the data governance program. After two or three months, you and your team review progress, and everything looks great. It's all working as you had envisioned.

LOL. Not a chance.

That was a bit of fiction writing on my part. The actual story is probably closer to this. You deploy the program and immediately hit unanticipated issues. Sure, some things are working okay, but many others are experiencing issues, and some are not working at all.

In reality, this isn't all bad. First, give yourself and your team credit for getting this far. Just designing and delivering the program on day one is a big deal.

But what you've discovered is that you didn't get everything right on day one and now it's time to review the issues, make modifications, and then update the program. As time passes and you continue to review and evolve the program, it will improve.

REMEMBER

Data governance should be considered a work in progress that is never complete. It will be in a constant state of evolution.

What I'm describing here is a contemporary management technique called *continuous improvement* (CI). At its core, CI is a culture that encourages team members to look for ways to enhance organizational operations no matter where they take place. It's about embracing ideas, evaluating current processes, and making incremental ongoing changes.

Data governance CI does just that. It considers data governance a candidate for regular improvements by enabling all stakeholders to provide suggestions and by the frequent testing and adoption of those that are approved.

CI typically follows these core principles:

>> **All team members can contribute ideas and identify problems:** The best suggestions and problem observations can come from anywhere. There must be a way to enable everyone to submit those ideas and have them reviewed. Embracing the views of all team members is a way to build a culture of CI and can greatly benefit collaboration and trust within the organization.

>> **Progress must be regularly reviewed:** For each adopted change, the organization must evaluate and determine if it has created the expected

improvement. Of course, CI will create change, but that doesn't mean it will be a positive change. That must be regularly monitored.

>> **Improvements are based on making small changes frequently:** Instead of identifying major structural changes that require a large effort and don't occur that often, CI favors regularly making lots of minor modifications.

>> **Changes must be communicated:** It is essential that all relevant stakeholders and team members are kept apprised before, during, and after the change. This principle aligns with the concept of ongoing communications that I explore in this chapter.

The PDCA framework

One of the most popular methods of continuous improvement in any business context is a four-step framework called PDCA: Plan, Do, Check, Act. PDCA in data governance takes place once a possible improvement has been identified (see Figure 11-2).

Plan: In this stage, a team creates the plan for the change. After determining feasibility, they design and develop what is required and prepare it for deployment.

Do: Next, the team takes the necessary steps to deploy a test version of the improvement. This is a chance to get feedback and ensure that the new change doesn't break an existing process.

Check: The change is deployed on a test basis and the team monitors performance and collects feedback. Any issues or comments that are raised are considered by the team. If the change doesn't seem to be working, it is withdrawn. However, if the signals are good, it's time to deploy the change for real.

Act: The last stage of this continuous improvement process is to make the change to the data governance program. It is now implemented, and the team can hope that it delivers the expected results. At the end of the act stage, the process returns to the plan step to prepare for the next improvement.

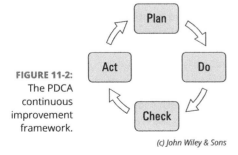

FIGURE 11-2:
The PDCA continuous improvement framework.

(c) John Wiley & Sons

Resolving data definition disputes

Managing data in small, simple organizations shouldn't present many issues. There are only a few systems and there's often a common understanding of business processes and vocabulary. But once an organization grows and increases in complexity and when there are lots of systems and departments, things get, let's just say, a little messier to manage.

Without explicit agreement on vocabulary, and particularly as it references a unit of data, system issues and tense disagreements between teams will occur.

For example, in one or more systems, a data entity called "customer" may be captured. Right away, it's possible you already have an idea of what the organization has defined as a "customer." You may be surprised. For the sales department, a customer might be the endpoint person who buys the product or service being sold. For an internal service department such as IT or HR, a customer might be a member of staff. For the warehouse, a customer might be the retailer. Right away, we have four departments who might define "customer" differently. That's a problem. In addition to being a communication barrier and the source of misunderstandings between people and teams, if customer data moves between systems without being correctly defined, everything from processes to reports to interfaces may produce errors or fail.

The "customer" entity is one example, but data definitions may be required on hundreds or even thousands of entities and attributes. You can quickly see how this may present conflicts from time to time, particularly when new systems are introduced or existing processes are modified.

Data definitions must be established and when disputes emerge, rapid resolutions are desirable for everyone involved and impacted.

Data definitions can— and should — be captured in what is called a *data glossary*. This glossary, like a dictionary, is a software application that contains all the data-related words, terms, phrases, and concepts, their context and relationships, and their definitions within an organization.

Fixing a data dispute is not as simple as everyone just agreeing on a definition. It's likely much more involved than just words. In all likelihood, resolving a data dispute will require modifications to entities, attributes, processes, and systems.

Turns out, perhaps unsurprisingly, that the data governance team is well-positioned to facilitate and help resolve data disputes. They may not be the first stop for stakeholders seeking a resolution, but with good marketing of the value of the data governance team, and visibility of the team across the data lifecycle, they can be seen as the right neutral arbiters.

The data governance team is also a good choice given that they have a thorough understanding of data policies and the agreed governance framework for managing data. For example, a data governance framework may include who makes decisions regarding different types of data, when they can be made, and how they are implemented and communicated.

Steps to data definition dispute resolution:

1. **Identify and gather stakeholders:** Data is at the heart of many people's jobs. It can be surprising how many people are impacted by data issues. You need to cast a wide net to include the producers and consumers of the data within scope. This might include people inside and outside the organization. Also, identify data and business process owners, and relevant IT and cybersecurity staff. In some instances, representation from legal and HR may be appropriate. At a minimum, a solid group of stakeholders will improve the collaboration and communication opportunities of the dispute.

2. **Analyze and evaluate the conflict:** At the point where stakeholders have been assembled, the tension and conflict may be at its peak. This means there is a lot of frustration, anxiety, and anger, and as a result the issue may have untangled into a hot mess that contains facts and untruths. Work collaboratively to correctly identify and quantify the issue. It's important not to judge anyone and to be open to rigorous discussion. Focus on the data and the benefits of finding a resolution for everyone. The outcome of this step is agreement on and scope of the issue.

3. **Seek a resolution:** You're now in a good place. It may have taken a little while to get here, but now you've moved on from identifying and understanding the issue, to the point of finding a fix. Agree on what success will look like. Elicit input on all possible solutions. Determine the pros and cons of each option including the costs, complexities, impacts, and trade-offs of each. The team should decide on the mechanism to evaluate each option. Through debate and deliberate analysis, work to reach consensus and choose a solution.

4. **Deploy the solution:** With the data governance framework as a guide, you can determine who needs to be involved in approving the change, who will implement the change, and how it will be communicated. Once the solution is deployed, it needs to be supported and monitored for some time. Assuming the fix is implemented, the dispute is resolved, and the success metrics are met, the team can enjoy their achievement.

TIP

With data governance as the independent lead in resolving data definition disputes, it's an ideal opportunity for the team to continuously demonstrate value.

Master data management

Imagine the following scenario. A sales representative takes an order over the phone from a new customer. The salesperson first creates a new record in the customer relationship management (CRM) system, which includes details such as name, address, phone number, and more. Next, they create a new order in the sales system. The customer's information is pulled in from the CRM. When finalizing the order, the salesperson enters a delivery address, which is the same as the home address of the customer, and inadvertently makes a typo in the Zip code. Instead of 33606, they enter 33602.

The order is submitted and makes its way to the warehouse for fulfilment. When preparing the shipping label, a warehouse associate notices the Zip code error and updates it in the shipping software. The order is then dispatched and makes its way to the customer.

This all sounds like a fairly routine business process. However, even in this small series of steps, a data problem has been introduced. In this scenario, there were three systems that contained the customer's contact details. Unfortunately, while the data should be identical, one of the systems now has wrong data, which means the systems are no longer in sync. A third party, for example, reviewing the customer's contact details in each system won't know which Zip code is correct.

In reality, organizations use many independent systems that capture the same information for different reasons. Each day a high volume of transactions are created and the likelihood of similar information being captured in dissimilar ways is almost guaranteed. Intuitively, you know this creates enormous challenges for organizations as the data flows into processes, gets shared with others, and is used for analytics and reports.

For example, will mail sent to customers go to the most current address? Will reports generate duplicates because entries for the same customer appear to be different customers? Will orders be submitted with current pricing? Oh, the humanity!

REMEMBER

Bottom line, without a solution, an organization — the bigger and more complex it becomes — has no way to know what the *single source of truth* (the definitive data source for a given data set that is accurate) is for their most valuable data. Bad data may be getting used and shared. That's bad news.

Fortunately, this isn't a new issue and organizations have been using master data management to solve it.

Master data management (MDM) is a combination of technology and processes to ensure that business critical data is kept accurate, consistent, and complete across an organization and with its partners.

To enable MDM, the organization must establish its master data. Master data, also known as the golden record or master record, is the source of truth for the organization's most important business data.

Typically, master data includes data about customers, products, suppliers, locations, and materials. Master data about a customer, for example, includes attributes such as contact name, business name, mailing address, email, and phone number.

Reference data

Another type of essential business data that must be managed as a source of truth is known as reference data. While master data is concerned with business transactions, reference data is used for classification and categorization of other data. It is often called "look-up" data and is a defined list when available as a value for an attribute. For example, a reference data attribute such as U.S. state would only have 50 options and they would be standardized either internally or from the U.S. Postal Service nomenclature.

While reference data is predominantly defined within an organization called internal reference data, it carries value in harmonizing data with outside data sources, called external reference data. Examples include country codes as defined by the International Organization for Standardization (ISO), product codes used by major vendors, and financial hierarchies and terms as defined by the financial industry.

MDM is a data quality discipline. You want master data to be uniform, accurate, complete, and consistent across the enterprise. In this way, systems and team members can use the master data with confidence and with results that can be trusted.

REMEMBER

Fundamentally, MDM is a function of data governance. In fact, it's a high priority requirement and expectation.

The tools available today for MDM provide a variety of solutions for creating, storing, processing, and disseminating master data. These tools can consume records from many different systems, rationalize and harmonize conflicting content, put it in a standard format, and then make it available for other systems to access. Some tools are highly automated in some of these processes and others require manual intervention.

To implement MDM, follow these basic steps. The data governance team must work with data owners and data stewards to complete many of these (see Figure 11-3).

1. **Determine your master data:** The data governance team, working with every department, finds agreement on what data is the most important for the organization.

2. **Find where master data is created:** Once the categories of master data have been determined, the data governance team, working with data owners, must identify the systems where the master data is created. For example, they may find that customer data is being entered manually in the CRM, the order system, the marketing system, and in the dispatch system.

3. **Identify what systems consume master data:** In this step, the team is determining what systems import master data from one of the sources in Step 2. Keep in mind, not all systems that use master data are creators of master data.

4. **Collect and organize the master data attributes:** If the team finds, say, five instances of supplier information, they need to create a list of common attributes and define them to ensure that the data captured is going to meet the needs of different master data consumers. For example, they determine what allowable values for a specific supplier attribute may be permissible.

5. **Develop the master data structure:** This step includes the broader data governance participants and leaders. Agreement must be established on each master data entity, including what attributes will be included, and the requirements and constraints of each attribute. It's also a good time to decide, for example, for each master data: who can edit, how often changes can be made, and what the rules are for adding new attributes.

6. **Choose an MDM solution:** Fortunately, the marketplace is competitive for innovation MDM solutions. There are many all-in-one packages, but you can also build your needs with specific tools. These will be choices for you and the data governance team working alongside IT and other relevant stakeholders. Your decision-making will be driven by your needs, complexity, and features available, and cost will likely be a factor (it always is). Always consider the ongoing maintenance needs, ongoing costs, and staffing requirements for complex toolsets such as MDM.

MDM requires careful monitoring and maintenance. Documenting and implementing processes for ongoing management is essential and it's a core responsibility of the data governance team to provide support and oversight. Managed well, it can provide a high degree of data integrity across your enterprise for your most important business data. You don't need to deploy it all at once, but your master data and management can be implemented incrementally. In this way, you can demonstrate early value to stakeholders without too much disruption. The long-term goal is to have all your master data managed this way.

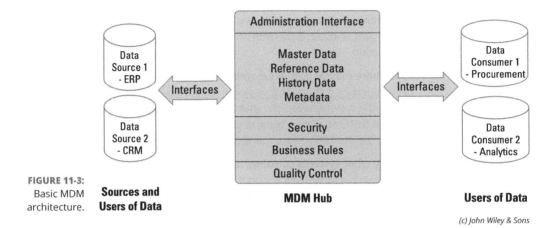

(c) John Wiley & Sons

FIGURE 11-3: Basic MDM architecture.

Automating a Data Governance Program

Fortunately, the power of software has reached data governance. As an existing or future data governance leader, you may already be overwhelmed with the scale and scope of responsibilities that are expected. In a world awash in data, it can seem like a losing battle to bring forward a modicum of essential governance processes and expect success.

But just like in so many other areas of life, software and automation is positively augmenting human efforts. Code is enabling scope and scale to increase exponentially while delivering even better results.

This is true too in data governance. With regularity, new solutions from big vendors, and a crop of promising startups are delivering remarkable new software tools. The solutions are sophisticated and intelligent and many, dependent on your budget and appetite for automation, can be real game-changers in the management of data.

Coupled with new software options, data governance itself continues to evolve as practitioners explore new approaches. The emergence of both DataOps and Data-GovOps are worth understanding and even exploring for use in your organization.

In this section, a combination of automation tools and the innovative, collaboration methods presented point to a whole new day for data governance leaders and teams.

Software tools for data governance

In general, the definition of a data governance tool is one that assists in the creation and maintenance of policies, procedures, and processes that control how data is stored, used, and managed.

No doubt, many aspects of data governance are complex, particularly in larger organizations. Fortunately, as expected from a competitive marketplace, where there is opportunity, you will find providers and their software solutions only too willing to help.

As data has grown in its significance to every organization, particularly in just the last few years during the Cambrian explosion of data, many innovative data tools have been introduced. Some of the software has emerged from the largest technology players such as Microsoft, Oracle, IBM, CA, Informatica, and SAP, but also mid-sized and even startups have entered this lucrative space.

I'm not going to list solutions here, as there's always a risk of implying some bias or leaving out an obvious player, plus, and this is probably the bigger reason, the marketplace is changing too fast and any list I provide will inevitably be dated quickly.

The quantity and quality of innovative data tools recently introduced have been game-changers. Figure 11-4 is illustrative of many of the areas now addressed with software tools.

With the increasing use of technologies such as artificial intelligence, data management, governance, and analytics — and frankly, all aspects of data science — have benefitted from increased automation, better decision-making, improved efficiencies and speed, higher data quality, greater compliance, and even the ability to contribute to increased revenue.

TIP

To achieve these potential benefits, it's certainly important for your organization to evaluate what tools may make sense.

Selecting data governance tools

Determining what tools you need, like so many things, depends on several factors. Considerations will often include:

>> Business priorities and requirements

>> The suite of data tools already available in the organization

>> The complexity of data environment

Data architecture

Data modeling and design

Data discovery

Data security

Data integration

Data storage

Document management

Master and reference data management

Metadata management

Business intelligence

FIGURE 11-4: Software tools serve all these data governance areas.

>> The complexity of IT infrastructure

>> Current maturity level of data governance

>> A narrow or broad focus of data governance objectives

>> Skill sets of data governance team and data staff across the organization

>> Available budget

>> Data governance team appetite for automation and system administration

Tool requirements may emerge out of an existing pain point, like so many solutions do. But deciding on a toolset may also be the product of a requirements-gathering process that considers the items in this list and others.

Some of the common features now found in data governance tools include:

>> **Data discovery, collation, and cataloging:** A mechanism to identify, collate, and support data set search.

>> **Data quality management:** Tools that identify and correct flaws, cleanse, validate, and transform data.

- » **Master data management (MDM):** This is covered earlier in the chapter in the "Master data management" section.

- » **Data analytics:** An application to enable the discovery of insights in data.

- » **Reporting platform:** A solution to generate all manner of business reports.

- » **Data visualization:** An application that uses graphical elements as a way to see and understand trends, outliers, and patterns in data.

- » **Data glossary and dictionary:** A repository that contains terms and definitions used to describe data and its usage context.

- » **Compliance tools:** Solutions that automate and facilitate processes and procedures that support industry, legal, security and regulatory and compliance requirements.

- » **Policy management:** A tool that helps in the creation policies, supports their review and approval, distributes to impacted staff, and can track that team members have received or viewed content.

- » **Data lineage:** A solution that identifies, maps, and explains the source and destination of data, including its origin and stops along the way. Data lineage is also known as *data provenance*.

Keep in mind that some tools are designed to do one or more of these tasks really well, while other solutions try to provide an entire suite of solutions. Needs, cost, and complexity are factors when determining whether to buy a single feature or full-suite solution.

DataOps

A defining characteristic of the early years of the 21st century is the need to innovate at speed. In an unforgiving marketplace, organizations that are slow to improve their internal processes or cannot bring products and services to the market are at a disadvantage, which can result in business failure.

In this context, greater emphasis has been placed on finding ways to accelerate innovation and produce more frequent deliverables.

With technology playing such a central role in innovation, it was observed that the relationship between teams that created solutions — primarily based on software — and those responsible for deploying and supporting the code, were not aligned. These two groups, the developers and the IT operations teams, for example, reported to different leaders and had dissimilar performance goals.

Around 2007, a movement started to better integrate development and operations that was aptly named *DevOps*.

DevOps is a reimaging of how to build and deliver solutions quickly. It incorporates automation, collaboration, communication, feedback, and iterative development cycles.

In a similar fashion, but on the premise that organizations were struggling with data volume and velocity, and the slow speed of deriving insights, it was observed that efficiencies could be gained in rethinking the lifecycle of data within the enterprise. Using the concepts and successes of DevOps, around 2014, a new approach to data analytics emerged called *DataOps*. Some called it DevOps for data science. Figure 11-5 shows the data management areas that are being automated — the shaded areas — with DataOps.

REMEMBER

Like DevOps, DataOps uses contemporary work approaches such as collaboration, tools, and automation to find efficiencies and deliver higher quality and quicker insights. You can think of DataOps as a way to kick data analytics into high gear.

Central to DataOps is the emphasis on collaboration between participants in the data value chain. This includes data analysts, data engineers, IT team members, quality control, and data governance. In addition, like DevOps, DataOps proposes an agile approach to delivering data solutions. Instead of long periods of requirements analysis, design, and then development, work is broken into smaller chunks and priority is given to delivering value quickly and often. Cycle times are compressed, and business users get the data they need sooner.

As an example of inefficiencies in the absence of DataOps, a marketing leader requests the development of a new monthly report. In traditional development lifecycle organization, it can take weeks and even months to elicit and validate the requirements for the report, design and develop it, receive feedback and make changes, and then deploy it. The long cycle times lead to disappointment and missed opportunities, and it deters data requestors from even making requests. DataOps changes the game on requests like these through a mix of agile methods, improved collaboration, and automation.

REMEMBER

Recent research revealed that many companies that embraced DataOps and agile practices were experiencing a 60 percent increase in revenues and profit growth.

DataOps can be implemented through team structuring and new processes. But it can also be facilitated through new supporting tools that include artificial intelligence and automation. A dynamic marketplace has emerged that will provide you with many options and new capabilities to accelerate your data analytics cycle times.

DataOps is a type of data governance in that it focuses on improved and faster methods to deliver more data value and quality while also considering risk. In addition, it requires the participation and support of the data governance team to help with policies, standards, quality control, and security considerations. DataOps tools can also give data governance teams new, actionable visibility to data use, flow, and challenges in the organization.

Some say DataOps is the future of data governance. The evidence is certainly pointing in that direction.

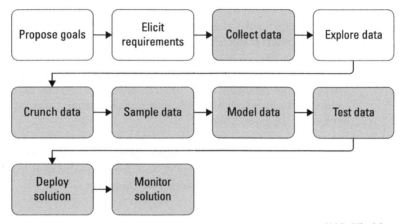

(c) John Wiley & Sons

FIGURE 11-5: More than half of data management operations can be automated (shaded areas) with DataOps.

DataGovOps

DataGovOps is a new approach to extending automation and *continuous governance* (CG) to the data lifecycle. CG means automated processes running without interruption instead of being manually applied periodically. DataGovOps builds on the concepts and success of DataOps. It seeks to eliminate many of the complex and manual processes associated with ensuring data is managed well, quality and compliance is maintained, and risks are reduced. In other words, it's an emerging approach to automating parts of data governance.

With CG, significant process efficiencies are achieved and data governance areas such as risk and compliance are improved. Rather than manual processes which, frankly, often cannot keep up with the volume and velocity of data today, automation across the data lifecycle and scaled across the entire enterprise is actually achievable.

CASE STUDY: DATA GOVERNANCE AUTOMATION BOOSTS INVESTMENT BANK PROCESSES

Background

The financial services industry is among the highest regulated areas in the business world. It's no surprise given that their members must maintain a high degree of trust with their clients while also operating in an environment that is a priority target for fraud and other crimes. Banks, investment houses, brokers, and others must meet government requirements and customer expectations by following specific processes and maintaining certain practices.

One common process for managing risk, referred to as *Know Your Customer* (KYC), is used by financial institutions to verify that customers are who they say they are. It involves checking methods of identification such as government-issued ID cards and a variety of acceptable documents.

A large, global investment bank had deployed KYC as part of their new customer on-boarding process. Implementing KYC helps reduce risk and meet legal compliance requirements such as anti-money laundering (AML) laws.

Problem Statement

As a result of hundreds of thousands of new customers being on-boarded at their branches and online all over the world annually, millions of KYC-related documents were generated that had to be processed.

With no global standards for proving identity, the bank was dealing with documents that contained structured, semi-structured, and unstructured data. Initially, the only way to manage the process was to incorporate a high degree of manual effort. Not only was this approach time-consuming and costly, but it was prone to errors and poor-quality data entry. Bad data meant risk exposure, revenue and cost implications, as well as an inferior customer experience.

The Solution

The solution was to turn to technology and experiment with an artificial intelligence system that could accurately identify and process the massive volume of variable documents. A good outcome was not guaranteed.

The bank decided to use a DataOps approach to reduce the cycle time to develop a proof-of-concept (POC), by emphasizing team collaboration across the enterprise and creating a unified technology and data architecture.

Results and Lessons Learned

Fortunately, the POC was a success, and the solution was subsequently deployed across the global organization. In addition to achieving a high degree of automation and data accuracy, the new process also created a unified KYC approach for the enterprise. Much less manual work was required, processing time decreased, and the quality of data increased.

For the bank, a DataOps approach to data governance became an enterprise standard for the development and deployment of mission-critical, data-related requirements.

Case study insights provided courtesy of Saker Ghani, Chief Strategist, Unlocked Ventures.

By automating some of the repetitive, yet important, parts of data governance, team members can focus on higher-value work. This also means that there's a better chance of data governance succeeding, particularly in environments where the scale of data management has skyrocketed in recent years. In addition, data laws, rules, and compliance requirements can change or be introduced that data governance teams take too long to address or, heaven-forbid, never get around to addressing. Automation is one of the answers here.

Any concept that can make data governance more efficient, less onerous, and even more valuable has a good chance of being embraced. I've said it before; data governance needs all the advantages it can get, as it's all too easy for an organization to jettison efforts if they become too burdensome.

REMEMBER

At its core, DataGovOps converts manual processes into code and script-based governance. It's sometimes referred to as "governance-as-code" and it focuses on codifying governance in order to automate it.

Using a governance-as-code approach with DataGovOps means that data governance can have greater coverage that includes not only the management of data within an enterprise, but data processes and uses that span between an organization and its external stakeholders such as suppliers. It may even provide a better user experience and interface between stakeholders and data governance.

DataGovOps tools can help notify and address areas such as:

>> Data breaches

>> Exposure of sensitive data

>> Team collaboration

>> Data misuse

>> Data management process enforcement

>> Privacy violations

>> Policy update requirements

>> Policy automation

DataGovOps is relatively new, so it should be evaluated in that context. The results are promising but a careful and deliberate adoption approach must be taken. For example, if DataGovOps is introduced not long after the data governance program is deployed, already stressed team members may be overwhelmed. It may not be a solution for smaller, less complex organizations and could, in fact, make data governance a lot worse. That said, a mature data culture with a large data team and healthy budget is a good candidate organization to evaluate and explore DataGovOps. An emerging marketplace of tools, including those already available for DataOps, will provide lots of options and a vendor community willing to experiment with you.

Cloud data governance

Historically, an organization's data lived metaphorically under the roof of that organization. It would reside on its own servers and administration and security of data was relatively straight-forward.

Of course, those easier days are largely over.

REMEMBER

Today's organization, in addition to storing and managing data on-premises, manages complex data pipelines that reach across the enterprise and in and out of a wide range of external entities such as providers and customers.

What has also become a dominant architecture for many organizations in the past few years is storing, accessing, and managing data at cloud providers. Many businesses are choosing to use providers such as Amazon AWS, Microsoft Azure, Oracle Cloud, and Google Cloud. In addition, many of the external data sources consumed by an organization are cloud-based.

All of this results in a complicated multi- and hybrid-cloud environment for many businesses.

While the principles of data governance still apply and are effective in these environments, cloud use increases complexity and risk in a number of areas. Example challenges may include:

>> **Ensuring the validity of data:** What controls are in place to validate that the data being accessed is authoritative and current? Who has the rights to make this determination?

>> **Cross-border requirements**: Cloud providers move data between their data centers for a variety of reasons such as optimization, and they may also place it in jurisdictions that could create security and compliance risks.

>> **Data protection**: Managing data in the cloud means outsourcing some degree of control over the cybersecurity environment. Controls, audits, processes, and special treatment for highly sensitive data in a cloud provider may be necessary.

>> **Provider support for compliance**: Can you be sure that the cloud provider is in compliance (both national and international) with all regulation and legal requirements?

The solution to cloud data governance?

>> Treat it with the same seriousness as all data in your environment. Your data governance program and teams must be fully engaged in all aspects.

>> Pay attention to its particular nuances such as those identified previously. This may mean special processes and policies.

>> Utilize the new generation of data governance software tools specifically built for managing data in multi- and hybrid-cloud environments.

Chapter **12**

Measuring and Monitoring a Data Governance Program

After your data governance program has been created and deployed, you need to measure its performance. This will be an ongoing responsibility. In the first few months, you and many stakeholders will be eager to understand whether the program is meeting any of its objectives and goals. By monitoring and measuring performance, you can modify the program and correct any issues. As time goes by, you'll also want to know if the goals and objectives that were identified at the initiation of the program are being met consistently, and whether they are underperforming or exceeding expectations.

In this chapter, I share many of the basics for identifying the right performance indicators and measuring and monitoring them, as well as some ways to increase enforcement.

Identifying Ways to Measure Program Success

A data governance program requires a robust post go-live measurement and monitoring effort. For you and your team's own satisfaction, you need to know whether the program is succeeding and where it needs to be adjusted. But you also need a way to communicate to a wide variety of stakeholders all manner of metrics on the program. Leadership will want to know if formal data governance is worthwhile and that its promise is being met.

No book can tell you precisely what metrics you need to measure for data governance. Your program is unique to your organization. Not only will the things you decide to measure be a reflection of strategic alignment, but the way they are measured will be specific too. For example, you'll determine whether a metric for a given performance item is best produced as a percentage or as a quantity count. You will also decide on dimensions such as frequency and granularity of measurement.

Determining how you'll measure and monitor the data governance program may be something you decide early on in the design and development phases. However, you might also make these decisions closer to the deployment date. You have many decisions to make in this important area.

Determining the right performance indicators

REMEMBER

There's no doubt that your data governance program is going to bring value to your organization. Just the rigor it demands and the attention it receives in a wide range of contexts will elevate the notion that data is important to your business and needs to be treated as such. This alone is an achievement, but of course, it's much more than that.

You and your team successfully sold the value of data governance to your organization based on an expectation of results. Leaders bought the idea, understood the motivation and desirable outcomes, and made resources and budget available.

It's a pretty good bet that these same leaders have asked to be regularly updated on the performance of the program. Many other stakeholders and staff, including you and your team, are also keen on timely and meaningful metrics to know whether the program is delivering results as expected. Relevant parties deserve to know whether the promises that were made are being achieved.

After the data governance program has been designed, built, and finally launched, will you know if it is working? In addition, do you know what needs attention so that you can continuously improve the program?

REMEMBER

To answer these questions, you need data governance performance indicators. These indicators — which need to be identified and defined — are measurements that evaluate organizational success.

Performance indicators, sometimes called *key performance indicators* or KPIs, measure all manner of essential business measurements. These include revenue growth, revenue per client, client retention rates, and client satisfaction.

WARNING

Don't think of performance indicators as optional. Measuring the data governance efforts and the benefits they produce must be considered a key requirement of any program.

Publishing, socializing, and debating your data governance metrics is the right conversation to be having with stakeholders. Rather than being consumed with the minutia of procedures and policies, leaders want to be talking about value creation.

There are plenty of indicators to choose from, but agreeing on the right ones and capturing the necessary data can be challenging. Sure, improvements in data quality, for example, is an obvious metric, but you need to capture much more. Great indicators mix operational and strategic performance. It is important to know how the organization is doing tactically on meeting some data objectives, but you want the metrics to also answer whether data efforts support the bigger strategic goals of your business.

For each performance indicator you can simply state its value. However, you might also include the goal for that metric and the gap to reach it. For example, data accuracy for a given system at a specific time might be 83 percent. The team may decide that 90 percent is the goal and state that alongside the current value. Observers can now see that there is a 7 percent difference. I suggest using a *sparkline* too, which is a small trend graphic, alongside the metric. It can more clearly show whether performance is improving.

You also need to strike the right balance between capturing metrics and the time spent on this activity. It can be labor-intensive and, in a world of limited time and competing priorities, you need to choose wisely where you spend your efforts. For example, metrics that simply capture individual compliance, say, with a required process, may not be as valuable as an indicator that demonstrates that the overall risk posture of the organization is being reduced.

TIP

Each KPI must benefit someone; otherwise, stop collecting and reporting on it.

Some measurements may be temporary too. For example, putting in place a data catalog that makes it easier for team members to discover and use valuable data sets is an achievement of data governance, but you may not have to measure how many searches are performed every day. It may be useful information early in the program, but after a while, it becomes meaningless. The value and objective have been achieved. Of course, some might disagree and there's likely a ton of great data catalog metrics that are valuable. That's just the thing about metrics: I can't tell you which ones you need. Each organization has to make that determination.

REMEMBER

Your performance indicators must reflect the goals of your organization.

Metrics can be determined by anyone. But finalizing agreement on what metrics to capture, who captures them, how they are captured, and who is the recipient of the metrics are all decisions for you, leadership, and the data governance team. KPI reporting can be as simple as a Word document, or you can explore any number of impressive reporting software tools.

The following data governance metrics are certainly not comprehensive but can be used to provide ideas and inspiration for your program.

As you read these lists, consider how you might capture the data to deliver these metrics. These metrics can be captured for specific, high-value data sets, or across all data sets in a domain, or other criteria. You also need to determine and describe what you're measuring. For example, will it be percentages, count, average, or something else?

Consider each of these metrics in a form that can be interpreted by the recipient. For example, see Figure 12-1.

FIGURE 12-1:
An example of a data governance performance indicator.

Data Quality Metric #1: Data Errors Discovered				
Data errors found in the following systems: XY01, XY02, and XY03	Found (Last Month)	Found (This Month)	Difference (Month over month)	Errors reported since July 1, 2020
	33	28	15% less	70% average reduction

Data quality

Since increasing data quality often dominates the business case for data governance, it's an important category to address. After all, one of the most visible results of data governance efforts is improved data quality.

The following list includes dimensions of data quality that you can measure. Again, the measurement scale and goals are yours to determine.

>> Accuracy

>> Completeness

>> Timeliness

>> Validity

>> Consistency

>> Integrity

>> Conformance

>> Issues identified

>> Issues corrected

>> Populated mandatory fields

>> Survey results on the quality of data from users

Strategic alignment

Measuring the contribution of data management to high-level strategy achievements may be exceptionally difficult, but it should not deter you from evaluating whether a linkage can be measured. Leadership would be excited by this possibility.

The following list includes dimensions of strategic alignment that you can measure. Decide on the measurement scale and goals as appropriate.

>> Business growth

>> Data usage in innovation

>> Data contribution toward profitability

>> Understanding the customer

>> Market insights

Governance

Reporting on the performance of specific data governance activities seems intuitive. But be selective. Some of these metrics will be useful early on and less so over the medium to long term. Consider, for example, standards and policies in terms of how many have been established.

The following list includes dimensions of data governance that you can measure. You need to determine your measurement scales and goals.

>> Standards

>> Policies

>> Procedures

>> Processes

>> Disputes resolved

>> Time to resolve issues

>> Compliance issues

>> Reduction in risk events

>> Adoption rates

>> Improvements in quality of reporting

People

Beyond capturing metrics on "things," you will benefit from understanding the degree that people are being integrated and succeeding in the program. Consider these metrics related to personnel:

>> Staff trained

>> Training sessions

>> Use of analytics tools

>> Number of data owners

>> Time spent on data governance activities

Technology

Technology as an enabler of data governance but also as the platform for data, in general, is a core area for performance measurement. Consider these metrics and adjust as needed:

>> Utilization of data tools

>> Information security incidents

>> Exception access requests

>> Data sets using master data

>> Data sets using reference data

>> Databases incorporating standards

>> Availability of systems and data

>> Accesses to the data catalog

>> Use of metadata

Building a management dashboard

In order to run a successful data governance program, different stakeholders are going to need performance indicators that are most relevant to them to make relevant and timely decisions. Reports and dashboards are both useful, but in different ways.

In many organizations, stakeholders receive predefined reports, and some have the power to generate reports. Reports are typically detailed and historical snapshots of a specific area of interest. For example, an HR leader may get a monthly report on the quality of on-boarding data for new hires. This contains a lot of domain-specific information as well as some history such as trends.

TIP

Data governance reports can be built within departments. The data governance team, stewards, and data owners may be utilized as subject matter experts to assist with their development.

A *management dashboard*, unlike a traditional report, is an online presentation of performance indicators that reflect real-time or close-to-real-time insights. It is presented in a visual manner to enable insights to be read and processed quickly. In the 21st century, speed is always a factor.

In addition, a dashboard presents a mix of indicators that give leaders a holistic view of the performance of a specific area or of the entire enterprise. The goal of a management dashboard is to deliver timely insights to leaders to help them make data-driven decisions. These dashboards can be customized to meet the needs of specific areas of the business, such as the C-suite, the data governance council, or the IT team.

REMEMBER

Sometimes, the result of reviewing a dashboard is to request a more detailed report. In this regard, a management dashboard and a reporting system should be considered both unique and complementary tools. They can both be considered valuable communication tools.

As part of the data governance program design and development, reports and dashboards must be in scope. They don't have to be elaborate on the first day of the program and, in fact, you should consider both as capabilities that will mature over a long period of time. What's essential though, is that you do provide a minimum amount of reporting and dashboard capabilities at the start of the program. After all, you do need a way for stakeholders, including you and your team, to be able to measure and report on progress.

Management dashboard best practices

The earliest iteration of the performance dashboard is created in collaboration with stakeholders. Remember, the metrics you capture and present must reflect the goals of the program. *Vanity metrics* — those that are interesting and nice-to-have but add no real value — should be avoided. Examples of vanity metrics include data anomalies that are interesting but don't suggest a pattern and the number of data catalog searches that have plateaued. These offer no additional insight. If you must, you can add a few of those in your end-of-year report.

Ideally, a high-quality management dashboard will extract and present data in real time from production systems. This might be possible for a small number of indicators, but my guess is that this will be difficult for your data governance metrics early on and should be your goal over a longer period of time. In the short term, you'll likely rely on team members uploading period data as necessary.

REMEMBER

A management dashboard should allow users to query, sort, and drill down on the data to a certain degree. Most users will reach a limit quickly on what they can do, and this is when they'll either stop exploring or request more data, likely in the form of a report.

Using a management dashboard

In addition to enabling leaders to understand performance levels quickly and to make necessary decisions, a management dashboard is well-suited for collaboration and sharing. A dashboard can be used in meetings to aid in a discussion and decision. A screenshot taken of a particular indicator at a specific time in support of either a question or assertion can be easily shared over social and email platforms.

Management dashboards are best-suited to support executive decision-making. They can turn complex ideas into actional insights. They provide a clear and factual picture for leaders to understand the state and performance of the organization.

REMEMBER

With a data governance management dashboard, the value of the program can be demonstrated, and decision-makers can ensure that the program is being steered in the direction of the best outcomes.

Check out these examples of performance dashboards:

>> www.smartsheet.com/sample-dashboard-templates-roundup

>> www.clicdata.com/examples/

>> www.geckoboard.com/dashboard-examples/

Using a data governance balanced scorecard

A specific and popular type of report for presenting a focused set of performance indicators and strategic progress is called a *balanced scorecard*. It's typically used by leaders to get a quick look at how strategic initiatives are progressing relative to goals and objectives, and to aid in decision-making. While the scorecard is most popularly used to manage strategic efforts, it can be used to monitor and respond to operational targets too.

A data governance balanced scorecard can be used by data governance stakeholders to measure and monitor program progress, successes, and challenges. A collection of performance indicators is first identified and agreed upon. At the time of initiation, a baseline metric is entered for each indicator. Then target metrics are chosen and entered. The interval of these will depend on your strategy. For example, for major goals, the target metrics may be annual. More tactical efforts could have quarterly targets. Figure 12-2 shows an example.

FIGURE 12-2:
An example of a data governance balance scorecard measurement.

Category	Objective	KPI	Baseline (June 2021)	By End of 2022	By End of 2023	By End of 2024	Current Status as of Dec 2022
People	Ensure that major systems and their datasets have data owners to provide oversight and accountability.	Percentage of core enterprise systems with formal data owners.	44	60	85	100	57

(c) John Wiley & Sons

Deploying Monitoring Processes

You've identified what you intend to measure and how you will present your performance indicators for the program. With these decisions made, you must also determine how you will monitor these metrics on an ongoing basis and when you'll be alerted to issues.

Performance indicators and monitoring are the two sides of the same coin. You can't have one without the other. The skills and manner in which you approach each, though, does differ. For example, you might identify system use of master data as a performance indicator. That's one important step. Next, however, is determining how that performance indicator will be monitored.

Today, monitoring data governance has matured considerably, particularly with the availability of sophisticated tools. Sure, manual efforts for some activities will continue to be required, but the emergence of, for example, artificial intelligence and vastly improved real-time monitoring, is providing data governance leaders with incredible new capabilities.

The role of monitoring in data governance

In general terms, the purpose of monitoring is to detect and alert issues in a project, program, system, or any number of organizational contexts. In monitoring data governance, you are interested in capturing and measuring its value, but also attaining notifications on issues related to procedures, policies, security, and compliance. With successful monitoring, you have the right amount of transparency relative to what's important to you, in order to understand any challenges and address them.

TIP

What gets monitored is your choice. Identifying the most important areas of interest and defining the right metrics is at the core getting results from monitoring.

The highest value of monitoring, like owning insurance, only becomes apparent when something isn't going right. It's a function of business that is largely invisible when everything is going well. Of course, when it is required, it's remarkably important and appreciated in the timely fixing of an issue and for maintaining continuous improvement.

Some level of monitoring and alerting is manual in organizations. For example, the inaccessibility of a specific data set may become apparent when a team member calls a help desk to report the issue. Support staff can then reactively evaluate the issue and respond. While this may ultimately get a good outcome, it can create a lot of unnecessary manual work as well as a support environment that is constantly fire-fighting.

Increasingly, organizations are implementing software-based monitoring for their data governance programs. In this environment, areas that are being monitoring proactively are operating 24/7 to alert appropriate team members when errors emerge, thresholds are exceeded, trends are identified, and other pattern anomalies are identified. These systems also contain insights like audit trails and logs that enable more rapid remediation.

Consider a large and complex environment that contains hundreds of priority data sets. Without a monitoring tool, it's not possible to be alerted in a timely manner if any of the systems begin to produce poor quality data. Perhaps one of the extract-transform-load (ETL) processes is failing. Bad data can now enter your data pipeline causing significant downstream issues. Rather than waiting for someone to notice, at which time the problem has snowballed, it may be best to get an automated alert as soon as possible, right?

Alerting is a powerful function in a data governance program.

Deciding what to monitor

A best practice with data governance is to start small and progressively build the program over time. It's a point I make many times in this book, because it's one of those learnings that can make a real difference to an organization that is beginning its data governance journey.

With this in mind, you don't need to monitor everything on day one. What you need to consider is what is worth monitoring at the outset to bring the most value. As time passes, you can expand your scope of monitoring.

The following items can help you decide, based on your program's goals, the types of areas to monitor and perhaps which ones to prioritize at the beginning of the program or those to add later.

Data quality

At the heart of data governance is managing data quality. It's a clear priority area for monitoring. The metrics for data quality earlier in this chapter are the right areas to consider (but you don't need to limit it to them). Depending on how each is being monitored, you can set triggers. Some can be as simple as creating alerts when data is missing or when there are duplicates. It may not be necessary to have alerts for every issue, but in some instances it may make sense for an alert to be sent when a pattern emerges. For example, for a field with missing data, an alert may only be sent when the same field in five consecutive records is noted.

Compliance

Ensuring that rules, policies, and laws regarding data are followed, including being up-to-date with changes, is a serious responsibility for every organization. Failure to comply can result in fines, leadership embarrassment, and even loss of business. As a result, monitoring compliance is non-discretionary. Remember, it's a central motivation for high-quality data governance.

WARNING

Among the many areas of data governance that require monitoring, compliance monitoring is often labor intensive. It can require varying degrees of intense oversight from auditors, legal, privacy, and security teams. In some industries, all staff are required to submit compliance confirmations. These may require review and follow-up. Your compliance leaders may also have to compile regular reports and submit them to relevant agencies.

Some level of automation is possible. For example, an organization may require all staff to take annual cybersecurity training. A system can track who has completed the training, send out notifications for those who are late or have not completed theirs, and notify leadership of issues.

Data governance program

I expect that you might be particularly interested in monitoring the progress and value of the data governance program. Not only is this of great importance to validate the work you and your team are doing, but it is an essential and expected insight that you must deliver to leadership as evidence that the program has succeeded.

REMEMBER

Monitoring results will inform your efforts to improve the program. If an area isn't meeting expectations, you can make timely adjustments. In addition, if it's unclear whether the program is performing in a certain area, it may mean new or modified performance indicators are required.

Data lineage

The journey of data from origin to destination and the stops it makes along the way is known as *data lineage*. It's a record of, for example, where data has been, where it's going, how it was used, who used it, and whether it was transformed. It's an important data aspect to govern. Managing data lineage helps with data integrity, reducing errors, policy compliance, security, and more. Having oversight for data lineage requires some form of monitoring. As data flows between systems, gets transformed, and is rendered in different forms such as reports and data extractions, there are any number of challenges it may confront. You need to decide, dependent on complexity and what's possible, where you will prioritize the monitoring of data lineage.

Cybersecurity

Protecting and ensuring the confidentiality, integrity, and availability of data is the main function of cybersecurity efforts. Unfortunately, organizations are increasingly the victims of cyberattacks. In addition to costing trillions of dollars to all types of businesses globally, attacks can be disabling and embarrassing, and they reduce brand confidence.

Monitoring data security is multidimensional in that it includes the engagement and utilization of technologies, processes, and people in many forms. Monitoring targets can include the network, data, servers, applications, human behavior, and identity management. Fortunately, as an advanced industry, cybersecurity provides an abundance of tools, support, and training in support of defensive needs and compliance requirements.

The topic of monitoring an organization's security is sizable and if it's an area of interest, I recommend studying it further, as it goes way beyond the scope of this book.

Automating monitoring

Fortunately, there is now a large marketplace for a variety of effective data governance monitoring tools. A quick online search will reveal many options for you and your organization. These tools can help you automate many monitoring tasks, as well as assist with analysis, alerts, auditing, and compliance management. The newest systems include artificial intelligence, which can detect anomalies, unusual patterns and behaviors, and even predict issues. The ability to monitor and alert in real time has expanded considerably too.

While building your own solution is an option, the sophistication of available tools, including open-source solutions, will make this avenue much less desirable.

Monitoring can be entirely owned and performed as an internal function, but it can also be outsourced. This includes not only an outside vendor providing the monitoring services and support but also the tools. While outsourcing to an external vendor may have a lot of benefits for many organizations (such as when insufficient talent exists internally), that does mean less control over the process and may end up more expensive and complicated than managing internally. Your teams need to weigh up the pros and cons to determine what approach makes the most sense for your organization.

Regardless of whether the system is managed internally or externally, it must be independent of the systems it is monitoring. For example, you don't want the performance or outage issue that you're monitoring to also affect the performance and availability of the monitoring tool. That just wouldn't be sensible. In addition, be careful to not create unnecessary performance burdens on the targets that are being monitored. Some of this can be expected since it is part of the cost of running additional layers of monitoring software against existing systems; however, taking special care can limit the impact.

Enforcing data governance

The work of getting approval, designing, developing, and then deploying your data governance program will be for nothing, if it doesn't achieve any of the results it promised, or if the organizational response is apathy and team members largely ignore the program. Both scenarios, however unlikely, are still possibilities. They may also be related, meaning that either one may cause the other.

I think you'll agree that you and your team have to make every effort to avoid these outcomes.

The risk of the first scenario can be reduced by designing and developing a program that aligns with business goals and engages a large number of participants in its crafting. Getting team members to have some skin in the game early can win advocates and supporters. You'll also want leadership support from the beginning. Actively communicating the benefits of the program well in advance of its deployment helps. In Chapter 10, I discuss these change management best practices in greater detail.

But I haven't discussed enforcing the program. It's time to do that.

WARNING

To be candid, discussing data governance in terms of enforcement is not the optimal way to approach this topic. In fact, for many, it may just reinforce the unhelpful notion that data governance is just a set of unpleasant processes that are painful, yet necessary.

Management science in the 21st century suggests that a "just do it and don't ask questions" approach to leadership garners little loyalty, compliance, and respect from team members.

REMEMBER

Ideally, data governance is a way to complement and accelerate the positives of a data culture. In this environment, the value of data is established, and team members are enthusiastic about all that it can bring to the organization if it's managed well.

Rather than think of data governance enforcement, it is better to consider how you can position the program for success. You want data governance to be understood and embraced, not because it's being enforced by some mandate, but rather because the organization is experiencing and recognizing its clear benefits. You're winning when team members believe in the merits of good data governance and take ownership and accountability for their role in it.

WARNING

Honestly, if the debate you're having with colleagues after data governance is deployed centers around how to enforce the policies, this may already represent a red flag that the program is in trouble.

Don't let it go there. Create the conditions for success so that, while enforcement challenges may come up from time-to-time (and they will), they are the exception, not the rule.

Garnering support for the program

Here are a few ways to assist with getting teams on board and reducing any friction that may result in adoption challenges.

Communication

The role of communications in data governance is multidimensional. It certainly includes creating awareness and selling the benefits of data governance before, during, and after the program is deployed (see Chapter 10). But it also means ensuring clear messaging on program guidance, directions on where to find policies, and understanding the responsibilities of each team member.

REMEMBER

Communications must also be ongoing, timely, and directed. This means data governance messaging doesn't end after the program is launched, what is communicated is meaningful and relevant when it's broadcast, and it reaches targeted employees.

Importantly, when communications are made, they must be consistent and in alignment with goals. What you want to avoid is one message regarding data governance from senior business leadership, and an entirely, even opposing view, coming from the cybersecurity team. Being on the same page demonstrates to team members that the organization is clear and in lock-step about the purpose and value of the data governance program.

Hearing from the voices of many different types of team members can help too. You want leaders such as the Chief Executive Officer (CEO), the program sponsor, and the Chief Data Officer (CDO) to be active, but it is also good to have department leaders and lower-level staff, using a mix of channels to advocate for the desired outcomes of the program.

Finally, good communications are a two-way street. While I've focused on top-down communications here, providing a way for team members to express their perspective and have it heard, and if appropriate, acted upon, is a healthy dynamic to foster.

Documentation

There's no hiding the fact that data governance is rather heavy on documentation. Remember, at the heart of data governance programs are policies that provide the necessary guidance for data management.

If you've spent any time in an organization, you'll quickly recognize that there is a wide spectrum of what people consider acceptable documentation. Documents that are hard to find, inaccessible, and difficult to understand are much less likely to inspire team members. Frankly, if a document doesn't make sense, a team member may abandon it without seeking help. That's an adoption and enforcement limiter right there.

Be careful with using technical language that hasn't been first explained. Always elaborate on and define acronyms and initialisms. Technical team members make this mistake often. Use plain language, as the audience for data governance covers people with all types of backgrounds and skills.

Bottom line: your data governance documentation should be easy to find, easy to access, and easy to understand.

Metrics

Earlier in this chapter, I covered the role of performance indicators for data governance. Using these metrics, everyone can understand what is being measured and the performance targets that are being pursued. The organization can also understand where it is doing well and where attention is needed.

Relevant metrics are a valuable communications tool that can quickly convey the meaningfulness of the data governance program.

When team members know what is important to their organization and how they can help to fulfil the mission, they are much more likely to be aligned and compliant. A popular refrain from employees is that they don't always know how their work is being measured and whether they are doing what is expected. Providing timely metrics that are relevant to teams can accelerate adoption of new policies and practices.

Take note though, that like policies, metrics must be clear and understandable. Make an effort to produce reports and build performance dashboards that have clarity and explanations. What you don't want is for team members to look at a data governance dashboard or glance at the executive summary of a report and not have any idea about what they're telling them.

Continuous improvement

Considering the data governance program a constantly evolving and improving effort helps to keep it current and relevant and provides it with a mechanism for challenges and issues to get addressed. This is the process of continuous improvement, or CI, a topic I discuss in Chapter 11.

CI can occur as a result of managing metrics, in that if some desired results or measurements are headed in the wrong direction, corrective action can be initiated. CI can also result from a healthy feedback mechanism. It's possible that team member compliance challenges may be occurring because a policy or process is broken. The provision of a mechanism that enables any employee to provide their feedback in a safe and receptive environment will encourage the surfacing of corrective actions. Free of unnecessary roadblocks, a meaningful change can validate the importance of the team member's feedback and eliminate a reason that some aspect of data governance is not being enforced.

Communicating how feedback for CI can be channeled is essential here. Consider how that may be achieved. It could it be as simple as a form on the data governance website, or team members could be instructed to make their supervisor or a data steward aware.

Chapter **13**

Responding to Data Governance Challenges and Risks

There's a lot about data governance that makes it a difficult program to design, develop, deploy, and maintain. It's a topic that many stakeholders are not familiar with and so you will spend some time explaining it to them and making the business case. Some will get it right away, but others will struggle, and with a small number, you'll experience outright resistance the whole time.

At the same time, most leaders and team members, when they take the time to consider it, do understand why data is an increasingly important topic for every organization. Given the right context, they may conclude that data governance is so obvious and urgent, that not hurrying to formalize it is a disservice to the business. This is the world in which you'll be operating as a data governance leader.

In this chapter, I explore why so much of data governance is hard, but I also contrast it with why you can be ultimately optimistic about success. Despite it being difficult, under the right conditions and planning, data governance can deploy in many areas with some ease.

Once your data governance is underway, you need some tips on ensuring it continues to run smoothly. In the second half of the chapter, I provide guidance on maintaining a successful program and anticipating issues.

Finally, I look into the future. Data governance is projected to grow in its importance in the enterprise. There will be a high demand for jobs and skills, and new technologies will support and improve data governance value and outcomes. Equally though, the complexity of managing data and the challenges organizations will face in governing data will add to the challenges and risks ahead.

Understanding these challenges and risks helps you prepare for a number of eventualities that will likely shape the future of data governance.

Exploring the Complexities of Data Governance

If you have no background in data governance, you're likely curious why so many organizations struggle to implement programs, particularly the first time around. Certainly, data governance is being deployed and getting results for all types of businesses, but it is all too often a difficult effort to get started and to maintain successfully. Every organization is going to be different, but in studying and researching many challenges, including my own personal experiences, I've identified a number of common issues.

But there's also good news here. There are plenty of reasons why data governance is a topic that can naturally succeed, and, in fact, the conditions are often ripe for its formal implementation. You need to understand the factors that will help you implement data governance well and leverage those to your advantage.

Data governance is hard

If your organization has decided to develop and deploy a data governance program, you're already in a better place than most. Despite all the remarkable advantages of a quality data governance program such as supporting new business opportunities, providing enhanced insights, and delivering better risk management, a sizable number of organizations have yet to make the leap. That said, current trends suggest increasing numbers of organizations are finally making the decision to move forward with a data governance program. That's good news.

But this good news must be balanced with a sobering statistic. Of those organizations that begin a data governance program for the first time, Gartner, a leading research and consulting firm, reports that up to 90 percent will struggle and even fail.

WARNING

It's a fact. Data governance is hard. But it's worth it. Don't let the fear of failure be a deterrent. A better way to move forward is to understand why data governance is hard to implement and then work to mitigate any anticipated issues.

The following sections discuss how to overcome some of the greatest challenges in implementing data governance.

Insufficient leadership and organizational support

There's a reason I bring this point up several times throughout this book: it really, really matters. Very little can succeed in an organization without commitment from its leaders. I'm not talking about a casual nod that suggests a leader has approved and supports an effort.

The leadership engagement I'm referring to here is support that is deep, sincere, and sustained.

REMEMBER

Leadership support is particularly important in a data governance program because it requires involvement from many leaders across the organization. They must be continuous champions and frequent communicators of the value of the program, and a team ready to approve the program budget as it progresses.

You and your team can help these leaders be the champions you need by providing them with insights and education. Don't forget, data literacy must generally be learned. Of course, this goes beyond leaders and applies to all team members.

TIP

It's through these leaders' overt and visible support that others in the organization will be inclined to give the program the attention necessary for its success.

You need enthusiastic cooperation and collaboration from team members across the organization. But it's not enough to get your colleagues to simply play nice with the program. What you're really striving for is eager participation. Helping your colleagues cross the chasm between indifference and keenness may end up being your greatest challenge. However, when you can make that happen, the data governance program has a great chance to produce results that may surprise and delight.

Too much (or too little ambition) at the start

After winning the hard-won case to leadership and getting the green light to move forward with a data governance program, there's a temptation to prove as much value as quickly as possible. This motivation comes from good intentions. After all, it makes sense that you and your team would want to covert the value pitch into results sooner than later.

That said, outside of exceptional circumstances, too much or even too little ambition early on is problematic.

With a large scope at the outset, team members across the organization may be overwhelmed. Every business has limited resources. Be mindful of the extra work that data governance may impose early in the program. Over time, this will improve as efficiencies emerge and team members bake any new procedures into their existing workloads. Some automation tools may be useful early too, but be mindful of how those can also be construed as more overhead. There's a balancing act here for sure.

Too many moving pieces introduced too quickly is a recipe for unmanageable complexity that will quickly backfire. But with too little ambition there's a risk that nothing will be achieved either. If leaders and team members don't see value, that will give them another reason to reject the program.

It's no easy task, but you have to find the right level of how much of the program to introduce on day one.

Keep in mind that this is a program and will likely be in place for many years to come. As a program, you and your team can ramp it up and evolve it over time. This contrasts with the notion of a project. Projects are almost always about delivering a finite amount in a finite time. With a program-based mindset, you can pace the deployment of program features. Identify initial sets of processes and data set candidates and exercise the program on those first. Once results begin to emerge, you are well positioned to expand to other areas and introduce more aspects of the program.

Poor communications and change management

Telling people what you're going to do, why you're going to do it, and what it means to them, and then preparing everyone for change are just some of the responsibilities a team has when implementing a project or program. I discuss these aspects of a data governance program in Chapter 10. I recommend paying particular attention to program communications and change management. Done well, they can be the difference between mediocrity and greatness. Done poorly, they almost guarantee failure.

REMEMBER

One of the recurrent themes you will experience before, during, and after launching a data governance program is countering the belief from many that data governance, while acknowledging some level being necessary, is an administrative burden that distracts from people's day jobs.

Communications and change management are tools designed to help make the case for data governance, help plan and prepare for everyone's success, and sustain a campaign that reinforces the benefits and demonstrates its value. Be clear on goals and objectives and clearly show how data governance aligns with the strategy of the organization.

TIP

Importantly, share metrics often, celebrate milestones being reached, and ensure that all leaders and staff are deeply engaged in the program. Remember, data governance isn't an IT program. It's an enterprise program.

Data challenges

A data governance program is designed to help bring discipline, control, and value to the organization's data environment. It assumes that data governance is bringing to the table leadership and organizational support; the right tools, policies, and procedures; and skilled team members ready to manage the program.

But a glaring challenge for any program is the state of the data environment in which it must exert its authority. Every organization will be different. Certainly, the bigger the business, the more the complexity, and the greater the resulting challenges. Factors include:

>> The volume, velocity, and variety of data being utilized

>> The number of systems and their interoperability

>> The number of system silos

>> The state of data quality

>> The technology infrastructure stability

>> The degree of data literacy

>> The quality of team collaboration across the enterprise

>> The maturity of cybersecurity architecture

>> The availability of data standards

>> The magnitude of compliance and regulatory requirements

>> The size of budget for data-related investments

Confronting these challenges and succeeding relies on good planning and setting the right expectations. A difficult data environment doesn't mean that a data governance program can't succeed. On the contrary, the program should help to make sense of data complexity and bring some oversight and controls to it.

TIP

Properly assess and evaluate the environment prior to developing data governance. Being honest with what the program is facing and planning accordingly will go a long way.

Data governance is easy

Clearly there are a lot of reasons why creating a data governance program is hard. But just because something is hard doesn't mean you shouldn't do it. In fact, some of the most rewarding experiences in life are the hardest. Ask someone who's climbed Mount Everest.

REMEMBER

Jumping headfirst into a difficult business problem and then succeeding in turning it around is not only a great outcome for an organization, but the work satisfaction derived is also hard to beat.

When faced with a daunting challenge, it's easy to focus on what makes it hard. In fact, a lot of innovation is never pursued because team members only see the difficulty. Those that succeed see all the challenges too and move forward regardless.

But they also see something else.

Even the most complex projects and programs we all face have characteristics that lend themselves toward good outcomes. The Mount Everest climber sees what appears to be an insurmountable climb, but also recognizes that they've had good training, they are carrying the right equipment, and that they are accompanied by experienced climbers.

Data governance is hard, but it also has many qualities that make the challenges just a little bit easier.

The following sections discuss ways that data governance can succeed despite its challenges.

Data governance is already happening

It would be fair to assume that since you've been tasked with implementing a data governance program, that nothing currently exists and that you're starting from scratch. The reality is that all organizations exhibit forms of data governance. Some to a small degree and others to a much greater extent.

Consider data security. Most organizations don't post all their data on external facing platforms for anyone to access. Instead, they store data on servers and cloud providers with access rules built in. Commonly, an organization needs to provide access and decide what level of access. This depends on who that person is. Some rules, tacit or otherwise, guide these access decisions. This is data governance.

Take any aspect of data such as risk management, quality, availability, privacy, and more, and you'll find some manner of governance in place. Of course, in the absence of formal, quality data governance, any rigor or consistency is likely missing. In fact, while data governance does exist in an informal way, it's the weak outcomes and growing risks that drive a formal program.

Knowing that data governance exists, albeit in a primitive state, is a great starting point for a dialogue with leaders and staff. The argument you can make is that you're not trying to introduce something completely new and without precedent. Instead, you're simply trying to implement something that will elevate what is already happening to enable much better results for the organization.

Big returns for low investment

What shouldn't be lost on anyone is that when data governance is done well, the benefits can be significant. This is a big reason why this topic is so important. It's a program that has the potential for far-reaching, positive impact. The returns for organizations have the potential to exceed expectations.

When first exposed to a proposal for a data governance program, executives may be reluctant for any number of reasons. These could include a lack of understanding of the topic and its value, a reluctance to deploy more administrative work, and given its scale across the organization, the view that it will be costly to deploy and maintain.

In the 30 years I've been working for organizations, I've always tried to make the argument, where appropriate and relevant, that costs should be viewed through the lens of the return. Specifically, if I ask for one million dollars for a project, it's true that this number alone may sound like a lot of money. However, if that million dollars either can reduce costs by 10 million dollars or generate 30 million dollars in new revenue, suddenly my one million dollar ask doesn't seem so much.

As you calculate the cost of your data governance program, if possible, try to communicate the dollar value of the benefits it will bring. I recognize it will be a harder ask, because many of the benefits of data governance, such as data quality and improved insights, are often hard to assign a dollar value.

Even small steps can produce results

That said, when budgets are limited and assigning dollar values to benefits is for one reason or another impractical, you have another route altogether. There can be a proposal for data governance that doesn't break the bank. Assuming an evolutionary deployment of data governance rather than a large, revolutionary change, it's possible to deploy some lightweight, low-to-no cost features early in the initial deployment.

If you assume that existing staff will take on data governance responsibilities, net new headcount is not required. This eliminates one of the costliest aspects of any organizational effort. Then, in the beginning of the program, the first capabilities of data governance can be the focus — for example, developing standards and data dispute management. Both of these are time-based efforts and overhead can be absorbed into existing operating costs. In time, more capabilities can be added and, as their value is recognized, leadership may be inclined to provide increasing levels of funding. On balance, research indicates that data governance programs that are more gradually introduced are more likely to succeed.

REMEMBER

While tools and system modifications may be important at some point, they may not be critical for many organizations on day one. Data governance is largely about governing how people behave, not how technology and data behaves.

This approach to data governance is not for everyone and in fact, would not be my first choice or recommendation. But it does provide the option for organizations that are both cost-restricted and less convinced of a larger data governance program to take some small steps and experience benefits.

Leaders and teams are more motivated than they appear

If you met with a colleague at work and told them that you're in charge of developing a program that will require most staff, including your colleague, to follow more rules on top of their existing work, it's likely their reaction may be less than enthusiastic. You might even tell them that it's important work and that it will be good for the organization. That may not sway the argument. Data governance introduced to those who don't know what it is, won't likely get the excited reaction you might desire.

However, you might approach your colleague in an entirely different way. Instead of telling them what you're going to do, you might ask how the data they are using for their work could be improved to help them. Answers will probably include the ability to find and access the data they need, the availability of information to help them to understand their data, and having the confidence that the data they have is current. Colleagues in legal will tell you that data privacy is important. C-suite executives will tell you that they want better and quicker insights from their data. Sales and marketing will want analytics that help them target and close more new customers.

REMEMBER

You see, your organization actually loves the idea of quality data governance. They just might not think of it in those terms.

Your job includes creating the conditions in which the value of data governance is understood by those who know managing data well is important but haven't considered the positive outcomes of better governance.

Your data governance program will be more successful and easier to deploy and maintain if the organization fully understands the benefits the program will bring to them. Even if the program does cause a slight increment in workload, for many it will be worth it, for all the improved outcomes.

Anticipating Ongoing Program Risks and Challenges

Overcoming the startup challenges of a data governance program and getting it to a steady state is an impressive accomplishment. You and your team deserve credit. But it's too soon to rest. With a data governance program now operational, you're moving into the maintenance phase. This means ensuring it will continue to run smoothly and be in a position to evolve as needs dictate.

As time passes too, you need to anticipate future needs. In some instances, you and your team can be proactive; at other times you'll be reacting to an environment that undoubtedly evolves in the months and years ahead. Understanding the possible future challenges, risks, and opportunities of data governance will help everyone in the organization be better prepared to respond and to take advantage of new possibilities.

Areas of data governance maintenance

Many years ago, I learned to fly a single-engine aircraft and earned my private pilot's license. Learning to fly was an incredible experience including understanding the science and regulations of flight. I attended flight school almost every weekend for over a year. Only when my instructor thought I was ready did he permit me to go solo. Soon after, I passed my exams and received my license. It's said that a new pilot flies at their most attentive and precise at that moment. I can attest to that. Eventually, as time passes, a pilot can get lax and forget important responsibilities. For that reason, pilots are required to take periodic tests to ensure they are up-to-date on rules and that their flying is still performed safely.

I share this story as an analog for the necessary ongoing maintenance required for an effective data governance program. Your team and the program will probably be at its best in the few months following its deployment. But as time passes, the program may face a series of challenges that can lower its effectiveness.

WARNING

A data governance program that is not maintained for the long term can raise risks. These risks include policies not being followed, increasing levels of bad data, and the overall gradual diminishing of the value data governance was supposed to bring in the first place.

The following sections discuss the areas of your data governance program that should be subject to regular review and remediation if necessary.

Staffing

In every organization, team members change as time passes. For example, some get new roles and some retire or leave for another organization. Of course, this is true for the roles within data governance too. If, for example, a data owner is no longer in the role they used to be in, you need to ensure that this fact is quickly identified, and a new candidate is put in place. Your team needs to be on top of this. The program will suffer quickly when data owners, data stewards, data governance council members, and others are not backfilled promptly. That new team member also needs to be trained fully and brought up to speed. Don't overlook this essential requirement.

Ongoing communications

I know, I know, I've said this several times already. That probably means it's really important. Ongoing communications are essential. Don't fall for a common mistake, which is to go heavy on communications before and during deployment, and then completely drop off the map afterward. Communicating program successes, progress, and metrics; reinforcing benefits; and making other announcements must continue indefinitely.

Aligning data strategy with data governance

One of the characteristics of good strategy management is to evolve it as conditions dictate. For example, a strategy that was created three years ago may not be as relevant today if major assumptions have changed and the strategy has remained the same. This may be the case for your organization's data strategy.

The role of data is evolving rapidly and it's likely your data strategy will need to respond accordingly. Given the tight relationship between strategy and governance, your data governance program needs to be in lockstep with the organization's data strategy. This is where strong collaboration between leaders is essential. In particular, the data governance leader, the chief data officer (CDO), and the chief information officer (CIO) can be most effective in ensuring data strategy and governance alignment.

Current regulations and policies

The laws, regulations, and industry requirements for data are constantly evolving. If your data governance program does not reflect current laws, then it's not possible for it to be effective. Risk can also escalate quickly, resulting in infractions and severe penalties. For example, if your state passes legislation that tightens (or loosens) data privacy rules, your program must be updated to reflect those changes. For sure, a close relationship with your compliance and legal teams is central here. Some larger organizations work with outside firms to ensure they are kept abreast of any updates in a timely manner. In a similar way, changes made to standards, such as external reference data, or the introduction of new systems and updates to data architecture must also be adopted and reflected in the data governance program. Inconsistent data standards, usage, and architecture across an organization will soon create painful issues.

Problem management

In the day-to-day operations of a data governance program, many issues will emerge. Given the range of possibilities, some issues will be resolved quickly while others will require days and even months to address.

Examples of problems include and range from the discovery that a data set has not been properly secured after a casual audit on a file server, to a compliance officer identifying a regulation that is not being completely enforced. To ensure that these problems are recorded and resolved requires some form of problem management system. While a system provides the mechanism for management, it's important to ensure that problems are being routed to the right people and that items are being addressed in a timely manner.

Some organizations put service level agreements (SLAs) in place between stakeholders. These provide a level of service expectation. For example, your organization might agree that issues related to data access must be resolved in four hours, whereas policy updates need to be made in four weeks. Ensuring that the entire problem management process is current and functioning must be a regular maintenance activity.

Periodic program reviews

A data governance program is multidimensional in nature. It includes procedures, policies, analytics, risk management, security, rules, tools, and much more. If you take my advice, you'll start modestly and build the program over time. Think of it as an evolution, not a revolution. However, after some months or perhaps a year or two — assuming the program is progressing well and adoption levels and positive results are high — the program will be firing on many cylinders. Depending on your organization's size and complexity, your data governance program may eventually be quite complex.

As the data environment changes, as degrees of stakeholder engagement shift, and as strategy needs evolve, the program will be stretched and squeezed. Parts of the program will work well, while other parts will falter. Issues within the program may not always be apparent. To ensure that the program is optimally working and to identify any latent issues, periodic reviews of the program's performance should be performed. The data governance team is well positioned to take the lead on this effort. How often the periodic review is conducted is entirely the choice of the organization. It may depend on the size and complexity of the program, or on the availability of team members to conduct the review. The review process should entail a comprehensive walkthrough of the entire program and an evaluation of how each part is performing. Based on the results, remediation can be recommended to the Data Governance Council.

The evolving data landscape

In the months and years ahead, the role of data governance is positioned to expand rapidly, both within organizations that have programs and into many more enterprises that haven't yet embraced it.

By 2026, the marketplace for data governance software tools alone is estimated to be more than $5 billion, with a compounding annual growth rate (CAGR) of 20 percent.

Data governance will move from being a niche, albeit an important area, into a major formal function within organizations. Since you're reading this book, you likely get it. If not, I hope my words are beginning to convince you. Great careers in data governance and related data science and management skills will see years of strong demand.

REMEMBER

Today, data is a big deal. It may, in fact, be the most important asset in your organization (after people, probably). Tomorrow, data will be an even bigger deal.

In the years ahead, a growing number of factors will increase the demand and challenges of data governance. I've assembled some of the areas in the next sections, under the categories of people, process, and technology.

People

In the following list, you can see how leaders and teams are driving increased demand for good data governance:

» Leaders are finally recognizing and embracing the power and value of data in much larger numbers. This epiphany for many is creating a momentum toward building data cultures. Many organizations are starting from scratch.

» Executives and teams are demanding more timely business insights. They want more effective tools and options to guide their organizations. In particular, data analytics is anticipated to be a major driver of customer experiences and innovation efforts. Leaders now understand that the hyper-competitive landscape of the 21st century requires data-driven decision-making.

» While recognizing the value of data, leaders are also waking up to the elevating data risk landscape. Increasing regulations and changing consumer and community expectations are driving a greater focus on areas such as privacy. For example, the General Data Protection Regulation (GDPR), a regulation in European Union law on data protection and privacy, and the California Consumer Privacy Act (CCPA) both emerged with far-reaching consequences for all types of organizations. Other countries are exploring similar regulations and laws.

» Anxious to leverage the power and value of data, demand for data-related skills is exploding. Needs span widely, including roles such as data analysts, data scientists, data engineers and architects, data governance analysts and managers, and beyond. The availability of talent is not keeping up with the demand.

» With greater emphasis on data, organizations must expand their data literacy at every level. For example, do team members have the skills to know what data questions to ask?

» The nature of how organizations are structured and the future of work is creating completely new challenges in managing data. For example, working from home, greater reliance on cloud providers, more integrated external partners, and a mix of full-time employees and temporary staff all require a different approach to how data is managed across the organization.

Process

In the following list, note how emerging organizational needs and attendant processes are drivers for good data governance:

>> Organizations are formalizing their data governance programs. They are seeking the right levels of formality, including identifying an appropriate data governance framework and maturity level.

>> Almost every business has become a technology organization in that utilizing technology and data has moved into the center of all activities. This creates new pressures and responsibilities to manage these resources well.

>> Many organizations are embracing a digital transformation that is reinventing how they produce their products and services and how they go to market. Within the core of this work is effectively managing data.

>> Organizational and consumer behavior is evolving to leverage online collaboration and sharing. These new social capabilities provide enormous freedoms but elevate a wide range of data-related risks, such as privacy, confidentiality, and intellectual capital. Processes are necessary to bring some stability to an area that can become chaotic.

>> Even data governance is subject to its own evolution. Many see data governance as the gateway to data intelligence. While these two areas greatly overlap, data intelligence suggests a maturing data governance competency that focuses on supporting capabilities for understanding, managing, and leveraging the value of data.

Technology

In the following list, you can see how the evolving technology and data environment is creating a need for good data governance:

>> Big data is massive. One estimate suggests that in 2025 alone, the world will create 163 zettabytes. Check out Chapter 2 to get a sense of how big this number is. This volume of data will continue to increase each year. The demands on organizations to be able to handle and manage larger and larger volumes, velocity, and variety of data will increase.

>> The days of all data being exclusively stored on-premises (at your physical facility) are over. Today, organizations must manage and govern data that is stored and moves between on-premises, colocation sites, cloud providers, endpoint devices such as sensors and machines, vendors, and many other locations.

» In a business environment that is increasingly operating online coupled with hyperconnectivity, the vectors for cybersecurity risks are rapidly growing. The cost of cybercrime globally in 2021 was estimated to be around $6 trillion. To manage and reduce risk, more investment and talent must be directed toward information security efforts.

» Digital and emerging technologies are more highly dependent on data. They consume and produce increasing volumes of data. Examples include cloud computing, artificial intelligence, blockchain, robotic process automation (RPA), and metaverse. In Chapter 10, I discuss the implications of data governance and some of these new technologies.

» With growing interest and increasing numbers of data governance programs being implemented, new software tools are emerging to support a high-demand marketplace. These tools are helping to support and even automate many areas of the data governance value chain. In Chapter 11, I discuss the growing capabilities of these tools in detail. More tools are a positive, but it does mean more demands on staff to be trained and skilled in taking advantage of their capabilities. These tools also incur annual maintenance and support costs.

5

The Part of Tens

Explore best practices for achieving data governance success in your organization

Identify the main stakeholders and their responsibilities in data governance programs

Chapter **14**

Ten Data Governance Best Practices

I ncreasing numbers of organizations are implementing data governance programs. It's a reflection of the growing importance of the topic in a world awash in ever-expanding volumes of data. It also suggests more awareness and education about the value of good data management practices. With more success stories to learn from, it's getting easier to understand some of the best practices that are helping enterprises deliver results with their programs.

To help you on the journey ahead, I've identified, through my own experience and research, a number of approaches that can make a difference. Some of these may seem obvious and others not so much. For the ones that seem intuitive, consider them friendly reminders. This list is in no particular order. They are all valuable, so I haven't prioritized them.

If you've already read through this book, you'll recognize many of these best practices, as I have addressed them in detail in many chapters. If you have just skipped to this section to get some quick tips, these will still be helpful.

I know I sound like a broken record when I say this, but implementing and maintaining quality data governance is hard. That's just reality. I want you to have all the advantages available to you. Enjoy these best practices and good luck in your own efforts.

Start Small and Progressively Build Your Program

After the difficult work of building the business case and gaining approval for a data governance program, there may be a tendency to move quickly to plan, design, and implement everything that you and your team promised.

Even for a large organization with plenty of resources, this may be a risky approach. Remember, you're introducing a program that is not only complex, but will find plenty of resistance as it requires changes across the whole organization. With the chance of failure already high, you want all the advantages possible to ensure a successful rollout.

The creation and operations of a data governance program involves significant implications for people, processes, and technologies. Each one of these areas requires careful attention and likely plenty of modifications as they are deployed and evaluated for effectiveness. Implementing these all at once, while not impossible, creates a hefty burden on you and your team, and imposes significant overhead on the organization.

Unlike so many other business initiatives that require all the parts to be assembled and ready on day one, data governance generally doesn't have that requirement. For example, it's possible just to focus on privacy at first. This may provide a big return quickly and build support as you begin to deploy other areas of the program.

It's reasonable to plan a data governance program as an initiative that is progressively implemented over a period of time. In determining an acceptable pace, you can consider the size of the organization, the resources at your disposal, the complexity of the program, and the urgency being placed on you and your team from leadership. Communicate your team's intentions and ensure that there is overall agreement in the approach.

REMEMBER

Starting small and implementing a data governance program over time can increase your chances of success, win over leaders and staff, and make for a more satisfying experience for everyone.

Ensure the Program Is Aligned with the Interests of the Organization

If you're like me, you understand the value of high-quality data and managing it well just seems like the right thing to do. But this view has been established because you and I live and breathe the data topic in detail every day. It's easier for us to understand the role data can play in running a successful organization.

The same can't be said for all leaders and team members. Of course, they understand that data is essential in a business today, and most use it in their everyday work. But while concepts such as quality data and data management are relatively intuitive, the same can't be said for data governance.

For an organization to see the value of data governance, this will require education about the topic for sure, but more importantly, leaders need to fully appreciate its value relative to the goals and needs of the organization.

The business case for data governance is made by identifying the benefits and opportunities that it can bring to the table. Typically, you have to speak in a language that organizations best understand. Leaders will be looking for how data governance can help to grow the business, increase revenue, improve customer satisfaction, lower risks, and make operations more efficient. It could be as specific as ensuring that all data compliance requirements are being met. In other words, alignment of data governance to the business goals means answering the question of "why?"

REMEMBER

When you succeed in identifying the right alignment between data governance and the business, you'll hopefully gain approval for the program. However, to sustain support and funding, you need to demonstrate evidence that the program is providing the benefits it promised. This is why managing metrics and communicating performance results are so essential.

Get Your Leaders to Advocate for the Program's Success

Researchers have concluded time and again that one of the most important criteria for a project's success is the degree of leadership support before, during, and after the effort. It's not enough to have a leader who supports a project at its initialization, but subsequently does not engage and is absent from the work. Full support through an initiative's lifecycle has been proven often to be the difference between success and failure. This has been my personal experience too.

While gaining at least one committed and passionate leader is a must, attaining the support from a number of leaders or the entire C-suite is optimal. Data governance isn't some sideshow that only the IT, compliance, or legal teams are concerned about. This topic is enterprise-wide and is the responsibility of all leaders and team members. This is why full C-suite support is encouraged.

After the case has been made, to help diminish any remaining reluctance from leaders, you can remind them of the following:

>> Governing data already takes place. This program improves outcomes by formalizing processes, creating structure, and providing real, tangible value.

>> The program doesn't need to cost a lot of money and time. These dimensions can be sized relative to business needs and budget.

>> Data governance doesn't need to be disruptive. There's a way to gradually implement and operationalize it that can be noninvasive.

Making the case and communicating the benefits to your leaders is more than half the battle. If you win that, you're well on your way. But you want more than just approval and administrative support. Aspire to get your leaders pumped up about the potential for managing the enterprise's data really well. Provide them with regular updates that show how the data governance program is producing high-performance results. If the program is making a difference, the metrics will demonstrate that, and leaders will get the investment validation that they require.

REMEMBER

When leaders are completely bought-in, they become advocates. They will periodically send strong, positive messages across the entire business that motivates positive action and reminds team members of the importance of the program. They'll also be your allies when major challenges arise and you and your team need some extra support.

Begin the Change Management Process Early

No matter how hard you might try to build a noninvasive data governance program, it will necessitate change that will impact people, processes, and technology. That change can be modest, or it can be quite disruptive. Whatever the case, data governance requires thoughtful and careful change management.

All initiatives benefit from good-quality planning and anticipation of needs and issues. When done well, a change management plan can result in materially better results for your efforts. For sure, the absence of good change management is often the source of project issues.

Change management must be considered in all phases of the data governance program, including design, deployment, operations, and support. You're transitioning an organization from one state to another. It's particularly valuable during the preparation phase — the months and weeks prior to the introduction of formal data governance.

You must prepare both stakeholders and the environment for the changes ahead. With data governance, there's simply no upside to surprises. Preparing for change includes ensuring that the program is aligned with leadership expectations, that the value and impact of the program is well understood across the organization, and that stakeholders know what to expect during each phase of the program implementation. It also includes listening and responding to stakeholder's concerns and ideas.

Factoring change management processes early into your data governance efforts will be rewarded as the effort proceeds. It can feel like yet another burden, but it greatly increases the possibility of better outcomes.

Establish Meaningful Metrics

As you design the data governance program, you must identify how you'll measure whether the program, when implemented, is performing as anticipated. Of course, you'll want to know whether it's doing better than expected, and perhaps most importantly, you'll want early evidence as to whether the program is failing to meet expectations.

Establishing meaningful metrics, those that provide a basis for timely decision-making and performance management, is essential to managing an effective data governance program. You need these metrics to communicate to a wide range of stakeholders whether the program is providing value and meeting its goals.

REMEMBER

Data governance needs data metrics to validate its existence and provide the basis for ongoing funding and support. Metrics are also at the heart of continuous improvement.

The most obvious metrics you'll want to focus on first are the ones directly aligned with the program's purpose. For example, if one of the program goals is to reduce the time needed to resolve data issues, you'll want to capture a baseline and then track resolution times over time. Ideally, you'll also have a target, such as a 70 percent time reduction from the baseline. Once the target is reached, you may choose to no longer track it. However, it's also not uncommon to measure the organization's ability to maintain that target and report when, for example, target resolution times are consistently not being met.

Beyond metrics that are strongly aligned with the program's goals, you might consider other measurements such as the number of team members trained in a particular data topic. Or you may work with the security team to collect a wide range of cybersecurity-related data metrics. As the organization's data maturity increases with the implementation of the data governance program, new metrics will emerge.

TIP

It's certainly not easy to establish metrics and then have an ongoing measurement program. Most teams find this part of a program quite difficult. Start small and add more metrics as you can. You don't need to measure everything right away.

Create Abundant Learning Opportunities for Team Members

While it would be great to assume that everyone understands how to extract and manipulate data, the reality is that many employees still struggle with basic spreadsheet skills. This is not a criticism of the individuals. It's often the result of not having the opportunity or being provided with the support to acquire more intermediate or expert level skills.

Fortunately, organizations are now recognizing the deficit in critical information-worker skills and more are investing in learning opportunities. There's never been a better time for acquiring new knowledge and skills. In addition to traditional in-person training, online learning has become a popular channel.

As you've discovered, or soon will, data governance requires a variety of skills, with varying complexity. It also comes with its own vocabulary and unique processes, and it often uses specialized software. It's hard to imagine deploying a data governance program without ensuring that the program is providing an abundance of learning options for those who will be impacted.

Be sure to account for training in your budget's calculations, both for the initial implementation and for ongoing learning needs.

Consider training as part of your change management efforts. Preparing teams for data governance requires skills building, and maintaining the program requires new and existing team members have timely learning opportunities. Training will build confidence and empower team members to succeed. It can also reduce the anxiety experienced as people anticipate change and modified expectations.

As you consider learning opportunities, be broad in your thinking. Today, gaining new skills can take many forms. In your training plan, include in-person and online training, on-demand options, and other modalities such as quality documentation, knowledge systems, and coaching.

Communicate Early and Often

Successful data governance programs create clear, consistent, and timely communications before, during, and after implementation. These communications inform team members about progress, expectations, requirements, impact, and a whole lot more. When it's done right, employees feel knowledgeable, confident, and ready for each milestone. They'll also understand the value of the program and understand its benefits, which is helpful in gaining champions across the enterprise.

Despite all the obvious advantages of executing a thoughtful and complete data governance communications campaign alongside training, it's often a poorly addressed area. You don't want an ad hoc, last-minute, email process, but rather a comprehensive plan that has one-off elements and recurring tasks such as a newsletter or progress updates. The plan should include objectives, audiences, and methods for each audience — you want to target the right people at the right time — and frequency.

Your data governance program needs a communications plan commensurate with its importance and its impact on the organization. Don't skimp in this area. In fact, your internal communications plan will cost the least in terms of dollars compared to your other program activities. The real costs are skills and time.

Someone needs to lead your data governance communications efforts. It might be you, but if you're lucky enough, your organization may have a Chief Communications Officer or equivalent to help. Sometimes a Chief Data Officer will be the voice too. You'll work with whatever makes most sense for your organization. Some of your communications need to come from someone senior, but ongoing communications can be a lower-level team member, or it could even come from the Data Governance Office.

It's also important to know each audience as you consider your messages. For example, don't send a technical email to people who don't need technical details. Ensure that a regular dose of data governance value is sprinkled into occasional communications. It's good to remind stakeholders why this work is important and how it is benefitting the organization. You might also consider a data governance program brand. This could include a unique logo and set of imagery that's consistent with the brand of the organization but also creates a distinctive look and feel to the program.

REMEMBER

Always remember that good communication is an opportunity to teach. Use it.

Remind Stakeholders This Is a Program, Not a Project

During my career I've worked on hundreds of projects. I've enjoyed most of them. Some of them I'm happy to forget. Projects are remarkably satisfying in that they are usually well-defined and have a measurable output. For example, if the project is to build a house, once the house is built, you can point to it and say, "There, we built a house." In many of the technology projects I've been involved with over several decades, I saw first-hand how the output benefited all types of people and organizations in the public and private sectors. Projects have a start and an end.

Planning, designing, and implementing data governance can look and feel like a project, but it's not a project. Data governance is a collection of long-term and ongoing efforts that can be referred to as a *program*. Unlike a project, a program focuses on business outcomes rather than outputs and may be continuous in its desire to meet business goals. Some refer to data governance as a practice. I prefer program. Both are appropriate and acceptable.

For you and me, this may be intuitive. The important takeaway here is that everyone in the organization needs to understand that data governance is an ongoing commitment and not a one-off project. You need to explain that when data governance is deployed, it will become part of how the organization operates and behaves. It may also evolve, sometimes abruptly, as requirements change, such as a newly introduced regulation or law.

When you make it clear that data governance is a program and not a project, employees understand that data governance is a long-term effort that becomes part of their daily work. They understand that it doesn't end at any point. There won't be a logical conclusion. Once the work gets underway, data governance becomes part of the organization.

Focus on People and Behaviors

It's easy to think of data solely in the context of processes and technologies. After all, data is created, collected, and stored in computer systems. All of us experience data in digital form. It's also fair to conclude that processes and technology are essential to the role of managing data.

That said, a more practical evaluation of data management makes it clear that people's behavior largely determines data outcomes. Simply put, people manage data.

At its core, data governance is about guiding and enforcing the way people work with data and its related technologies. Reminding yourself and your teams of this periodically can help reorientate if there's an indication that the focus is shifting. For example, if there's a lot of blame being placed on a tool, perhaps it's worth determining whether it's a training issue or a usability problem. Replacing the tool may not be the right approach. Rather, providing better learning opportunities may be better.

In data governance, emphasis is placed on stewardship and ownership of data, both deeply human functions. People who care about the data they are entrusted with will likely be more diligent and responsive to needs.

Data governance is also about compliance. While processes and technologies can help, each person has the opportunity to do the right thing, or they can create risks for themselves and the organization.

In addition, from writing policies to choosing technology, determining priorities, responding to issues, and establishing security rules, each of these areas is the product of human decisions. In the end, the people in an organization are responsible for data governance, not some abstract black box.

REMEMBER

For a data governance program to be successful, the "people" dynamics must become the focus.

Understand What Data Matters to the Organization

Not all data is equal. The important data in your organization may only be 10-20 percent of all data that is created, captured, and stored. That other 80 percent may have value in some context, but it doesn't drive the business forward. For example, a subset of the *data domain* (a logical grouping of data) on customers is likely going to be characterized as important, whereas data stored as a by-product of operational back-office processes is not likely to be considered critical.

Unless your plan is to apply the rigor of data governance to every data domain in the business — not a practical or necessary approach — you need to work with stakeholders to identify the data domains and the data within them that truly matter.

TIP

Prioritizing data domains also enables you to start small by managing scope and progressively deploying the data governance program:

The first step in understanding what data will be included in the data governance program is to know what data the organization has and what data sets are important. Examples of data domains include customers, sales, finance, procurement, and inventory.

Another way to categorize data is to consider collections of common data sets that together have unique value. These are called *information assets.* One example is product information. Whether you look through the lens of data domains or information assets, you have to know what exists and what's truly critical.

Once you have identified the critical data, it can be categorized into one or more areas of data governance concern. For example: compliance, business growth, security sensitivity, or quality. In addition, data domains have owners that you can engage early as stakeholders. You'll also likely learn which data domains don't have owners, which will help you determine areas of weakness.

Knowing what data is important allows you and your team to prioritize and focus efforts, enables the program to start small, categorizes the focus for each data domain or information asset, and identifies the data owners.

Chapter **15**

Ten Essential Data Governance Stakeholders

This chapter contains a quick reference, and a summarized description, of the types of people and teams that are required for a good data governance program.

Recall that data governance is people-centric and people-driven. In some organizations, data governance is implemented exclusively as a set of expected behaviors through processes and policies, without an investment in tools and systems. This keeps the costs negligible, while getting the work done. Of course, for many organizations, it's much more than that. The point here is that at a basic level, data governance is achieved by the right people doing the right things at the right time.

The stakeholders discussed in this chapter are essential to data governance. But don't be alarmed if it seems like a lot. In large, complex organizations, there's likely to be additional staffing requirements. On the other hand, in medium-sized businesses, many of these roles and responsibilities are performed by the same person. Also keep in mind that many data governance roles are fulfilled by people who have other responsibilities. The data steward, for example, can be anyone with an interest in data and some basic data skills.

Use this chapter as a quick reference. If you want more detail, turn to the table of contents to find a deeper discussions of these roles, including their responsibilities and the context in which these roles support the goals of data governance.

Data Owner

A *data owner* is a team member who is accountable to a particular data set. This person cares for the data, including whether it is up-to-date, accurate, compliant, and complete. They are tasked with ensuring data quality and defining the security requirements of their data sets. Without a data owner, there's nobody tending to the data.

REMEMBER

While it's unintuitive given their title, data owners are only accountable for data sets; they don't own them.

To ensure that your organization's data is well managed, every data set should have an official owner. Certain team members will be responsible for a large number of data sets based on their role and responsibilities. For example, someone like the Chief Information Officer (CIO) will likely own (or designate to someone on their team) a lot of back-office-related data sets.

Some data governance practitioners support the concept of federated data ownership. Rather than an individual being assigned a data set, a data steward or similar will be accountable for the outcome of a data process. While there are advantages to this approach, I find that eventually there is a need to have someone accountable to each data set.

What you might discover as you begin your planning is that the formality of data ownership is not common. Data governance changes that, because it requires that these owners be data subject matter experts that other stakeholders can rely on.

TIP

Establishing data owners for all applicable data sets should be an early priority in your planning activities.

Data Steward

The *data steward* role is most central to the operations of a data governance program. Data stewards are responsible for the data governance processes that drive quality and value.

Depending on the size and complexity of your organization, there will be one or more data stewards. In a sophisticated data governance environment, there are many data stewards representing the main data domains. They work together and with other data stakeholders, such as data owners, to drive and enforce data strategy and to ensure that the program is successful.

The organization's data stewards will collaborate to focus on creating data policies and procedures, ensure data quality, set up compliance areas, resolve data issues, and make data-related decisions. Each is an expert in their designated data domains and business units. While they don't need to be technically savvy, they are expected to have some data-related skills. They serve as a communications channel between various data governance stakeholders such as data owners, the information technology (IT) department, and the Data Governance Council.

Data Custodian

A data steward and a data custodian share some common responsibilities, such as ensuring data security and appropriate handling of data. However, the *data custodian* is typically someone in the IT department responsible for implementing the technical requirements specified by the data steward.

This person often performs or has oversight of systems-specific tasks such as database administration and data backups. They lead the implementation of technical requirements. Increasingly, as more technology migrates to the cloud, this role focuses on how an organization's data is hosted and managed in the cloud environment.

Data custodians are also experts in the lifecycle of data in their domain. For example, they know its lineage, its security requirements, and its data schema, and they have detailed knowledge of how the data is processed through its relevant pipeline. While they may understand the business domain and value of the data, this is not their focus.

People in this role collaborate closely with other data governance stakeholders, particularly data stewards.

Data User

It's easy to focus on all the leadership roles responsible for handling data and ensuring it is managed well. But what about people who just use data in their daily roles by entering, accessing, manipulating, and analyzing it? Without such employees, there would be little need for data governance. Of course, data users are also data governance stakeholders.

Data users represent every function of an organization. They are customer service representatives, salespeople, engineers, cashiers, hiring managers, budget analysts, and every other type of business role you can imagine. In their daily work, they input, create, and rely on data.

Being directly engaged with data, these users need to understand their responsibilities relative to acceptable use and retention, the legal, security, privacy aspects, as well as other areas of data governance. In many instances, knowledge of data standards is important. Data users need to attend training and keep apprised through various communications channels of evolving expectations.

Some data users represent their teams in ongoing data governance committees and projects.

Data Governance Manager

The *data governance manager* is the person responsible for managing the day-to-day operations of the data governance program. It's a hands-on role requiring leadership, planning, oversight, and decision-making. Depending on the size and complexity of the organization, this may be a full-time role or may be an additional set of responsibilities for a senior team member. In some instances, the Chief Data Officer (CDO) fulfils this role and has overall responsibility for leadership of the program.

REMEMBER

The role belongs to a person who is passionate about data and deeply believes in the data vision and strategy of the organization. They may even have helped create that vision and strategy. Could this be you?

Responsibilities cover the entire spectrum of data governance. The data governance manager helps plan, design, deploy, support, and enforce all aspects. The organization views this role as the central contact and face of data governance. This person is required to work at every level and be comfortable working with the C-suite and external stakeholders.

Chief Data Officer (CDO)

As data has grown in critical importance in increasing numbers of organizations, a relatively new executive role has been established. The *Chief Data Officer* (CDO) is the most senior person in the business with responsibility for all aspects of data. Intuitively, data governance is within the scope of the CDO.

As a C-suite occupant, the CDO must lead and advise about data use in support of the organization's strategy, look for ways to create value from data, and manage security, compliance, and regulatory concerns. The role must ensure that data is treated as a valuable asset and all attendant risks are managed. The role works closely and collaborates with other C-suite peers, such as the Chief Executive Officer, the Chief Information Officer, and the Chief Operations Officer.

The CDO has a central role in helping to create the data culture. This means investing in data-related tools and training, as well as encouraging the organization to use data as a strategic asset, glean insights from it, and embrace data-driven decision-making. A mature data culture goes hand-in-hand with maturing data governance.

There are few leadership roles as important as the CDO — when an organization is fortunate enough to have one — in enabling the success of data governance. This person must be a champion of managing data well. This quality is at the heart of why the role exists.

Chief Information Officer (CIO)

There's always a risk in placing too much emphasis on the technological aspects of data governance. Although the IT department is important, data governance is not exclusively its domain. All too often, data governance is reduced to a security function that lives in the technology department. For a few organizations, this might be appropriate. Hopefully, if this book has achieved anything, it's convinced you that data governance is an enterprise-wide concern.

That said, the IT team has important responsibilities when it comes to managing and governing data. The *Chief Information Officer* (CIO) is the senior executive with oversight of the technology in an organization. With the elevated role of technology now driving businesses forward, the CIO is essential to supporting the organization's strategy, including its use of data.

Beyond the role of overseeing data custodian responsibilities in IT, the CIO works closely with the other C-suite executives, and particularly with the CDO, in ensuring data is managed well, is appropriately secure, and is high quality. In other words, the CIO is a partner in data governance leadership. In the absence of a CDO, the CIO may perform many of these responsibilities.

Chief Executive Officer (CEO)

The leader of an organization, the *Chief Executive Officer* (CEO) or equivalent, has an enormous influence on its culture and behavior. Every day this person sets the tone and models expectations by what they say and do.

Assuming the CEO recognizes data as one of the most important — if not the most important — assets of the organization, they are ultimately responsible for driving the success of all data efforts. Even though the CIO and CDO are central to helping build a data culture, the CEO must take the lead. This person must champion the necessary message and actions across the C-suite and into the leadership ranks. The CIO, CDO, and other executives will carry and execute the data vision, which includes data governance, on the CEO's behalf.

In considering a data governance sponsor, the CEO is sometimes a good choice, although there's a risk that this person may not have the capacity to be the champion you need. The data governance sponsor must have the time, knowledge, and passion for data. They also have to be prepared for a long-term commitment. At a minimum, the CEO can designate and hold accountable an executive sponsor of the data governance program.

WARNING

Achieving full commitment from the CEO to your data governance program is critical. It's a proven best practice, and in my view, it's essential. Without it, success will elude you.

Data Governance Council (DGC)

The *Data Governance Council* (DGC), sometimes called the Data Governance Board (DGB) or Data Governance Committee (DGC), is a group of representative stakeholders who confer regularly to govern and guide the strategy of the data governance program. The council prioritizes initiatives and approves a wide range of data-related elements, such as policies and standards.

Through its oversight and leadership, the DGC supports high-quality data, while also helping to manage and reduce its risk.

Specific responsibilities of the DGC include reviewing and approving data tools, resolving enterprise-level data issues, communicating program value to the enterprise, enforcing various policies, and approving funds.

Often a senior executive, such as the program sponsor or the CDO, is the council's chairperson. Whoever leads the council should have advanced data knowledge and skills. They must understand the dynamics of data management and governance.

Members of the DGC can include representatives from major business units, the CIO, representatives of the data stewards and data owners, security analysts, legal managers, and auditors.

Data Governance Program Office (DGPO)

While the Data Governance Council has strategic oversight for the data governance program and meets periodically, the *Data Governance Program Office* (DGPO), or simply the Data Governance Office (DGO), is focused on day-to-day management, operations, and support.

Members of the DGPO have tactical and operational responsibilities for data governance. They include data analysts, project managers, security analysts, reporting associates, IT associates, and data users.

The team is managed by the data governance manager or equivalent. Outside of large organizations, the DGPO largely exists as a virtual team. Members spend a portion of their time on efforts, since this work is only part of their overall responsibilities.

Primarily, the DGPO works on the administrative and operational aspects of the program. In this mode, their activities include monitoring and capturing results of data governance activities, providing assistance to decision-making, creating performance reports, identifying and delivering training, and scheduling and facilitating the agendas for the DGC and other related stakeholder groups. Some DGPO teams are empowered to develop standards, policies, and procedures, thereby working with data stewards and other stakeholders.

Index

I

IBM (International Business Machines), 35
icons, explained, 3–4
Identify function, in NIST cybersecurity
    framework, 101
identifying
    business case for data governance, 78–84
    business strategy, 142
    data assets, 142–143
    roles and responsibilities, 71, 121–138
    roles of data, 41–49
    stakeholders, 140–141, 194
    techniques for measuring success, 210–217
implementing data governance programs,
    158–171
improving
    financial bottom line, 83
    outcomes with data, 49–54
inclusiveness, ensuring, 111–112
incremental growth, 115–116
industry, data strategy and, 70
information assets, 11
information governance, data governance
    compared with, 11
information technology (IT) department, role of
    data governance for, 175
insight management, as a role of data, 46–47
insights, converting into data, 27–29, 61–62
intangible assets, 49
integrity
    as a central area of data governance, 102
    in CIA triad, 133
International Business Machines (IBM), 35
International Organization for Standardization
    (ISO), 196
Internet of Things (IoT)
    about, 37, 79, 177
    architecture, 181
    role of data governance in, 179–180
interviews, as an analysis technique, 145
investment, returns compared with, 233
IoT (Internet of Things)

about, 37, 79, 177
architecture, 181
role of data governance in, 179–180
IP (digital intellectual property), 179
ISACA, Control Objectives for Information and
    Related Technologies (COBIT) IT governance
    framework, 14–15
ISO (International Organization for
    Standardization), 196
IT (information technology) department, role of
    data governance for, 175

K

key performance indicators (KPIs), 211–212
knowledge graphs, 148–150
KPIs (key performance indicators), 211–212

L

language, clarity of, 167
Last Updated section, policy document, 154
leadership
    advocacy from, 247–248
    creating groups, 134–138
    in data governance framework, 15–16
    insufficiency of, 229
learning delivery methods, 170–171
learning opportunities, creating, 250–251
lifecycle, of data, 33–34
logical data models, 147

M

maintenance, in data governance, 235–238
management dashboards
    best practices for, 216
    building, 215–217
    using, 216–217
managing
    data strategy, 73
    day-to-day of data governance programs,
        186–198
market value approach, 65

running
- about, 185–186
- automating data governance programs, 198–207
- data governance programs, 185–207
- managing day-to-day of data governance programs, 186–198
- programs, 115

S

sales department, role of data governance for, 172–173

Sales Manager, role of data governance for, 172–173

Schmidt, Eric (CEO), 37

Scope section, policy document, 154

security, as a central area of data governance, 100–101

seeking resolution, 194

SEICMM (Software Institute Capability Maturity Model), 117–119

selecting data governance tools, 199–201

semi-structured data, 25

service level agreements (SLAs), 237

simplicity, in communication, 167

single source of truth, 195

size, data strategy and, 70

SLAs (service level agreements), 237

small data, 38

smart data, 39

Software Institute Capability Maturity Model (SEICMM), 117–119

software tools, for data governance, 199

solutions, deploying, 194

staff costs, 90

staffing, ongoing maintenance in, 236

stakeholders
- about, 255–256
- analyzing needs of, 140–150
- Chief Data Officer (CDO), 259
- Chief Executive Officer (CEO), 260
- Chief Information Officer (CIO), 259–260
- collecting requirements of, 144–145
- data custodian, 257
- Data Governance Council (DGC), 260–261
- data governance manager, 258
- Data Governance Program Office (DGPO), 261
- data owner, 256
- data steward, 256–257
- in data strategy proposal, 84–86
- data user, 257–258
- essential, 255–261
- gathering, 194
- identifying, 140–141, 194
- reminders for, 252–253

standardization
- as an approach to data governance, 94–95
- case study on, 95–96

standards, in data governance framework, 16

status, reporting on, 189–190

storage, of data, 27

Storage stage, in lifecycle of data, 33

strategic alignment metric, 213

strategic participation, 123

strategy
- in data governance framework, 15–16
- as a role of data, 43

structure, improving usability with, 99

structured data, 25

success, measuring, 115

summary, in proposal, 88

supporting
- data governance, 80–83
- gathering for programs, 223–225

T

Tabulating Machine Company, 35

tactical participation, 123

tangible assets, 49

technical metadata, 58

techniques
- for data governance programs, 141–145
- identifying for measuring success, 210–217

technology
- data governance and, 240–241
- metric for, 214–215

third industrial revolution, 36

timeliness, data quality and, 104

timing, for communication, 251–252

Tip icon, 3

tool costs, 90

tools

  in data governance framework, 17

  improving usability with, 99

  selecting for data governance, 199–201

training, providing, 168–171

transforming through data, 55–73

transparency, as an approach to data governance, 92–93

U

uniqueness, data quality and, 104

unstructured data, 25

U.S. Census, 35

usability, as a central area of data governance, 99

Usage stage, in lifecycle of data, 33

utilizing voices, 166–167

V

validity, data quality and, 104

value

  of change management, 160

  of data, 31, 56–67

of data governance, 97–104

driving through data, 41–54

of monitoring, 218

Variability, as a characteristic of big data, 36

Variety, as a characteristic of big data, 36

Velocity, as a characteristic of big data, 36

Veracity, as a characteristic of big data, 36

vision statement, in proposal, 87

voices, utilizing, 166–167

Volume, as a characteristic of big data, 36

W

W3C (World Wide Web Consortium), 150

Wanamaker, John (retailer), 38

Warning icon, 4

websites

  Cheat Sheet, 4

  data catalog example, 59

  management dashboards, 217

  NIST cybersecurity framework, 102

with-and-without method, 65

workshops, as an analysis technique, 145

World Wide Web Consortium (W3C), 150

Z

zettabyte, 25–27

About the Author

Dr. Jonathan Reichental is the founder of Human Future, a global business and technology advisory, investment, and education firm. His previous roles have included senior software engineering manager, director of technology innovation, and he has served as chief information officer (CIO) at both O'Reilly Media and the City of Palo Alto, California.

In 2013 he was recognized as one of the 25 doers, dreamers, and drivers in government in America. In 2016, he was named a top influential CIO in the United States and in 2017, he was named one of the top 100 CIOs in the world. He has also won a best CIO in Silicon Valley award and a national IT leadership prize.

Reichental is a recognized global thought leader, keynote speaker, and a business and government adviser on a number of emerging trends including urban innovation, smart cities, sustainability, blockchain technology, data governance, the fourth industrial revolution, digital transformation, and many more.

He is an adjunct professor in the School of Management at the University of San Francisco and instructs at several other universities. Reichental regularly creates online educational video courses for LinkedIn Learning, which include a highly successful series on data governance.

Reichental has written several books, including *Smart Cities for Dummies, Exploring Smart Cities Activity Book for Kids,* and *Exploring Cities Bedtime Rhymes.*

You can learn more about his work at www.reichental.com and you can follow him on LinkedIn and Twitter.

Dedication

This book is dedicated to the American composer, conductor, and pianist John Williams. From the theme music of *Star Wars* to *Saving Private Ryan* and hundreds of others, his compositions continue to bring me remarkable joy and remain the soundtrack of my life.

Acknowledgments

Thank you to everyone who has made this book possible. I'm grateful to each of you and I hope I've made you proud with this contribution to the body of knowledge on data.

In particular, I'd like to thank Hari Kalahasti, Steve Weiss, Paul Kuchina, Saker Ghani, Sahil Naqvi, Myles Suer, Alation, Monica Guedes, and LinkedIn Learning.

Special appreciation to the whole Wiley team, including Steven Hayes and Kezia Endsley.

Finally, big hugs and thanks to my mom and dad, Evanne and Tomi.

There are others to thank who I can't recall right now. Don't worry, I'll call you.

Publisher's Acknowledgments

Acquisitions Editor: Steven Hayes

Senior Project Editor: Kristie Pyles

Copy Editor: Kezia Endsley

Technical Editor: Mark Friedlich

Production Editor: Tamilmani Varadharaj

Cover Image: © fizkes/Shutterstock

Printed and bound by CPI Group (UK) Ltd, Croydon, CR0 4YY

20/06/2023

03228555-0001